Laravel: Up and Running
A Framework for Building Modern PHP Apps

Matt Stauffer

Beijing · Boston · Farnham · Sebastopol · Tokyo

Laravel: Up and Running

by Matt Stauffer

Copyright © 2017 Matt Stauffer. All rights reserved.

Printed in the United States of America.

Published by O'Reilly Media, Inc., 1005 Gravenstein Highway North, Sebastopol, CA 95472.

O'Reilly books may be purchased for educational, business, or sales promotional use. Online editions are also available for most titles (*http://oreilly.com/safari*). For more information, contact our corporate/institutional sales department: 800-998-9938 or *corporate@oreilly.com*.

Editor: Allyson MacDonald	**Indexer:** Angela Howard
Production Editor: Colleen Lobner	**Interior Designer:** David Futato
Copyeditor: Rachel Head	**Cover Designer:** Randy Comer
Proofreader: Kim Cofer	**Illustrator:** Rebecca Demarest

December 2016:   First Edition

Revision History for the First Edition
2016-11-14:   First Release

See *http://oreilly.com/catalog/errata.csp?isbn=9781491936085* for release details.

978-1-491-93608-5

[LSI]

This book is dedicated to my gracious and inspiring wife, Tereva, my joyful and courageous son, Malachi, and my beautiful daughter, Mia, who spent the majority of this book's creation in her mama's belly.

Table of Contents

Preface

The story of how I got started with Laravel is a common one: I had written PHP for years, but I was on my way out the door, pursuing the power of Rails and other modern web frameworks. Rails in particular had a lively community, a perfect combination of opinionated defaults and flexibility, and the power of Ruby Gems to leverage prepackaged common code.

Something kept me from jumping ship, and I was glad for that when I found Laravel. It offered everything I was drawn to in Rails, but it wasn't just a Rails clone; this was an innovative framework with incredible documentation, a welcoming community, and clear influences from many languages and frameworks.

Since that day I've been able to share my journey of learning Laravel through blogging and speaking at conferences; I've written dozens of apps in Laravel for side and work projects, and I've met thousands of Laravel developers online and in person. I have plenty of tools in my toolkit at our consultancy, but I am honestly happiest when I sit down in front of a command line and type `laravel new project`.

What This Book Is About

This is not the first book about Laravel, and it won't be the last. I don't intend for this to be a book that covers every line of code or every implementation pattern. I don't want this to be the sort of book that goes out of date when a new version of Laravel is released. Instead, its primary purpose is to provide developers with a high-level overview and concrete examples to learn what they need to get started, as quickly as possible. Rather than mirroring the docs, I want to help you understand the foundational concepts behind Laravel.

Laravel is a powerful and flexible PHP framework. It has a thriving community and a wide ecosystem of tools, and as a result it's growing in appeal and reach. This book is for developers who already know how to make websites and applications and want to quickly learn how to do so in Laravel.

Laravel's documentation is thorough and excellent. If you find that I don't cover any particular topic deeply enough for your liking, I encourage you to visit the online documentation (*http://laravel.com/docs*) and dig deeper into that particular topic.

I think you will find the book a comfortable balance between high-level introduction and concrete application, and by the end you should feel comfortable writing an entire application in Laravel, from scratch. And, if I did my job well, you'll be excited to try.

Who This Book Is For

This book assumes knowledge of basic object-oriented programming practices, PHP (or at least the general syntax of C-family languages), and the basic concepts of the Model–View–Controller (MVC) pattern and templating. If you've never made a website before, you may find yourself in over your head. But as long as you have some programming experience, you don't have to know anything about Laravel before you read this book—we'll cover everything you need to know, from the simplest "Hello, world!"

Laravel can run on any operating system, but there will be some Bash (shell) commands in the book that are easiest to run on Linux/Mac OS. Windows users may have a harder time with these commands and with modern PHP development, but if you follow the instructions to get Homestead (a Linux virtual machine) running, you'll be able to run all of the commands from there.

How This Book Is Structured

This book is structured in what I imagine to be a chronological order: if you're building your first web app with Laravel, the early chapters cover the foundational components you'll need to get started, and the later chapters cover less foundational or more esoteric features.

Each section of the book can be read on its own, but for someone new to the framework, I've tried to structure the chapters so that it's actually very reasonable to start from the beginning and read until the end.

Where applicable, each chapter will end with two sections: "Testing" and "TL;DR." If you're not familiar, TL;DR means "too long; didn't read." These final sections will show you how to write tests for the features covered in each chapter and give a high-level overview of what was covered.

The book is written for Laravel 5.3, but because Laravel 5.1 is the latest LTS release, any features that are new in 5.2 or 5.3 will be identified.

Conventions Used in This Book

The following typographical conventions are used in this book:

Italic
> Indicates new terms, URLs, email addresses, filenames, and file extensions.

`Constant width`
> Used for program listings, as well as within paragraphs to refer to program elements such as variable or function names, databases, data types, environment variables, statements, and keywords.

`Constant width bold`
> Shows commands or other text that should be typed literally by the user.

`Constant width italic`
> Shows text that should be replaced with user-supplied values or by values determined by context.

 This element signifies a tip or suggestion.

 This element signifies a general note.

 This element indicates a warning or caution.

O'Reilly Safari

 *Safari* (formerly Safari Books Online) is membership-based training and reference platform for enterprise, government, educators, and individuals.

Members have access to thousands of books, training videos, Learning Paths, interactive tutorials, and curated playlists from over 250 publishers, including O'Reilly

Media, Harvard Business Review, Prentice Hall Professional, Addison-Wesley Professional, Microsoft Press, Sams, Que, Peachpit Press, Adobe, Focal Press, Cisco Press, John Wiley & Sons, Syngress, Morgan Kaufmann, IBM Redbooks, Packt, Adobe Press, FT Press, Apress, Manning, New Riders, McGraw-Hill, Jones & Bartlett, and Course Technology, among others.

For more information, please visit *http://oreilly.com/safari*.

How to Contact Us

Please address comments and questions concerning this book to the publisher:

> O'Reilly Media, Inc.
> 1005 Gravenstein Highway North
> Sebastopol, CA 95472
> 800-998-9938 (in the United States or Canada)
> 707-829-0515 (international or local)
> 707-829-0104 (fax)

We have a web page for this book, where we list errata, examples, and any additional information. You can access this page at *http://bit.ly/laravel-up-and-running*.

To comment or ask technical questions about this book, send email to *bookquestions@oreilly.com*.

For more information about our books, courses, conferences, and news, see our website at *http://www.oreilly.com*.

Find us on Facebook: *http://facebook.com/oreilly*

Follow us on Twitter: *http://twitter.com/oreillymedia*

Watch us on YouTube: *http://www.youtube.com/oreillymedia*

Acknowledgments

This book would not have happened without the gracious support of my amazing wife Tereva or the understanding ("Daddy's writing, buddy!") of my son Malachi. And while she wasn't explicitly aware of it, my daughter Mia was around for almost the entire creation of the book, so this book is dedicated to the whole family. There were many, many long evening hours and weekend Starbucks trips that took me away from my family, and I couldn't be more grateful for their support and also their presence just making my life awesome.

Additionally, the entire Tighten Co. family has supported and encouraged me through the writing of the book, several even editing (Keith Damiani, editor extraordinaire) and helping me with challenging code samples (Adam Wathan, King of the Collection Pipeline). Dan Sheetz, my partner in Tighten crime, has been gracious enough to watch me while away many a work hour cranking on this book and was nothing but supportive and encouraging; and Dave Hicking, our operations manager, helped me arrange my schedule and work responsibilities around writing time.

Taylor Otwell deserves thanks and honor for creating Laravel—and therefore creating so many jobs and helping so many developers love our lives that much more. He deserves appreciation for how he's focused on developer happiness and how hard he's worked to have empathy for developers and to build a positive and encouraging community. But I also want to thank him for being a kind, encouraging, and challenging friend. Taylor, you're a boss.

Thanks to Jeffrey Way, who I still contend to be one of the best teachers on the Internet. He originally introduced me to Laravel and still introduces more people every day. He's also, unsurprisingly, a fantastic human being whom I'm glad to call a friend.

Thank you to Jess D'Amico, Shawn McCool, Ian Landsman, and Taylor for seeing value in me as a conference speaker early on and giving me a platform to teach from. Thanks to Dayle Rees for making it so easy for so many to learn Laravel in the early days.

Thanks to every person who put their time and effort into writing blog posts about Laravel, especially early on: Eric Barnes, Chris Fidao, Matt Machuga, Jason Lewis, Ryan Tablada, Dries Vints, Maks Surguy, and so many more.

And thanks to the entire community of friends on Twitter, IRC, and Slack who've interacted with me over the years. I wish I could name every name, but I would miss some and then feel awful about missing them. You all are brilliant, and I'm honored to get to interact with you on a regular basis.

Thanks to my O'Reilly editor, Ally MacDonald, and all of my technical editors: Keith Damiani, Michael Dyrynda, Adam Fairholm, and Myles Hyson.

And, of course, thanks to the rest of my family and friends, who supported me directly or indirectly through this process—my parents and siblings, the Gainesville community, other business owners and authors, other conference speakers, and the inimitable DCB. I need to stop writing because by the time I run out of space here I'll be thanking my Starbucks baristas.

## CHAPTER 1

Why Laravel?

In the early days of the dynamic web, writing a web application looked a lot different than it does today. Developers then were responsible for writing the code for not just the unique business logic of our applications, but also each of the components that are so common across sites—user authentication, input validation, database access, templating, and more.

Today, programmers have dozens of application development frameworks and thousands of components and libraries easily accessible. It's a common refrain among programmers that, by the time you learn one framework, three newer (and purportedly better) frameworks have popped up intending to replace it.

"Just because it's there" might be a valid justification for climbing a mountain, but there are better reasons to choose to use a specific framework—or to use a framework at all. It's worth asking the question: why frameworks? More specifically, why Laravel?

Why Use a Framework?

It's easy to see why it's beneficial to use the individual components, or packages, that are available to PHP developers. With packages, someone else is responsible for developing and maintaining an isolated piece of code that has a well-defined job, and in theory that person has a deeper understanding of this single component than you have time to have.

Frameworks like Laravel—and Symfony, Silex, Lumen, and Slim—prepackage a collection of third-party components together with custom framework "glue" like configuration files, service providers, prescribed directory structures, and application bootstraps. So, the benefit of using a framework in general is that someone has made decisions not just about individual components for you, but also about *how those components should fit together*.

"I'll Just Build It Myself"

Let's say you start a new web app without the benefit of a framework. Where do you begin? Well, it should probably route HTTP requests, so you now need to evaluate all of the HTTP request and response libraries available and pick one. Then a router. Oh, and you'll probably need to set up some form of routes configuration file. What syntax should it use? Where should it go? What about controllers? Where do they live, and how are they loaded? Well, you probably need a dependency injection container to resolve the controllers and their dependencies. But which one?

Furthermore, what if you do take the time to answer all those questions and successfully create your application—what's the impact on the next developer? What about when you have four such custom-framework–based applications, or a dozen, and you have to remember where the controllers live in each, or what the routing syntax is?

Consistency and Flexibility

Frameworks address this issue by providing a carefully considered answer to the question "Which component should we use here?" and ensuring that the particular components chosen work well together. Additionally, frameworks provide conventions that reduce the amount of code a developer new to the project has to understand—if you understand how routing works in one Laravel project, for example, you understand how it works in all Laravel projects.

When someone prescribes rolling your own framework for each new project, what they're really advocating is the ability to *control* what does and doesn't go into your application's foundation. That means the best frameworks will not only provide you with a solid foundation, but also give you the freedom to customize to your heart's content. And this, as I'll show you in the rest of this book, is part of what makes Laravel so special.

A Short History of Web and PHP Frameworks

An important part of being able to answer the question "Why Laravel?" is understanding Laravel's history—and understanding what came before it. Prior to Laravel's rise in popularity, there were a variety of frameworks and other movements in PHP and other web development spaces.

Ruby on Rails

David Heinemeier Hansson released the first version of Ruby on Rails in 2004, and it's been hard to find a web application framework since then that hasn't been influenced by Rails in some way.

Rails popularized MVC, RESTful JSON APIs, convention over configuration, Active-Record, and many more tools and conventions that had a profound influence on the way web developers approached their applications—especially with regard to rapid application development.

The Influx of PHP Frameworks

It was clear to most developers that Rails, and similar web application frameworks, were the wave of the future, and PHP frameworks, including those admittedly imitating Rails, starting popping up quickly.

CakePHP was the first in 2005, and it was soon followed by Symfony, CodeIgniter, Zend Framework, and Kohana (a CodeIgniter fork). Yii arrived in 2008, and Aura and Slim in 2010. 2011 brought FuelPHP and Laravel, both of which were not quite CodeIgniter offshoots, but instead proposed as alternatives.

Some of these frameworks were more Rails-y, focusing on database object-relational mappers (ORMs), MVC structures, and other tools targeting rapid development. Others, like Symfony and Zend, focused more on enterprise design patterns and ecommerce.

The Good and the Bad of CodeIgniter

CakePHP and CodeIgniter were the two early PHP frameworks that were most open about how much their inspiration was drawn from Rails. CodeIgniter quickly rose to fame and by 2010 was arguably the most popular of the independent PHP frameworks.

CodeIgniter was simple, easy to use, and boasted amazing documentation and a strong community. But its use of modern technology and patterns advanced slowly, and as the framework world grew and PHP's tooling advanced, CodeIgniter started falling behind in terms of both technological advances and out-of-the-box features. Unlike many other frameworks, CodeIgniter was managed by a company, and they were slow to catch up with PHP 5.3's newer features like namespaces and the moves to GitHub and later Composer. It was in 2010 that Taylor Otwell, Laravel's creator, became dissatisfied enough with CodeIgniter that he set off to write his own framework.

Laravel 1, 2, and 3

The first beta of Laravel 1 was released in June 2011, and it was written completely from scratch. It featured a custom ORM (Eloquent); closure-based routing (inspired by Ruby Sinatra); a module system for extension; and helpers for forms, validation, authentication, and more.

Early Laravel development moved quickly, and Laravel 2 and 3 were released in November 2011 and February 2012, respectively. They introduced controllers, unit testing, a command-line tool, an inversion of control (IoC) container, Eloquent relationships, and migrations.

Laravel 4

With Laravel 4, Taylor rewrote the entire framework from the ground up. By this point Composer, PHP's now-ubiquitous package manager, was showing signs of becoming an industry standard and Taylor saw the value of rewriting the framework as a collection of components, distributed and bundled together by Composer.

Taylor developed a set of components under the code name *Illuminate* and, in May 2013, released Laravel 4 with an entirely new structure. Instead of bundling the majority of its code as a download, Laravel now pulled in the majority of its components from Symfony (another framework that released its components for use by others) and the Illuminate components through Composer.

Laravel 4 also introduced queues, a mail component, facades, and database seeding. And because Laravel was now relying on Symfony components, it was announced that Laravel would be mirroring (not exactly, but soon after) the six-monthly release schedule Symfony follows.

Laravel 5

Laravel 4.3 was scheduled to release in November 2014, but as development progressed, it became clear that the significance of its changes merited a major release, and Laravel 5 was released in February 2015.

Laravel 5 featured a revamped directory structure, removal of the form and HTML helpers, the introduction of the contract interfaces, a spate of new views, Socialite for social media authentication, Elixir for asset compilation, Scheduler to simplify cron, dotenv for simplified environment management, form requests, and a brand new REPL (read–evaluate–print loop).

What's So Special About Laravel?

So what is it that sets Laravel apart? Why is it worth having more than one PHP framework at any time? They all use components from Symfony anyway, right? Let's talk a bit about what makes Laravel "tick."

The Philosophy of Laravel

You only need to read through the Laravel marketing materials and READMEs to start seeing its values. Taylor uses light-related words like "Illuminate" and "Spark."

And then there are these: "Artisans." "Elegant." Also, these: "Breath of fresh air." "Fresh start." And finally: "Rapid." "Warp speed."

The two most strongly communicated values of the framework are to increase developer speed and developer happiness. Taylor has described the "Artisan" language as intentionally contrasting against more utilitarian values. You can see the genesis of this sort of thinking in his 2011 question on StackExchange (*http://bit.ly/2dT5kmS*) in which he stated, "Sometimes I spend ridiculous amounts of time (hours) agonizing over making code look pretty"—just for the sake of a better experience of looking at the code itself. And he's often talked about the value of making it easier and quicker for developers to take their ideas to fruition, getting rid of unnecessary barriers to creating great products.

Laravel is, at its core, about equipping and enabling developers. Its goal is to provide clear, simple, and beautiful code and features that help developers quickly learn, start, and develop, and write code that's simple, clear, and will last.

The concept of targeting developers is clear across Laravel materials. "Happy developers make the best code" is written in the documentation. "Developer happiness from download to deploy" was the unofficial slogan for a while. Of course, any tool or framework will say it wants developers to be happy. But having developer happiness as a *primary* concern, rather than secondary, has had a huge impact on Laravel's style and decision-making progress. Where other frameworks may target architectural purity as their primary goal, or compatibility with the goals and values of enterprise development teams, Laravel's primary focus is on serving the individual developer.

How Laravel Achieves Developer Happiness

Just saying you want to make developers happy is one thing. Doing it is another, and it requires you to question what in a framework is most likely to make developers unhappy and what is most likely to make them happy. There are a few ways Laravel tries to make developers' lives easier.

First, Laravel is a rapid application development framework. That means it focuses on a shallow (easy) learning curve and on minimizing the steps between starting a new app and publishing it. All of the most common tasks in building web applications, from database interactions to authentication to queues to email to caching, are made simpler by the components Laravel provides. But Laravel's components aren't just great on their own; they provide a consistent API and predictable structures across the entire framework. That means that, when you're trying something new in Laravel, you're more than likely going to end up saying, "… and it just works."

This doesn't end at the framework itself, either. Laravel provides an entire ecosystem of tools for building and launching applications. You have Homestead and Valet for local development, Forge for server management, and Envoyer for advanced deployment. And there's a suite of add-on packages: Cashier for payments and subscriptions, Echo for WebSockets, Scout for search, Passport for API authentication, Socialite for social login, and Spark to bootstrap your SaaS. Laravel is trying to take the repetitive work out of developers' jobs so they can do something unique.

Next, Laravel focuses on "convention over configuration"—meaning that if you're willing to use Laravel's defaults, you'll have to do much less work than with other frameworks that require you to declare all of your settings even if you're using the recommended configuration. Projects built on Laravel take less time than those built on most other PHP frameworks.

Laravel also focuses deeply on simplicity. It's possible to use dependency injection and mocking and the Data Mapper pattern and repositories and Command Query Responsibility Segregation and all sorts of other more complex architectural patterns with Laravel, if you want. But while other frameworks might suggest using those tools and structures on every project, Laravel and its documentation and community lean toward starting with the simplest possible implementation—a global function here, a facade there, ActiveRecord over there. This allows developers to create the simplest possible application to solve for their needs.

An interesting source of how Laravel is different is that its creator and its community are more connected to and inspired by Ruby and Rails and functional programming languages than by Java. There's a strong current in modern PHP to lean toward verbosity and complexity, embracing the more Java-esque aspects of PHP. But Laravel tends to be on the other side, embracing expressive, dynamic, and simple coding practices and language features.

The Laravel Community

If this book is your first exposure to the Laravel community, you have something special to look forward to. One of the distinguishing elements of Laravel, which has contributed to its growth and success, is the welcoming, teaching community that surrounds it. From Jeffrey Way's Laracasts (*https://laracasts.com/*) video tutorials to Laravel News (*https://laravel-news.com/*) to Slack and IRC channels, from Twitter friends to bloggers to the Laracon conferences, Laravel has a rich and vibrant community full of folks who've been around since day one and folks who are on their own day one. And this isn't an accident:

> From the very beginning of Laravel, I've had this idea that all people want to feel like they are part of something. It's a natural human instinct to want to belong and be accepted into a group of other like-minded people. So, by injecting personality into a web framework and being really active with the community, that type of feeling can grow in the community.
>
> —Taylor Otwell, *Product and Support interview*

Taylor understood from the early days of Laravel that a successful open source project needed two things: good documentation and a welcoming community. And those two things are now hallmarks of Laravel.

How It Works

Up until now, everything I've shared here has been entirely abstract. What about the code, you ask? Let's dig into a simple application (Example 1-1) so you can see what working with Laravel day-to-day is actually like.

Example 1-1. "Hello, World" in routes/web.php

```
// File: routes/web.php
<?php

Route::get('/', function() {
    return 'Hello, World!';
});
```

The simplest possible action you can take in a Laravel application is to define a route and return a result any time someone visits that route. If you initialize a brand new Laravel application on your machine, define the route in Example 1-1, and then serve the site from the *public* directory, you'll have a fully functioning "Hello, World" example (see Figure 1-1).

Hello, World!

Figure 1-1. Returning "Hello, World!" with Laravel

It looks very similar to do the same with controllers, as you can see in Example 1-2.

Example 1-2. "Hello, World" with controllers

```
// File: routes/web.php
<?php

Route::get('/', 'WelcomeController@index');

// File: app/Http/Controllers/WelcomeController.php
<?php
namespace app\Http\Controllers;
```

```
class WelcomeController
{
    public function index()
    {
        return 'Hello, World!';
    }
}
```

And if we're storing our greetings in the database, it'll also look pretty similar (see Example 1-3).

Example 1-3. Multigreeting "Hello, World" with database access

```
// File: routes/web.php
<?php

Route::get('/', function() {
    return Greeting::first()->body;
});

// File: app/Greeting.php
<?php

use Illuminate\Database\Eloquent\Model;

class Greeting extends Model {}

// File: database/migrations/2015_07_19_010000_create_greetings_table.php
<?php

use Illuminate\Database\Migrations\Migration;
use Illuminate\Database\Schema\Blueprint;

class CreateGreetingsTable extends Migration
{
    public function up()
    {
        Schema::create('greetings', function (Blueprint $table) {
            $table->increments('id');
            $table->string('body');
            $table->timestamps();
        });
    }

    public function down()
    {
        Schema::drop('greetings');
    }
}
```

Example 1-3 might be a bit overwhelming, and if so, just skip over it. We'll learn about everything that's happening here in later chapters, but you can already see that with just a few lines of code, we've set up database migrations and models and pulled records out. It's just that simple.

Why Laravel?

So—why Laravel?

Because Laravel helps you bring your ideas to reality with no wasted code, using modern coding standards, surrounded by a vibrant community, with an empowering ecosystem of tools.

And because you, dear developer, deserve to be happy.

## CHAPTER 2

Setting Up a Laravel Development Environment

Part of PHP's success has been because it's hard to find a web server that *can't* serve PHP. However, modern PHP tools have stricter requirements than those of the past. The best way to develop for Laravel is to ensure a consistent local and remote server environment for your code, and thankfully, the Laravel ecosystem has a few tools for this.

System Requirements

Everything we'll cover in this chapter is possible with Windows machines, but you'll need dozens of pages of custom instructions and caveats. I'll leave those instructions and caveats to actual Windows users, so the examples here and in the rest of the book will focus on Unix/Linux/Mac OS developers.

Whether you choose to serve your website by installing PHP and other tools on your local machine, serve your development environment from a virtual machine via Vagrant, or rely on a tool like MAMP/WAMP/XAMPP, your development environment will need to have all of the following installed in order to serve Laravel sites:

- PHP >= 5.6.4 for Laravel 5.3 or PHP >= 5.5.9 for 5.1 and 5.2
- OpenSSL PHP extension
- PDO PHP extension
- Mbstring PHP extension
- Tokenizer PHP extension

Composer

Whatever machine you're developing on will need to have Composer (*https://getcom poser.org/*) installed globally. If you're not familiar with Composer, it's a tool that's at the foundation of most modern PHP development. Composer is a dependency manager for PHP, much like NPM for Node or RubyGems for Ruby. You'll need Composer to install Laravel, update Laravel, and bring in external dependencies.

Local Development Environments

For many projects, hosting your development environment using a simpler tool set will be enough. If you already have MAMP or WAMP or XAMPP installed on your system, that will likely be fine to run Laravel. You can also just run Laravel with PHP's built-in web server, assuming your system PHP is the right version.

All you really need *to get started* is the ability to run PHP. Everything past that is up to you.

However, Laravel offers two tools for local development, Valet and Homestead, and we'll cover both briefly. If you're unsure of which to use, I'd recommend using Valet and just skimming the Homestead section; however, both tools are valuable and worth understanding.

Laravel Valet

If you want to use PHP's built-in web server, your simplest option is to serve every site from a *localhost* URL. If you run `php -S localhost:8000 -t public` from your Laravel site's root folder, PHP's built-in web server will serve your site at *http://local host:8000/*. You can also run `php artisan serve` once you have your application set up to easily spin up an equivalent server.

But if you're interested in tying each of your sites to a specific development domain, you'll need to get comfortable with your operating system's hosts file and use a tool like dnsmasq (*http://bit.ly/2eNPJ5T*). Let's instead try something simpler.

If you're a Mac user (there are also unofficial forks for Windows and Linux), Laravel Valet (*https://laravel.com/docs/valet*) takes away the need to connect your domains to your application folders. Valet installs dnsmasq and a series of PHP scripts that make it possible to type `laravel new myapp && open myapp.dev` and for it to *just work*. You'll need to install a few tools using Homebrew, which the documentation will walk you through, but the steps from initial installation to serving your apps are few and simple.

Install Valet (see the docs (*https://laravel.com/docs/valet*) for the latest installation instruction—it's under very active development at this time of writing), and point it at one or more directories where your sites will live. I ran `valet park` from my *~/Sites* directory, which is where I put all of my under-development apps. Now, you can just add *.dev* to the end of the directory name and visit it in your browser.

Valet makes it easy to serve all folders in a given folder as "FOLDERNAME.dev" using `valet park`, to serve just a single folder using `valet link`, to open the Valet-served domain for a folder using `valet open`, to serve the Valet site with HTTPS using `valet secure`, and to open an ngrok tunnel so you can share your site with others with `valet share`.

Laravel Homestead

Homestead is another tool you might want to use to set up your local development environment. It's a configuration tool that sits on top of Vagrant and provides a pre-configured virtual machine image that is perfectly set up for Laravel development, *and* mirrors the most common production environment that many Laravel sites run on.

Setting up Homestead

If you choose to use Homestead, it's going to take a bit more work to set up than something like MAMP or Valet. The benefits are myriad, however: configured correctly, your local environment can be incredibly close to your remote working environment; you won't have to worry about updating your dependencies on your local machine; and you can learn all about the structure of Ubuntu servers from the safety of your local machine.

What Tools Do Homestead Offer?

You can always upgrade the individual components of your Homestead virtual machine, but here are a few important tools Homestead comes with by default:

- To run the server and serve the site, Ubuntu, PHP, and Nginx (a web server similar to Apache).
- For database/storage and queues, MySQL, Postgres, Redis, Memcached, and *beanstalkd*.
- For build steps and other tools, Node.

Installing Homestead's dependencies

First, you'll need to download and install either VirtualBox (*https://www.virtual box.org/wiki/Downloads*) or VMWare. VirtualBox is most common because it's free.

Next, download and install Vagrant (*https://www.vagrantup.com/downloads.html*).

Vagrant is convenient because it makes it easy for you to create a new local virtual machine from a precreated "box," which is essentially a template for a virtual machine. So, the next step is to run `vagrant box add laravel/homestead` from your terminal to download the box.

Installing Homestead

Next, let's actually install Homestead. You can install multiple instances of Homestead (perhaps hosting a different Homestead box per project), but I prefer a single Homestead virtual machine for all of my projects. If you want one per project, you'll want to install Homestead in your project directory; check the Homestead documentation online (*https://laravel.com/docs/5.3/homestead*) for instructions. If you want a single virtual machine for all of your projects, install Homestead in your user's home directory using the following command:

```
git clone https://github.com/laravel/homestead.git ~/Homestead
```

Now, run the initialization script from wherever you put the *Homestead* directory:

```
bash ~/Homestead/init.sh
```

This will place Homestead's primary configuration file, *Homestead.yaml*, in a new *~/.homestead* directory.

Configuring Homestead

Open up *Homestead.yaml* and configure it how you'd like. Here's what it looks like out of the box:

```
ip: "192.168.10.10"
memory: 2048
cpus: 1
provider: virtualbox

authorize: ~/.ssh/id_rsa.pub

keys:
    - ~/.ssh/id_rsa

folders:
    - map: ~/Code
      to: /home/vagrant/Code

sites:
    - map: homestead.app
      to: /home/vagrant/Code/Laravel/public

databases:
    - homestead
```

```
# blackfire:
#     - id: foo
#       token: bar
#       client-id: foo
#       client-token: bar

# ports:
#     - send: 50000
#       to: 5000
#     - send: 7777
#       to: 777
#       protocol: udp
```

You'll need to tell it your provider (likely `virtualbox`), point it to your public SSH key (by default `~/.ssh/id_rsa.pub`; if you don't have one, GitHub (*http://bit.ly/ 2e7Auof*) has a great tutorial on creating SSH keys), map folders and sites to their local machine equivalents, and provision a database.

Mapping folders in Homestead allows you to edit files on your local machine and have those files show up in your Vagrant box so they can be served. For example, if you have a *~/Sites* directory where you put all of your code, you'd map the folders in Homestead by replacing the folders section in *Homestead.yaml* with the following:

```
folders:
    - map: ~/Sites
      to: /home/vagrant/Sites
```

You've now just created a directory in your Homestead virtual machine at */home/ vagrant/Sites* that will mirror your computer's directory at *~/Sites*.

Top-level domains for development sites

You can choose any convention for local development sites' URLs, but *.app* and *.dev* are the most common. Homestead suggests `.app`, so if I'm working on a local copy of *symposiumapp.com*, I'll develop at *symposiumapp.app*.

Now, let's set up our first example website. Let's say our live site is going to be *project-Name.com*. In *Homestead.yaml*, we'll map our local development folder to *project-Name.app*, so we have a separate URL to visit for local development:

```
sites:
    - map: projectName.app
      to: /home/vagrant/Sites/projectName/public
```

As you can see, we're mapping the URL *projectName.app* to the virtual machine directory */home/vagrant/Sites/projectName/public*, which is the *public* folder within our Laravel install. We'll learn more about that later.

Finally, you're going to need to teach your local machine that, when you try to visit *projectName.app*, it should look at your computer's local IP address to resolve it. Mac and Linux users should edit */etc/hosts*, and Windows users *C:\Windows\System32\drivers\etc\hosts*. Add a line to this file that looks like this:

```
192.168.10.10  projectName.app
```

Once you've provisioned Homestead, your site will be available to browse (on your machine) at *http://projectName.app/*.

Creating databases in Homestead

Just like you can define a site in *Homestead.yaml*, you can also define a database. Databases are a lot simpler, because you're only telling the provisioner to *create* a database with that name, nothing else. We do this as follows:

```
databases:
    - projectname
```

Provisioning Homestead

The first time you actually turn on a Homestead box, you need to tell Vagrant to initialize it. Navigate to your *Homestead* directory and run `vagrant up`:

```
cd ~/Homestead
vagrant up
```

Your Homestead box is now up and running; it's mirroring a local folder, and it's serving it to a URL you can visit in any browser on your computer. It also has created a MySQL database. Now that you have that environment running, you're ready to set up your first Laravel project—but first, a quick note about using Homestead day-to-day.

Using Homestead day-to-day

It's common to leave your Homestead virtual machine up and running at all times, but if you don't, or if you have recently restarted your computer, you'll need to know how to spin the box up and down.

Since Homestead is based on Vagrant commands, you'll just use basic Vagrant commands for most Homestead actions. Change to the directory where you installed Homestead (using `cd`) and then run the following commands as needed:

- `vagrant up` spins up the Homestead box.
- `vagrant suspend` takes a snapshot of where the box is and then shuts it down; like "hibernating" a desktop machine.
- `vagrant halt` shuts the entire box down; like turning off a desktop machine.

- `vagrant destroy` deletes the entire box; like formatting a desktop machine.

- `vagrant provision` re-runs the provisioners on the preexisting box.

Connecting to Homestead databases from desktop applications

If you use a desktop application like Sequel Pro, you'll likely want to connect to your Homestead MySQL databases from your host machine. These settings will get you going:

- **Connection type:** Standard (non-SSH)

- **Host:** 127.0.0.1

- **Username:** homestead

- **Password:** secret

- **Port:** 33060

Creating a New Laravel Project

There are two ways to create a new Laravel project, but both are run from the command line. The first option is to globally install the Laravel installer tool (using Composer); the second is to use Composer's `create-project` feature.

You can learn about both options in more detail on the Installation documentation page (*http://laravel.com/docs/installation*), but I'd recommend the Laravel installer tool.

Installing Laravel with the Laravel Installer Tool

If you have Composer installed globally, installing the Laravel installer tool is as simple as running the following command:

```
composer global require "laravel/installer=~1.1"
```

Once you have the Laravel installer tool installed, spinning up a new Laravel project is simple. Just run this command from your command line:

```
laravel new projectName
```

This will create a new subdirectory of your current directory named *projectName* and install a bare Laravel project in it.

Installing Laravel with Composer's create-project Feature

Composer also offers a feature called `create-project` for creating new projects with a particular skeleton. To use this tool to create a new Laravel project, issue the following command:

```
composer create-project laravel/laravel projectName --prefer-dist
```

Just like the installer tool, this will create a subdirectory of your current directory named *projectName* that contains a skeleton Laravel install, ready for you to develop.

Laravel's Directory Structure

When you open up a directory that contains a skeleton Laravel application, you'll see the following files and directories:

```
app/
bootstrap/
config/
database/
public/
resources/
routes/
storage/
tests/
vendor/
.env
.env.example
.gitattributes
.gitignore
artisan
composer.json
composer.lock
gulpfile.js
package.json
phpunit.xml
readme.md
server.php
```

Let's walk through them one by one to get familiar.

The Folders

The root directory contains the following folders by default:

- *app* is where the bulk of your actual application will go. Models, controllers, route definitions, commands, and your PHP domain code all go in here.

- *bootstrap* contains the files that the Laravel framework uses to boot every time it runs.

- *config* is where all the configuration files live.
- *database* is where database migrations and seeds live.
- *public* is the directory the server points to when it's serving the website. This contains *index.php*, which is the front controller that kicks off the bootstrapping process and routes all requests appropriately. It's also where any public-facing files like images, stylesheets, scripts, or downloads go.
- *resources* is where non-PHP files that are needed for other scripts live. Views, language files, and (optionally) Sass/LESS and source JavaScript files live here.
- *routes* is where all of the route definitions live, both for HTTP routes and "console routes," or Artisan commands.
- *storage* is where caches, logs, and compiled system files live.
- *tests* is where unit and integration tests live.
- *vendor* is where Composer installs its dependencies. It's Git-ignored (marked to be excluded from your version control system), as Composer is expected to run as a part of your deploy process on any remote servers.

The Loose Files

The root directory also contains the following files:

- *.env* and *.env.example* are the files that dictate the environment variables (variables that are expected to be different in each environment and are therefore not committed to version control). *.env.example* is a template that each environment should duplicate to create its own *.env* file, which is Git-ignored.
- *artisan* is the file that allows you to run Artisan commands (see Chapter 7) from the command line.
- *.gitignore* and *.gitattributes* are Git configuration files.
- *composer.json* and *composer.lock* are the configuration files for Composer; *composer.json* is user-editable and *composer.lock* is not. These files share some basic information about this project and also define its PHP dependencies.
- *gulpfile.js* is the (optional) configuration file for Elixir and Gulp. This is for compiling and processing your frontend assets.
- *package.json* is like *composer.json* but for frontend assets.
- *phpunit.xml* is a configuration file for PHPUnit, the tool Laravel uses for testing out of the box.
- *readme.md* is a Markdown file giving a basic introduction to Laravel.

- *server.php* is a backup server that tries to allow less-capable servers to still preview the Laravel application.

Configuration

The core settings of your Laravel application—database connection, queue and mail settings, etc.—live in files in the *config* folder. Each of these files returns an array, and each value in the array will be accessible by a config key that is comprised of the filename and all descendant keys, separated by dots (`.`)

So, if you create a file at *config/services.php* that looks like this:

```
// config/services.php
return [
    'sparkpost' => [
        'secret' => 'abcdefg'
    ]
];
```

you will now have access to that config variable using `config('services.spark post.secret')`.

Any configuration variables that should be distinct for each environment (and therefore not committed to source control) will instead live in your *.env* files. Let's say you want to use a different Bugsnag API key for each environment. You'd set the config file to pull it from *.env*:

```
// config/services.php
return [
    'bugsnag' => [
        'api_key' => env('BUGSNAG_API_KEY')
    ]
];
```

This `env()` helper function pulls a value from your *.env* file with that same key. So now, add that key to your *.env* (settings for this environment) and *.env.example* (template for all environments) files:

```
BUGSNAG_API_KEY=oinfp9813410942
```

Your *.env* file already contains quite a few environment-specific variables needed by the framework, like which mail driver you'll be using and what your basic database settings are.

Up and Running

You're now up and running with a bare Laravel install. Run `git init`, commit the bare files with `git add .` and `git commit`, and you're ready to start coding. That's it!

And if you're using Valet, you can run the following commands and instantly see your site live in your browser:

```
laravel new myProject && cd myProject && valet open
```

Every time I start a new project, these are the steps I take:

```
laravel new myProject
cd myProject
git init
git add .
git commit -m "Initial commit"
```

I keep all of my sites in a *~/Sites* folder, which I have set up as my primary Valet directory, so in this case I'd instantly have *myProject.dev* accessible in my browser with no added work. I can edit *.env* and point it to a particular database, add that database in my MySQL app, and I'm ready to start coding.

Lambo

I perform the this set of steps so often that I created a simple global Composer package to do it for me. It's called Lambo, and you can learn more about it on GitHub (*https://github.com/tightenco/lambo*).

Testing

In every chapter after this, the "Testing" section at the end of the chapter will show you how to write tests for the feature or features that were covered. Since this chapter doesn't cover a testable feature, let's talk tests quickly. (To learn more about writing and running tests in Laravel, head over to Chapter 12.)

Out of the box, Laravel brings in PHPUnit as a dependency and is configured to run the tests in any file in the *tests* directory whose name ends with *Test.php* (for example, *tests/UserTest.php*).

So, the simplest way to write tests is to create a file in the *tests* directory with a name that ends with *Test.php*. And the easiest way to run them is to run `./vendor/bin/phpunit` from the command line (in the project root).

If any tests require database access, be sure to run your tests from the machine where your database is hosted—so if you're hosting your database in Vagrant, make sure to `ssh` into your Vagrant box to run your tests from there. Again, you can learn about this and much more in Chapter 12.

TL;DR

Since Laravel is a PHP framework, it's very simple to serve it locally. Laravel also provides two tools for managing your local development: a simpler tool called Valet that uses your local machine to provide your dependencies, and a preconfigured Vagrant setup named Homestead. Laravel relies on, and can be installed by, Composer, and comes out of the box with a series of folders and files that reflect both its conventions and its relationship with other open source tools.

## CHAPTER 3

Routing and Controllers

The essential function of any web application framework is to take requests from a user and deliver responses, usually via HTTP(S). This means defining an application's routes is the first and most important project to tackle when learning a web framework; without routes, you have no ability to interact with the end user.

In this chapter we will examine routes in Laravel and show how to define them, how to point them to the code they should execute, and how to use Laravel's routing tools to handle a diverse array of routing needs.

Route Definitions

In a Laravel application, you will define your "web" routes in *routes/web.php* and your "API" routes in *routes/api.php*. Web routes are those that will be visited by your end users; API routes are those for your API, if you have one. For now, we'll primarily focus on the routes in *routes/web.php*.

> In projects running versions of Laravel prior to 5.3, there will be only one routes file, located at *app/Http/routes.php*.

The simplest way to define a route is to match a path (e.g., /) with a closure, as seen in Example 3-1.

Example 3-1. Basic route definition

```
// routes/web.php
Route::get('/', function () {
    return 'Hello, World!';
});
```

What's a Closure?

Closures are PHP's version of anonymous functions. A closure is a function that you can pass around as an object, assign to a variable, pass as a parameter to other functions and methods, or even serialize.

You've now defined that, if anyone visits / (the root of your domain), Laravel's router should run the closure defined there and return the result. Note that we `return` our content and don't `echo` or `print` it.

A quick introduction to middleware

You might be wondering, "Why am I returning 'Hello, World!' instead of echoing it?"

There are quite a few answers, but the simplest is that there are a lot of wrappers around Laravel's request and response cycle, including something called middleware. When your route closure or controller method is done, it's not time to send the output to the browser yet; returning the content allows it to continue flowing through the response stack and the middleware before it is returned back to the user.

Many simple websites could be defined entirely within the web routes file. With a few simple GET routes combined with some templates as illustrated in Example 3-2, you can can serve a classic website easily.

Example 3-2. Sample website

```
Route::get('/', function () {
    return view('welcome');
});

Route::get('about', function () {
    return view('about');
});

Route::get('products', function () {
```

```
    return view('products');
});

Route::get('services', function () {
    return view('services');
});
```

 Static calls

If you have much experience developing PHP, you might be surprised to see static calls on the Route class. This is not actually a static method per se, but rather service location using Laravel's facades, which we'll cover in Chapter 11.

If you prefer to avoid facades, you can accomplish these same definitions like this:

```
$router->get('/', function () {
    return 'Hello, World!';
});
```

HTTP Methods

If you're not familiar with the idea of HTTP methods, read on in this chapter for more information, but for now, just know that every HTTP request has a "verb," or action, along with it. Laravel allows you to define your routes based on which verb was used; the most common are GET and POST, followed by PUT, DELETE, and PATCH. Each method communicates a different thing to the server, and to your code, about the intentions of the caller.

Route Verbs

You might've noticed that we've been using Route::get in our route definitions. This means we're telling Laravel to only match for these routes when the HTTP request uses the GET action. But what if it's a form POST, or maybe some JavaScript sending PUT or DELETE requests? There are a few other options for methods to call on a route definition, as illustrated in Example 3-3.

Example 3-3. Route verbs

```
Route::get('/', function () {
    return 'Hello, World!';
});

Route::post('/', function () {});

Route::put('/', function () {});
```

```
Route::delete('/', function () {});

Route::any('/', function () {});

Route::match(['get', 'post'], '/', function () {});
```

Route Handling

As you've probably guessed, passing a closure to the route definition is not the only way to teach it how to resolve a route. Closures are quick and simple, but the larger your application gets, the clumsier it becomes to put all of your routing logic in one file. Additionally, applications using route closures can't take advantage of Laravel's route caching (more on that later), which can shave up to hundreds of milliseconds off of each request.

The other common option is to pass a controller name and method as a string in place of the closure, as in Example 3-4.

Example 3-4. Routes calling controller methods

```
Route::get('/', 'WelcomeController@index');
```

This is telling Laravel to pass requests to that path to the index() method of the App \Http\Controllers\WelcomeController controller. This method will be passed the same parameters and treated the same way as a closure you might've alternatively put in its place.

Route Parameters

If the route you're defining has parameters—segments in the URL structure that are variable—it's simple to define them in your route and pass them to your closure (see Example 3-5).

Example 3-5. Route parameters

```
Route::get('users/{id}/friends', function ($id) {
    //
});
```

The Naming Relationship Between Route Parameters and Closure/Controller Method Parameters

As you can see in Example 3-5, it's most common to use the same names for your route parameters ({id}) and the method parameters they inject into your route definition (function ($id)). But is this necessary?

Unless you're using route/model binding, no. The only thing that defines which route parameter matches with which method parameter is their order (left to right), as you can see here:

```
Route::get('users/{userId}/comments/{commentId}', function (
    $thisIsActuallyTheRouteId,
    $thisisReallyTheCommentId
    ) {
    //
});
```

That having been said, just because you *can* make them different doesn't mean you *should*. I recommend keeping them the same for the sake of future developers, who could get tripped up by inconsistent naming.

You can also make your route parameters optional by including a question mark (?) after the parameter name, as illustrated in Example 3-6. In this case, you should also provide a default value for the route's corresponding variable.

Example 3-6. Optional route parameters

```
Route::get('users/{id?}', function ($id = 'fallbackId') {
    //
});
```

And you can use regular expressions (regexes) to define that a route should only match if a parameter meets particular requirements, as in Example 3-7.

Example 3-7. Regular expression route constraints

```
Route::get('users/{id}', function ($id) {
    //
})->where('id', '[0-9]+');

Route::get('users/{username}', function ($username) {
    //
})->where('username', '[A-Za-z]+');

Route::get('posts/{id}/{slug}', function ($id, $slug) {
```

```
    //
})->where(['id' => '[0-9]+', 'slug' => '[A-Za-z]+']);
```

As you've probably guessed, if you visit a path that matches a route string, but the regex doesn't match the parameter, it won't be matched. Since routes are matched top to bottom, `users/abc` would skip the first closure in Example 3-7, but it would be matched by the second closure, so it would get routed there. On the other hand, `posts/abc/123` wouldn't match any of the closures, so it would return a 404 Not Found error.

Route Names

The simplest way to refer to these routes elsewhere in your application is just by their path. There's a `url()` helper to simplify that linking in your views, if you need it; see Example 3-8 for an example. The helper will prefix your route with the full domain of your site.

Example 3-8. URL helper

```
<a href="<?php echo url('/'); ?>">
// outputs <a href="http://myapp.com/">
```

However, Laravel also allows you to name each route, which enables you to refer to it without explicitly referencing the URL. This is helpful because it means you can give simple nicknames to complex routes, and also because linking them by name means you don't have to rewrite your frontend links if the paths change (see Example 3-9).

Example 3-9. Defining route names

```
// Defining a route with name in routes/web.php:
Route::get('members/{id}', 'MembersController@show')->name('members.show');

// Link the route in a view using the route() helper
<a href="<?php echo route('members.show', ['id' => 14]); ?>">
```

This example illustrates a few new concepts. First, we're using fluent route definition to add the name, by chaining the `name()` method after the `get()` method. This method allows us to name the route, giving it a short alias to make it easier to reference elsewhere.

Defining custom routes in Laravel 5.1

Fluent route definitions don't exist in Laravel 5.1. You'll need to instead pass an array to the second parameter of your route definition; check the Laravel docs to see more about how this works. Here's Example 3-9 in Laravel 5.1:

```
Route::get('members/{id}', [
    'as' => 'members.show',
    'uses' => 'MembersController@show'
]);
```

In our example, we've named this route `members.show`; *resourcePlural.action* is a common convention within Laravel for route and view names.

Route Naming Conventions

You can name your route anything you'd like, but the common convention is to use the plural of the resource name, then a period, then the action. So, here are the routes most common for a resource named `photo`:

```
photos.index
photos.create
photos.store
photos.show
photos.edit
photos.update
photos.destroy
```

To learn more about these conventions, see "Resource Controllers" on page 41.

We also introduced the `route()` helper. Just like `url()`, it's intended to be used in views to simplify linking to a named route. If the route has no parameters, you can simply pass the route name: (`route('members.index')`) and receive a route string `http://myapp.com/members/index`). If it has parameters, pass them in as an array as the second parameter like we did in this example.

In general, I recommend using route names instead of paths to refer to your routes, and therefore using the `route()` helper instead of the `url()` helper. Sometimes it can get a bit clumsy—for example, if you're working with multiple subdomains—but it provides an incredible level of flexibility to later change the application's routing structure without major penalty.

Passing Route Parameters to the route() Helper

When your route has parameters (e.g., `users/{id}`), you need to define those parameters when you're using the `route()` helper to generate a link to the route.

There are a few different ways to pass these parameters. Let's imagine a route defined as `users/{userId}/comments/{commentId}`. If the user ID is 1 and the comment ID is 2, let's look at a few options we have available to us:

Option 1:

```
route('users.comments.show', [1, 2])
// http://myapp.com/users/1/comments/2
```

Option 2:

```
route('users.comments.show', ['userId' => 1, 'commentId' => 2])
// http://myapp.com/users/1/comments/2
```

Option 3:

```
route('users.comments.show', ['commentId' => 2, 'userId' => 1])
// http://myapp.com/users/1/comments/2
```

Option 4:

```
route('users.comments.show', ['userId' => 1, 'commentId' => 2, 'opt' => 'a'])
// http://myapp.com/users/1/comments/2?opt=a
```

As you can see, nonkeyed array values are assigned in order; keyed array values are matched with the route parameters matching their keys, and anything left over is added as a query parameter.

Route Groups

Often a group of routes share a particular characteristic—a certain authentication requirement, a path prefix, or perhaps a controller namespace. Defining these shared characteristics again and again on each route not only seems tedious but also can muddy up the shape of your routes file and obscure some of the structures of your application.

Route groups allow you to group several routes together, and apply any shared configuration settings once to the entire group, to reduce this duplication. Additionally, route groups are visual cues to future developers (and to your own brain) that these routes are grouped together.

To group two or more routes together, you "surround" the route definitions with a route group, as shown in Example 3-10. In reality, you're actually passing a closure to the group definition, and defining the grouped routes within that closure.

Example 3-10. Defining a route group

```
Route::group([], function () {
    Route::get('hello', function () {
        return 'Hello';
    });
    Route::get('world', function () {
        return 'World';
    });
});
```

By default, a route group doesn't actually do anything. There's no difference between the group in Example 3-10 and separating a segment of your routes with code comments. The empty array that's the first parameter, however, allows you to pass a variety of configuration settings that will apply to the entire route group.

Middleware

Probably the most common use for route groups is to apply middleware to a group of routes. We'll learn more about middleware in Chapter 10, but, among other things, they're what Laravel uses for authenticating users and restricting guest users from using certain parts of a site.

In Example 3-11, we're creating a route group around the `dashboard` and `account` views and applying the `auth` middleware to both. In this example, it means users have to be logged in to the application to view the dashboard or the account page.

Example 3-11. Restricting a group of routes to logged-in users only

```
Route::group(['middleware' => 'auth'], function () {
    Route::get('dashboard', function () {
        return view('dashboard');
    });
    Route::get('account', function () {
        return view('account');
    });
});
```

Applying middleware in controllers

Often it's clearer and more direct to attach middleware to your routes in the controller instead of at the route definition. You can do this by calling the middleware() method in the constructor of your controller. The string you pass to the middleware() method is the name of the middleware, and you can optionally chain modifier methods (only() and except()) to define which methods will receive that middleware:

```
class DashboardController extends Controller
{
    public function __construct()
    {
        $this->middleware('auth');

        $this->middleware('admin-auth')
            ->only('admin');

        $this->middleware('team-member')
            ->except('admin');
    }
}
```

Note that, if you're doing a lot of "only" and "except" customizations, that's often a sign that you should break out a new controller for the exceptional routes.

Path Prefixes

If you have a group of routes that share a segment of their path—for example, if your site's API is prefixed with /api—you can use route groups to simplify this structure (see Example 3-12).

Example 3-12. Prefixing a group of routes

```
Route::group(['prefix' => 'api'], function () {
    Route::get('/', function () {
        // Handles the path /api
    });
    Route::get('users', function () {
        // Handles the path /api/users
    });
});
```

Note that each prefixed group also has a / route that represents the root of the prefix —in Example 3-12 that's /api.

Subdomain Routing

Subdomain routing is the same as route prefixing, but it's scoped by subdomain instead of route prefix. There are two primary uses for this. First, you may want to present different sections of the application (or entirely different applications) to different subdomains. Example 3-13 shows how you can achieve this.

Example 3-13. Subdomain routing

```
Route::group(['domain' => 'api.myapp.com'], function () {
    Route::get('/', function () {
        //
    });
});
```

Second, you might want to set part of the subdomain as a parameter, as illustrated in Example 3-14. This is most often done in cases of multitenancy (think Slack or Harvest, where each company gets its own subdomain, like *tighten.slack.co*).

Example 3-14. Parameterized subdomain routing

```
Route::group(['domain' => '{account}.myapp.com'], function () {
    Route::get('/', function ($account) {
        //
    });
    Route::get('users/{id}', function ($account, $id) {
        //
    });
});
```

Note that any parameters for the group get passed into the grouped routes' methods as the first parameter(s).

Namespace Prefixes

When you're grouping routes by subdomain or route prefix, it's likely their controllers have a similar PHP namespace. In the API example, all of the API routes' controllers might be under an `API` namespace. By using the route group namespace prefix, as shown in Example 3-15, you can avoid long controller references in groups like `"API/ControllerA@index"` and `"API/ControllerB@index"`.

Example 3-15. Route group namespace prefixes

```
// App\Http\Controllers\ControllerA
Route::get('/', 'ControllerA@index');

Route::group(['namespace' => 'API'], function () {
```

```
// App\Http\Controllers\API\ControllerB
    Route::get('api/', 'ControllerB@index');
});
```

Name Prefixes

The prefixes don't stop there. It's common that route names will reflect the inheritance chain of path elements, so `users/comments/5` will be served by a route named `users.comments.show`. In this case, it's common to use a route group around all of the routes that are beneath the `users.comments` resource.

Just like we can prefix URL segments and controller namespaces, we can also prefix strings to the route name. With route group name prefixes, we can define that every route within this group should have a given string prefixed to its name. In this context, we're prefixing `"users."` to each route name, then `"comments."` (see Example 3-16).

Example 3-16. Route group name prefixes

```
Route::group(['as' => 'users.', 'prefix' => 'users'], function () {
    Route::group(['as' => 'comments.', 'prefix' => 'comments'], function () {
        // Route name will be users.comments.show
        Route::get('{id}', function () {
            //
        })->name('show');
    });
});
```

Views

In a few of the route closures we've looked at so far, we've seen something along the lines of `return view('account')`. What's going on here?

If you're not familiar with the Model–View–Controller (MVC) pattern, *views* (or templates) are files that describe what some particular output should look like. You might have views for JSON or XML or emails, but the most common views in a web framework output HTML.

In Laravel, there are two formats of view you can use out of the box: plain PHP, or Blade templates (see Chapter 4). The difference is in the filename: *about.php* will be rendered with the PHP engine, and *about.blade.php* will be rendered with the Blade engine.

Three ways to load a view()

There are three different ways to return a view. For now, just concern yourself with `view()`, but if you ever see `View::make()`, it's the same thing, and you could also inject the `Illuminate\View\View Factory` if you prefer.

Once you've loaded a view, you have the option to simply return it (as in Example 3-17), which will work fine if the view doesn't rely on any variables from the controller.

Example 3-17. Simple view() usage

```
Route::get('/', function () {
    return view('home');
});
```

This code looks for a view in *resources/views/home.blade.php* or *resources/views/home.php*, and loads its contents and parses any inline PHP or control structures until you have just the view's output. Once you return it, it's passed on to the rest of the response stack and eventually returned to the user.

But what if you need to pass in variables? Take a look at Example 3-18.

Example 3-18. Passing variables to views

```
Route::get('tasks', function () {
    return view('tasks.index')
        ->with('tasks', Task::all());
});
```

This closure loads the *resources/views/tasks/index.blade.php* or *resources/views/tasks/index.php* view and passes it a single variable named `tasks`, which contains the result of the `Task::all()` method. `Task::all()` is an Eloquent database query we'll learn about in Chapter 8.

Using View Composers to Share Variables with Every View

Sometimes it can become a hassle to pass the same variables over and over. There may be a variable that you want accessible to every view in the site, or to a certain class of views or a certain included subview—for example, all views related to tasks, or the header partial.

It's possible to share certain variables with every template or just certain templates, like in the following code:

```
view()->share('variableName', 'variableValue');
```

To learn more, check out "View Composers and Service Injection" on page 64.

Controllers

I've mentioned controllers a few times, but until now most of the examples have shown route closures. If you're not familiar with the MVC pattern (Figure 3-1), controllers are essentially classes that organize the logic of one or more routes together in one place. Controllers tend to group similar routes together, especially if your application is structured along a traditionally CRUD-like format; in this case, a controller might handle all the actions that can be performed on a particular resource.

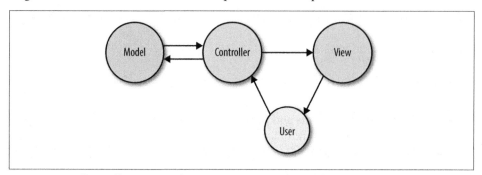

Figure 3-1. A basic illustration of MVC

What is CRUD?

CRUD stands for *create*, *read*, *update*, *delete*, which are the four primary operations that web applications most commonly provide on a resource. For example, you can create a new blog post, you can read that post, you can update it, or you can delete it.

It may be tempting to cram all of the application's logic into the controllers, but it's better to think of controllers as the traffic cops that route HTTP requests around your application. Since there are other ways requests can come into your application —cron jobs, Artisan command-line calls, queue jobs, etc.—it's wise to not rely on controllers for much behavior. This means a controller's primary job is to capture the intent of an HTTP request and pass it on to the rest of the application.

So, let's create a controller. One easy way to do this is with an Artisan command, so from the command line run the following:

```
php artisan make:controller TasksController
```

Artisan and Artisan generators

Laravel comes bundled with a command-line tool called Artisan. Artisan can be used to run migrations, create users and other database records manually, and perform many other manual, one-time tasks.

Under the `make` namespace, Artisan provides tools for generating skeleton files for a variety of system files. That's what allows us to run `php artisan make:controller`.

To learn more about this and other Artisan features, see Chapter 7.

This will create a new file named *TasksController.php* in *app/Http/Controllers*, with the contents shown in Example 3-19.

Example 3-19. Default generated controller

```php
<?php

namespace App\Http\Controllers;

use Illuminate\Http\Request;

use App\Http\Requests;

class TasksController extends Controller
{
}
```

Modify this file as shown in Example 3-20, creating a new public method called `home()`. We'll just return some text there.

Example 3-20. Simple controller example

```php
<?php

use App\Http\Controllers\Controller;

class TasksController extends Controller
{
    public function home()
    {
        return 'Hello, World!';
    }
}
```

Then like we learned before, we'll hook up a route to it, as shown in Example 3-21.

Example 3-21. Route for the simple controller

```
// routes/web.php
<?php

Route::get('/', 'TasksController@home');
```

That's it. Visit the / route and you'll see the words "Hello, World!"

Controller Namespacing

In Example 3-21 we referenced a controller with the fully qualified class name of `App\Http\Controllers\TasksController`, but we only used the class name. This isn't because we can simply reference controllers by their class name. Rather, we can ignore the `App\Http\Controllers\` when we reference controllers; by default, Laravel is configured to look for controllers within that namespace.

This means that if you have a controller with the fully qualified class name of `App\Http\Controllers\API\ExercisesController`, you'd reference it in a route definition as `API\ExercisesController`.

The most common use of a controller method, then, will be something like Example 3-22.

Example 3-22. Common controller method example

```
// TasksController.php
...
public function index()
{
    return view('tasks.index')
        ->with('tasks', Task::all());
}
```

This controller method loads the *resources/views/tasks/index.blade.php* or *resources/views/tasks/index.php* view and passes it a single variable named `tasks`, which contains the result of the `Task::all()` Eloquent method.

Generating resource controllers

If you ever used `php artisan make:controller` in Laravel prior to 5.3, you might be expecting it to autogenerate methods for all of the basic resource routes like `create()` and `update()`. You can bring this behavior back in Laravel 5.3 by passing the `--resource` flag when you create the controller:

```
php artisan make:controller TasksController --resource
```

Getting User Input

The second most common action to perform in a controller method is to take input from the user and act on it. That introduces a few new concepts, so let's take a look at a bit of sample code and walk through the new pieces.

First, let's bind it quickly; see Example 3-23.

Example 3-23. Binding basic form actions

```
// routes/web.php
Route::get('tasks/create', 'TasksController@create');
Route::post('tasks', 'TasksController@store');
```

Notice that we're binding the GET action of tasks/create (which shows the form) and the POST action of tasks/ (which is where we POST when we're creating a new task). We can assume the create() method in our controller just shows a form, so let's look at the store() method in Example 3-24.

Example 3-24. Common form input controller method

```
// TasksController.php
...
public function store()
{
    $task = new Task;
    $task->title = Input::get('title');
    $task->description = Input::get('description');
    $task->save();

    return redirect('tasks');
}
```

This example makes use of Eloquent models and the redirect() functionality, and we'll talk about them more later, but you can see what we're doing here: we create a new Task, pull data out of the user input and set it on the task, save it, and then redirect back to the page that shows all tasks.

There are two main ways to get user input from a POST: the Input facade, which we used here, and the Request object, which we'll talk about next.

Importing facades

If you follow any of these examples, whether in controllers or any other PHP class that is namespaced, you might find errors showing that the facade cannot be found. This is because they're not present in *every* namespace, but rather they're made available in the root namespace.

So, in Example 3-24, we'd need to import the Input facade at the top of the file. There are two ways to do that: either we can import \Input, or we can import Illuminate\Support\Facades\Input. For example:

```php
<?php

namespace App\Http\Controllers;

use Illuminate\Support\facades\Input;

class TasksController
{
    public function store()
    {
        $task = new Task;
        $task->title = Input::get('title');
        $task->description = Input::get('description');
        $task->save();

        return redirect('tasks');
    }
}
```

As you can see, we can get the value of any user-provided information, whether from a query parameter or a POST value, using Input::get('fieldName'). So our user filled out two fields on the "add task" page: "title" and "description." We retrieve both using the Input facade, save them to the database, and then return.

Injecting Dependencies into Controllers

Laravel's facades present a simple interface to the most useful classes in Laravel's codebase. You can get information about the current request and user input, the session, caches, and much more.

But if you prefer to inject your dependencies, or if you want to use a service that doesn't have a facade, you'll need to find some way to bring instances of these classes into your controller.

This is our first exposure to Laravel's service container. For now, if this is unfamiliar, you can think about it as a little bit of Laravel magic; or, if you want to know more about how it's actually functioning, you can skip ahead to Chapter 11.

All controller methods (including the constructors) are resolved out of Laravel's container, which means anything you typehint that the container knows how to resolve will be automatically injected.

As a nice example, what if you'd prefer having an instance of the `Request` object instead of using the facade? Just typehint `Illuminate\Http\Request` in your method parameters, like in Example 3-25.

Example 3-25. Controller method injection via typehinting

```
// TasksController.php
...
public function store(\Illuminate\Http\Request $request)
{
    $task = new Task;
    $task->title = $request->input('title');
    $task->description = $request->input('description');
    $task->save();

    return redirect('tasks');
}
```

So, you've defined a parameter that must be passed into the `store()` method. And since you typehinted it, and since Laravel knows how to resolve that class name, you're going to have the `Request` object ready for you to use in your method with no work on your part. No explicit binding, no anything else—it's just there as the `$request` variable.

By the way, this is actually how I and many other Laravel developers prefer to get the user input: inject an instance of the `Request` and read the user input from there, instead of relying on the `Input` facade.

Resource Controllers

Sometimes naming the methods in your controllers can be the hardest part of writing a controller. Thankfully, Laravel has some conventions for all of the routes of a traditional REST/CRUD controller (called a "resource controller" in Laravel); additionally, it comes with a generator out of the box and a convenience route definition that allows you to bind an entire resource controller at once.

To see the methods that Laravel expects for a resource controller, let's generate a new controller from the command line:

```
php artisan make:controller MySampleResourceController --resource
```

Now open *app/Http/Controllers/MySampleResourceController.php*. You'll see it comes prefilled with quite a few methods. Let's walk over what each represents. We'll use a `Task` as an example.

The methods of Laravel's resource controllers

For each, you can see the HTTP verb, the URL, the controller method name, and the "name." Table 3-1 shows the HTTP verb, the URL, the controller method name, and the "name" for each of these default methods.

Table 3-1. The methods of Laravel's resource controllers

Verb	URL	Controller method	Name	Description
GET	tasks	index()	tasks.index	Show all tasks
GET	tasks/create	create()	tasks.create	Show the create task form
POST	tasks	store()	tasks.store	Accept form submission from the create task form
GET	tasks/{task}	show()	tasks.show	Show one task
GET	tasks/{task}/edit	edit()	tasks.edit	Edit one task
PUT/PATCH	tasks/{task}	update()	tasks.update	Accept form submission from the edit task form
DELETE	tasks/{task}	destroy()	tasks.destroy	Delete one task

Binding a resource controller

So, we've seen that these are the conventional route names to use in Laravel, and also that it's easy to generate a resource controller with methods for each of these default routes. Thankfully, you don't have to generate routes for each of these controller methods by hand, if you don't want to. Instead, there's a trick for that, and it's called "resource controller binding." Take a look at Example 3-26.

Example 3-26. Resource controller binding

```
// routes/web.php
Route::resource('tasks', 'TasksController');
```

This will automatically bind all of the routes for this resource to the appropriate method names on the specified controller. It'll also name these routes appropriately; for example, the index() method on the tasks resource controller will be named tasks.index.

artisan route:list

If you ever find yourself in a situation where you're wondering what routes your current application has available, there's a tool for that: from the command line, run php artisan route:list and you'll get a listing of all of the available routes (see Figure 3-2).

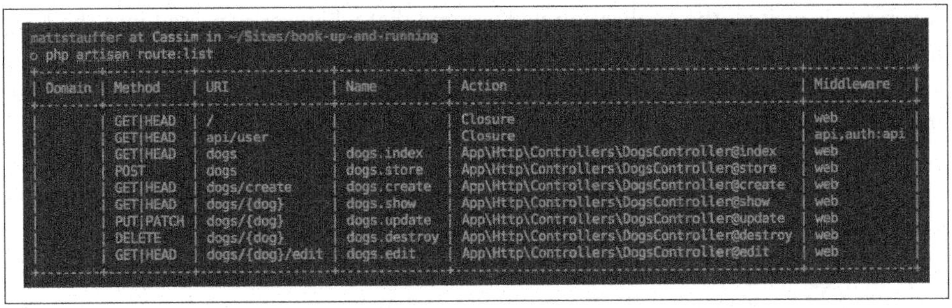

```
mattstauffer at Cassim in ~/Sites/book-up-and-running
o php artisan route:list
+--------+-----------+-------------------+--------------+-----------------------------------------------+--------------+
| Domain | Method    | URI               | Name         | Action                                        | Middleware   |
+--------+-----------+-------------------+--------------+-----------------------------------------------+--------------+
|        | GET|HEAD  | /                 |              | Closure                                       | web          |
|        | GET|HEAD  | api/user          |              | Closure                                       | api,auth:api |
|        | GET|HEAD  | dogs              | dogs.index   | App\Http\Controllers\DogsController@index     | web          |
|        | POST      | dogs              | dogs.store   | App\Http\Controllers\DogsController@store     | web          |
|        | GET|HEAD  | dogs/create       | dogs.create  | App\Http\Controllers\DogsController@create    | web          |
|        | GET|HEAD  | dogs/{dog}        | dogs.show    | App\Http\Controllers\DogsController@show      | web          |
|        | PUT|PATCH | dogs/{dog}        | dogs.update  | App\Http\Controllers\DogsController@update    | web          |
|        | DELETE    | dogs/{dog}        | dogs.destroy | App\Http\Controllers\DogsController@destroy   | web          |
|        | GET|HEAD  | dogs/{dog}/edit   | dogs.edit    | App\Http\Controllers\DogsController@edit      | web          |
+--------+-----------+-------------------+--------------+-----------------------------------------------+--------------+
```

Figure 3-2. php artisan route:list example

Route Model Binding

One of the most common routing patterns is that the first line of any controller method tries to find the resource with the given ID, like in Example 3-27.

Example 3-27. Getting a resource for each route

```
Route::get('conferences/{id}', function ($id) {
    $conference = Conference::findOrFail($id);
});
```

Laravel provides a feature that simplifies this pattern called "route model binding." This allows you to define that a particular parameter name (e.g., `{conference}`) will indicate to the route resolver that it should look up an Eloquent record with that ID and then pass it in as the parameter *instead* of just passing the ID.

There are two kinds of route model binding: implicit and custom (or explicit).

Implicit Route Model Binding

The simplest way to use route model binding is to name your route parameter something unique to that model (e.g., name it `$conference` instead of `$id`), then typehint that parameter in the closure/controller method and use the same variable name there. It's easier to show than to describe, so take a look at Example 3-28.

Example 3-28. Using an explicit route model binding

```
Route::get('conferences/{conference}', function (Conference $conference) {
    return view('conferences.show')->with('conference', $conference);
});
```

Because the route parameter (`{conference}`) is the same as the method parameter (`$conference`), and the method parameter is typehinted with a `Conference` model (`Conference $conference`), Laravel sees this as a route model binding. Every time this route is visited, the application will assume that whatever is passed into the URL in place of {conference} is an ID that should be used to look up a `Conference`, and then that resulting model instance will be passed in to your closure or controller method.

Customizing the route key for an Eloquent model

Any time an Eloquent model is looked up via a URL segment (usually because of route model binding), the default column Eloquent will look it up by is its primary key (ID).

To change the column your Eloquent model uses for URL lookups, add a method to your model named `getRouteKeyName()`:

```
public function getRouteKeyName()
{
    return 'slug';
}
```

Now, a URL like `conferences/{conference}` will expect to get the slug instead of the ID, and will perform its lookups accordingly.

Implicit route model binding was added in Laravel 5.2, so you won't have access to it in 5.1.

Custom Route Model Binding

To manually configure route model bindings, add a line like the one in Example 3-29 to the `boot()` method in `App\Providers\RouteServiceProvider`.

Example 3-29. Adding a route model binding

```
public function boot(Router $router)
{
    // Just allows the parent's boot() method to still run
    parent::boot($router);

    // Perform the binding
    $router->model('event', Conference::class);
}
```

You've now defined that whenever a route has a parameter in its definition named {event}, as demonstrated in Example 3-30, the route resolver will return an instance of the `Conference` class with the ID of that URL parameter.

Example 3-30. Using an explicit route model binding

```
Route::get('events/{event}', function (Conference $event) {
    return view('events.show')->with('event', $event);
});
```

Route Caching

If you're looking to squeeze every millisecond out of your load time, you may want to take a look at route caching. One of the pieces of Laravel's bootstrap that can take anywhere from a few dozen to a few hundred milliseconds is parsing the *routes/** files, and route caching speeds up this process dramatically.

To cache your routes file, you need to be using all controller and resource routes (no route closures). If your app isn't using any route closures, you can run php artisan route:cache, Laravel will serialize the results of your *routes/** files. If you want to delete the cache, run php artisan route:clear.

Here's the drawback: Laravel will now match routes against that cached file instead of your actual *routes/** files. You can make endless changes to those files, and they won't take effect until you run route:cache again. This means you'll have to recache every time you make a change, which introduces a lot of potential for confusion.

Here's what I would recommend instead: since Git ignores the route cache file by default anyway, consider only using route caching on your production server, and run the php artisan route:cache command every time you deploy new code (whether via a Git post-deploy hook, a Forge deploy command, or as a part of whatever other deploy system you use). This way you won't have confusing local development issues, but your remote environment will still benefit from route caching.

Form Method Spoofing

Sometimes, you need to manually define which HTTP verb a form should send as. HTML forms only allow for GET or POST, so if you want any other sort of verb, you'll need to specify that yourself.

An Introduction to HTTP Verbs

We've talked about the GET and POST HTTP verbs already. If you're not familiar with HTTP verbs, the other two most common ones are PUT and DELETE, but there's also HEAD, OPTIONS, PATCH, and two others that are pretty much never used in normal web development, TRACE and CONNECT.

Here's the quick rundown: GET requests a resource and HEAD asks for a headers-only version of the GET, POST creates a resource, PUT overwrites a resource and PATCH modifies a resource, DELETE deletes a resource, and OPTIONS asks the server which verbs are allowed at this URL.

HTTP Verbs in Laravel

As we've shown already, you can define which verbs a route will match in the route definition using Route::get(), Route::post(), Route::any(), or Route::match(). You can also match with Route::patch(), Route::put(), and Route::delete().

But how does one send a request other than GET with a web browser? First, the method attribute in an HTML form determines its HTTP verb: if your form has a method of "GET", it will submit via query parameters and a GET method; if the form has a method of "POST", it will submit via the post body and a POST method.

JavaScript frameworks make it easy to send other requests, like DELETE and PATCH. But if you find yourself needing to submit HTML forms in Laravel with verbs other than GET or POST, you'll need to use form method spoofing, which is spoofing the HTTP method in an HTML form.

HTTP Method Spoofing in HTML Forms

To inform Laravel that the form you're currently submitting should be treated as something other than POST, add a hidden variable named _method with the value of either "PUT", "PATCH", or "DELETE", and Laravel will match and route that form sub-mission as if it were actually a request with that verb.

The form in Example 3-31, since it's passing Laravel the method of "DELETE", will match routes defined with Route::delete() but not those with Route::post().

Example 3-31. Form method spoofing

```
<form action="/tasks/5" method="POST">
    <input type="hidden" name="_method" value="DELETE">
</form>
```

CSRF Protection

If you've tried to create and submit a form in a Laravel application already—including the form in Example 3-31—you've likely run into the dreaded TokenMismatchExcep tion.

By default, all routes in Laravel except "read-only" routes (those using GET, HEAD, or OPTIONS) are protected against cross-site request forgery (CSRF) attacks by requiring a token, in the form of an input named _token, to be passed along with each request. This token is generated at the start of every session, and every non–read-only route compares the submitted _token against the session token.

What is CSRF?

A cross-site request forgery is when one website pretends to be another. The goal is for someone to hijack your users' access to your website, by submitting forms from *their* website to *your* website via the logged-in user's browser.

The best way around CSRF attacks is to protect all inbound routes —POST, DELETE, etc.—with a token, which Laravel does out of the box.

You have two options for getting around this. The first, and preferred, method is to add the _token input to each of your submissions. In HTML forms, that's simple; look at Example 3-32.

Example 3-32. CSRF tokens

```
<form action="/tasks/5" method="POST">
    <?php echo csrf_field(); ?>
    <!-- or: -->
    <input type="hidden" name="_token" value="<?php echo csrf_token(); ?>">
</form>
```

In JavaScript applications, it's a bit more work, but not much. The most common solution for sites using JavaScript frameworks is to store the token on every page in a <meta> tag like this one:

```
<meta name="csrf-token" content="<?php echo csrf_token(); ?>" id="token">
```

Storing the token in a <meta> tag makes it easy to bind it to the correct HTTP header, which you can do once globally for all requests from your JavaScript framework, like in Example 3-33.

Example 3-33. Globally binding a header for CSRF

```
// in jQuery:
$.ajaxSetup({
    headers: {
        'X-CSRF-TOKEN': $('meta[name="csrf-token"]').attr('content')
    }
});

// in Vue:
Vue.http.interceptors.push((request, next) => {
```

```
request.headers['X-CSRF-TOKEN'] =
    document.querySelector('#token').getAttribute('content');

    next();
});
```

Laravel will check the X-CSRF-TOKEN on every request, and valid tokens passed there will mark the CSRF protection as satisfied.

Note that the Vue syntax for CSRF in this example is not necessary if you're working with the 5.3 Vue bootstrap; it already does this work for you.

Redirects

So far the only things we've returned from a controller method or route definition have been views. But there are a few other structures we can return to give the browser instructions on how to behave.

First, let's cover the redirect. There are two common ways to generate a redirect; we'll use the redirect global helper here, but you may prefer the facade. Both create an instance of Illuminate\Http\RedirectResponse, perform some convenience methods on it, and then return it. You can also do this manually, but you'll have to do a little more work yourself. Take a look at Example 3-34 to see a few ways you can return a redirect.

Example 3-34. Different ways to return a redirect

```
// Using the global helper to generate a redirect response
Route::get('redirect-with-helper', function () {
    return redirect()->to('login');
});

// Using the global helper shortcut
Route::get('redirect-with-helper-shortcut', function () {
    return redirect('login');
});

// Using the facade to generate a redirect response
Route::get('redirect-with-facade', function () {
    return Redirect::to('login');
});
```

Note that the redirect() helper exposes the same methods as the Redirect facade, but it also has a shortcut; if you pass parameters directly to the helper, instead of chaining methods after it, it's a shortcut to the to() redirect method.

redirect()->to()

The method signature for the to() method for redirects looks like this:

```
function to($to = null, $status = 302, $headers = [], $secure = null)
```

$to is a valid internal path; $status is the HTTP status (defaulting to 302 FOUND); $headers allows you to define which HTTP headers to send along with your redirect; and $secure allows you to override the default choice of http versus https (which is normally set based on your current request URL). Example 3-35 shows another example of its use.

Example 3-35. redirect()->to()

```
Route::get('redirect', function () {
    return redirect()->to('home');

    // or same, using the shortcut:

    return redirect('home');
});
```

redirect()->route()

The route() method is the same as the to() method, but rather than pointing to a particular path, it points to a particular route name (see Example 3-36).

Example 3-36. redirect()->route()

```
Route::get('redirect', function () {
    return redirect()->route('conferences.index');
});
```

Note that, since some route names require parameters, its parameter order is a little different. route() has an optional second parameter for the route parameters:

```
function route($to = null, $parameters = [], $status = 302, $headers = [])
```

So, using it might look a little like Example 3-37.

Example 3-37. redirect()->route() with parameters

```
Route::get('redirect', function () {
    return redirect()->route('conferences.show', ['conference' => 99]);
});
```

redirect()->back()

Because of some of the built-in conveniences of Laravel's session implementation, your application will always have knowledge of what the user's previously visited page was. That opens up the opportunity for a `redirect()->()` redirect, which simply redirects the user to whatever page she came from. There's also a global shortcut for this: `back()`.

Other Redirect Methods

The redirect service provides other methods that are less commonly used, but still available:

- `home()` redirects to a route named `home`.
- `refresh()` redirects to the same page the user is currently on.
- `away()` allows for redirecting to an external URL without the default URL validation.
- `secure()` is like `to()` with the `secure` parameter set to `"true"`.
- `action()` allows you to link to a controller and method like this: `redirect()->action('MyController@myMethod')`.
- `guest()` is used internally by the auth system (discussed in Chapter 9); when a user visits a route he's not authenticated for, this captures the "intended" route and then redirects the user (usually to a login page).
- `intended()` is also used internally by the auth system; after a successful authentication, this grabs the "intended" URL stored by the `guest()` method and redirects the user there.

redirect()->with()

When you're redirecting users to different pages, you often want to pass certain data along with them. You could manually flash the data to the session, but Laravel has some convenience methods to help you with that.

Most commonly, you can pass along either an array of keys and values or a single key and value using `with()`, like in Example 3-38.

Example 3-38. Redirect with data

```
Route::get('redirect-with-key-value', function () {
    return redirect('dashboard')
        ->with('error', true);
});
```

```
Route::get('redirect-with-array', function () {
    return redirect('dashboard')
        ->with(['error' => true, 'message' => 'Whoops!']);
});
```

Chaining methods on redirects

As with many other facades, most calls to the `Redirect` facade can accept fluent method chains, like the `with()` calls in Example 3-38. Learn more about fluency in "What Is a Fluent Interface?" on page 146.

You can also use `withInput()`, as in Example 3-39, to redirect with the user's form input flashed; this is most common in the case of a validation error, where you want to send the user back to the form she just came from.

Example 3-39. Redirect with form input

```
Route::get('form', function () {
    return view('form');
});

Route::post('form', function () {
    return redirect('form')
        ->withInput()
        ->with(['error' => true, 'message' => 'Whoops!']);
});
```

The easiest way to get the flashed input that was passed with `withInput()` is using the `old()` helper, which can be used to get all old input (`old()`) or just the value for a particular key (`old('username')`, with the second parameter as the default if there is no old value). You'll commonly see this in views, which allows this HTML to be used both on the "create" and the "edit" view for this form:

```
<input name="username" value="<?=
    old('username', 'Default username instructions here');
?>">
```

Speaking of validation, there is also a useful method for passing errors along with a redirect response: `withErrors()`. You can pass it any "provider" of errors, which may be an error string, an array of errors, or, most commonly, an instance of the Illuminate `Validator`, which we'll cover in Chapter 10. Example 3-40 shows an example of its use.

Example 3-40. Redirect with errors

```
Route::post('form', function () {
    $validator = Validator::make($request->all()), $this->validationRules);

    if ($validator->fails()) {
        return redirect('form')
            ->withErrors($validator)
            ->withInput();
    }
});
```

withErrors() automatically shares an $errors variable with the views of the page it's redirecting to, for you to handle however you'd like.

The validate() shortcut in controller methods

Like how Example 3-40 looks? If you're defining your routes in a controller, there's a simple and powerful tool that cleans up that code. Read more in "validate() in the Controller Using ValidatesRequests" on page 103.

Aborting the Request

Aside from returning views and redirects, the most common way to exit a route is to abort. There are a few globally available methods (abort(), abort_if(), and abort_unless()), which optionally take HTTP status codes, a message, and a headers array as parameters.

As Example 3-41 shows, abort_if() and abort_unless() take a first parameter that is evaluated for its truthiness, and perform the abort depending on the result.

Example 3-41. 403 Forbidden aborts

```
Route::post('something-you-cant-do', function (Illuminate\Http\Request) {
    abort(403, 'You cannot do that!');
    abort_unless($request->has('magicToken'), 403);
    abort_if($request->user()->isBanned, 403);
});
```

Custom Responses

There are a few other options available for us to return, so let's go over the most common responses after views, redirects, and aborts. Just like with redirects, you can either use the response() helper or the Response facade to run these methods on.

response()->make()

If you want to create an HTTP response manually, just pass your data into the first parameter of `response()->make()`: e.g., `return response()->make('Hello, World!')`. Once again, the second parameter is the HTTP status code and the third is your headers.

response()->json() and ->jsonp()

To create a JSON-encoded HTTP response manually, pass your JSON-able content (arrays, collections, or whatever else) to the `json()` method: e.g., `return response()->json(User::all());`. It's just like `make()`, except it `json_encodes` your content and sets the appropriate headers.

response()->download() and ->file()

To send a file for the end user to download, pass either an `SplFileInfo` instance or a string filename to `download()`, with an optional second parameter of the filename: e.g., `return response()->download('file501751.pdf', 'myFile.pdf')`.

To display the same file in the browser (if it's a PDF or an image or something else the browser can handle), use `response()->file()` instead, which takes the same parameters.

Testing

In some other communities, the idea of unit testing controller methods is common, but within Laravel (and most of the PHP community), it's most common to rely on *application testing* to test the functionality of routes.

For example, to verify that a POST route works correctly, we can write a test like Example 3-42.

Example 3-42. Writing a simple POST route test

```php
// AssignmentTest.php
public function test_post_creates_new_assignment()
{
    $this->post('/assignments', [
        'title' => 'My great assignment'
    ]);

    $this->seeInDatabase('assignments', [
        'title' => 'My great assignment'
    ]);
}
```

Did we directly call the controller methods? No. But we ensured that the goal of this route—to receive a POST and save its important information to the database—was met.

You can also use similar syntax to visit a route and verify that certain text shows up on the page, or that clicking certain buttons does certain things (see Example 3-43).

Example 3-43. Writing a simple GET route test

```
// AssignmentTest.php
public function test_list_page_shows_all_assignments()
{
    $assignment = Assignment::create([
        'title' => 'My great assignment'
    ]);

    $this->visit('assignments')
        ->dee(['My great assignment']);
}
```

TL;DR

Laravel's routes are defined in *routes/web.php* and *routes/api.php*, where you can define the expected path for each route, which segments are static and which are parameters, which HTTP verbs can access the route, and how to resolve it. You can also attach middleware to routes, group them, and give them names.

What is returned from the route closure or controller method dictates how Laravel responds to the user. If it's a string or a view, it's presented to the user; if it's other sorts of data, it's converted to JSON and presented to the user; and if it's a redirect, it forces a redirect.

Laravel provides a series of tools and conveniences to simplify common routing-related tasks and structures. These include resource controllers, route model binding, and form method spoofing.

## CHAPTER 4

Blade Templating

Compared to most other backend languages, PHP actually functions relatively well as a templating language. But it has its shortcomings, and it's also just ugly to be using <?php inline all over the place, so you can expect most modern frameworks to offer a templating language.

Laravel offers a custom templating engine called Blade, which is inspired by .NET's Razor engine. It boasts a concise syntax, a shallow learning curve, a powerful and intuitive inheritance model, and easy extensibility.

For a quick look at what writing Blade looks like, check out Example 4-1.

Example 4-1. Blade samples

```
<h1>{{ $group->title }}</h1>
{!! $group->heroImageHtml() !!}

@forelse ($users as $user)
    • {{ $user->first_name }} {{ $user->last_name }}<br>
@empty
    No users in this group.
@endforelse
```

As you can see, Blade introduces a convention in which its custom tags, called "directives," are prefixed with an @. You'll use directives for all of your control structures and also for inheritance and any custom functionality you want to add.

Blade's syntax is clean and concise, so at its core it's just more pleasant and tidy to work with than the alternatives. But the moment you need anything of any complexity in your templates—nested inheritance, complex conditionals, or recursion—Blade starts to really shine. Just like the best Laravel components, it takes complex application requirements and makes them easy and accessible.

Additionally, since all Blade syntax is compiled into normal PHP code and then cached, it's fast and it allows you to use native PHP in your Blade files if you want. However, I'd recommmend avoiding usage of PHP if at all possible—usually if you need to do anything that you can't do with Blade or a custom Blade directive, it doesn't belong in the template.

Using Twig with Laravel

Unlike many other Symfony-based frameworks, Laravel doesn't use Twig by default. But if you're just in love with Twig, there's a Twig Bridge (*https://github.com/rcrowe/TwigBridge*) package that makes it easy to use Twig instead of Blade.

Echoing Data

As you can see in Example 4-1, {{ and }} are used to wrap sections of PHP that you'd like to echo. {{ $variable }} is similar to <?= $variable ?> in plain PHP.

It's different in one way, however, and you might've guessed this already: Blade escapes all echoes by default using PHP's htmlentities() to protect your users from malicious script insertion. That means {{ $variable }} is functionally equivalent to <?= htmlentities($variable) ?>. If you want to echo without the escaping, use {!! and !!} instead.

{{and }} When Using a Frontend Templating Framework

You might've noticed that the echo syntax for Blade ({{ }}) is similar to the echo syntax for many frontend frameworks. So, how does Laravel know when you're writing Blade versus Handlebars?

Blade will ignore any {{ that's prefaced with an @. So, it will parse the first of the following examples, but the second will be echoed out directly:

```
// Parsed as Blade; the value of $bladeVariable is echoed to the view
{{ $bladeVariable }}

// @ is removed, and "{{ handlebarsVariable }}" echoed to the view directly
@{{ handlebarsVariable }}
```

Control Structures

Most of the control structures in Blade will be very familiar. Many directly echo the name and structure of the same tag in PHP.

There are a few convenience helpers, but in general, the control structures just look cleaner than they would in PHP.

Conditionals

First, let's take a look at the control structures that allow for logic.

@if

Blade's `@if ($condition)` compiles to `<?php if ($condition): ?>`. `@else`, `@elseif`, and `@endif` also compile to the exact same syntax in PHP. Take a look at Example 4-2 for some examples.

Example 4-2. @if, @else, @elseif, and @endif

```
@if (count($talks) === 1)
    There is one talk at this time period.
@elseif (count($talks) === 0)
    There are no talks at this time period.
@else
    There are {{ count($talks) }} talks at this time period.
@endif
```

Just like with the native PHP conditionals, you can mix and match these how you want. They don't have any special logic; there's literally a parser looking for something with the shape of `@if ($condition)` and replacing it with the appropriate PHP code.

@unless and @endunless

`@unless`, on the other hand, is a new syntax that doesn't have a direct equivalent in PHP. It's the direct inverse of `@if`. `@unless ($condition)` is the same as `<?php if (! $condition)`. See it in use in Example 4-3.

Example 4-3. @unless and @endunless

```
@unless ($user->hasPaid())
    You can complete your payment by switching to the payment tab.
@endunless
```

Loops

Next, let's take a look at the loops.

@for, @foreach, and @while

`@for`, `@foreach`, and `@while` work the same in Blade as they do in PHP; see Examples 4-4, 4-5, and 4-6.

Example 4-4. @for and @endfor

```
@for ($i = 0; $i < $talk->slotsCount(); $i++)
    The number is {{ $i }}<br>
@endfor
```

Example 4-5. @foreach and @endforeach

```
@foreach ($talks as $talk)
    • {{ $talk->title }} ({{ $talk->length }} minutes)<br>
@endforeach
```

Example 4-6. @while and @endwhile

```
@while ($item = array_pop($items))
    {{ $item->orSomething() }}<br>
@endwhile
```

@forelse

`@forelse` is a `@foreach` that also allows you to program in a fallback if the object you're iterating over is empty. We saw it in action at the start of this chapter; Example 4-7 shows another example.

Example 4-7. @forelse

```
@forelse ($talks as $talk)
    • {{ $talk->title }} ({{ $talk->length }} minutes)<br>
@empty
    No talks this day.
@endforelse
```

$loop Within @foreach and @forelse

The @foreach and @forelse directives in Laravel 5.3 add one feature that's not available in PHP foreach loops: the $loop variable. Used within a @foreach or @forelse loop, this variable will return a stdClass object with the following properties:

index
: The 0-based index of the current item in the loop; 0 would mean "first item"

iteration
: The 1-based index of the current item in the loop; 1 would mean "first item"

remaining
: How many items remain in the loop; if the current item is the first of three, this will be 2

count
: The count of items in the loop

first
: A boolean indicating whether this is the first item in the loop

last
: A boolean indicating whether this is the last item in the loop

depth
: How many "levels" deep this loop is: 1 for a loop, 2 for a loop within a loop, etc.

parent
: A reference to the $loop variable for the parent loop item; if this loop is within another @foreach loop otherwise, null

Here's an example of how to use it:

```
<ul>
@foreach ($pages as $page)
    <li>{{ $loop->iteration }}: {{ $page->title }}
        @if ($page->hasChildren())
        <ul>
        @foreach ($page->children() as $child)
            <li>{{ $loop->parent->iteration }}.
                {{ $loop->iteration }}:
                {{ $child->title }}</li>
        @endforeach
        </ul>
        @endif
    </li>
@endforeach
</ul>
```

or

If you're ever unsure whether a variable is set, you're probably used to checking `isset()` on it before echoing it, and echoing something else if it's not set. Blade has a convenience helper, or, that does this for you and lets you set a default fallback: `{{ $title or "Default" }}` will echo the value of `$title` if it's set, or "Default" if not.

Template Inheritance

Blade provides a structure for template inheritance that allows views to extend, modify, and include other views.

Here's how inheritance is structured with Blade.

Defining Sections with @section/@show and @yield

Let's start with a top-level Blade layout, like in Example 4-8. This is the definition of the generic page wrapper that we'll later place page-specific content into.

Example 4-8. Blade layout

```
<!-- resources/views/layouts/master.blade.php -->
<html>
    <head>
        <title>My Site | @yield('title', 'Home Page')</title>
    </head>
    <body>
        <div class="container">
            @yield('content')
        </div>
        @section('footerScripts')
            <script src="app.js"></script>
        @show
    </body>
</html>
```

This looks a bit like a normal HTML page, but you can see we've *yielded* in two places (`title` and `content`), and we've defined a *section* in a third (`footerScripts`).

We have three Blade directives here that each look a little different: `@yield('title', 'Home Page')` alone, `@yield('content')` with a defined default, and `@section ... @show` with actual content in it.

All three function essentially the same. All three are defining that there's a section with a given name (which is the first parameter). All three are defining that the section *can* be extended later. And all three are defining what to do if the section isn't extended, either by providing a string fallback ('Home Page'), no fallback (which will just not show anything if it's not extended), or an entire block fallback (in this case, `<script src="app.js"></script>`).

What's different? Well, clearly, `@yield('content')` has no default content. But additionally, the default content in `@yield('title')` *only* will be shown if it's never extended. If it is extended, its child sections will not have programmatic access to the default value. `@section ... @show`, on the other hand, is both defining a default *and* doing so in a way that its default contents will be available to its children, through `@parent`.

Once you have a parent layout like this, you can extend it like in Example 4-9.

Example 4-9. Extending a Blade layout

```
<!-- resources/views/dashboard.blade.php -->
@extends('layouts.master')

@section('title', 'Dashboard')

@section('content')
    Welcome to your application dashboard!
@endsection

@section('footerScripts')
    @parent

    <script src="dashboard.js"></script>
@endsection
```

@show versus @endsection

You may have noticed that Example 4-8 uses `@section ... @show`, but Example 4-9 uses `@section ... @endsection`. What's the difference?

Use `@show` when you're defining the place for a section, in the parent template. Use `@endsection` when you're defining the content for a template in a child template.

This child view will actually allow us to cover a few new concepts in Blade inheritance.

@extends

First, with `@extends('layouts.master')`, we define that this view should not be rendered on its own, but that it instead *extends* another view. That means its role is to define the content of various sections, but not to stand alone. It's almost more like a series of buckets of content, rather than an HTML page. This line also defines that the view it's extending lives at *resources/views/layouts/master.blade.php*.

Each file should only extend one other file, and the `@extends` call should be the first line of the file.

@section and @endsection

Second, with `@section('title', 'Dashboard')`, we provide our content for the first section, `title`. Since the content is so short, instead of using `@section` and `@end section` we're just using a shortcut. This allows us to pass the content in as the second parameter of `@section` and then move on. If it's a bit disconcerting to see `@section` without `@endsection`, you could just use the normal syntax.

Third, with `@section('content')` and on, we use the normal syntax to define the contentsx of the `content` section. We'll just throw a little greeting in for now. Note, however, that when you're using `@section` in a child view, you end it with `@end section` (or its alias `@stop`), instead of `@show`, which is reserved for defining sections in parent views.

@parent

Fourth, with `@section('footerScripts')` and on, we use the normal syntax to define the contents of the `footerScripts` section.

But remember, we actually defined that content (or, at least, its "default") already in the master layout. So this time, we have two options: we can either *overwrite* the content from the parent view, or we can *add* to it.

You can see that we have the option to include the content from the parent by using the `@parent` directive within the section. If we didn't, the content of this section would entirely overwrite anything defined in the parent for this section.

@include

Now that we've established the basics of inheritance, there are a few more tricks we can perform.

What if we're in a view and want to pull in another view? Maybe we have a call-to-action "Sign up" button that we want to re-use around the site. And maybe we want to customize its button text every time we use it. Take a look at Example 4-10.

Example 4-10. Including view partials with @include

```
<!-- resources/views/home.blade.php -->
<div class="content" data-page-name="{{ $pageName }}">
    <p>Here's why you should sign up for our app: <strong>It's Great.</strong></p>

    @include('sign-up-button', ['text' => 'See just how great it is'])
</div>

<!-- resources/views/sign-up-button.blade.php -->
<a class="button button--callout" data-page-name="{{ $pageName }}">
    <i class="exclamation-icon"></i> {{ $text }}
</a>
```

@include pulls in the partial and, optionally, passes data into it. Note that not only can you *explicitly* pass data to an include via the second parameter of @include, but you can also reference any variables within the included file that are available to the including view ($pageName, in this example). Once again, you can do whatever you want, but I would recommend you consider always explicitly passing every variable that you intend to use, just for clarity.

@each

You can probably imagine some circumstances in which you'd need to loop over an array or collection and @include a partial for each item. There's a directive for that: @each.

Let's say we have a sidebar composed of modules, and we want to include multiple modules, each with a different title. Take a look at Example 4-11.

Example 4-11. Using view partials in a loop with @each

```
<!-- resources/views/sidebar.blade.php -->
<div class="sidebar">
    @each('partials.module', $modules, 'module', 'partials.empty-module')
</div>

<!-- resources/views/partials/module.blade.php -->
<div class="sidebar-module">
    <h1>{{ $module->title }}</h1>
</div>

<!-- resources/views/partials/empty-module.blade.php -->
<div class="sidebar-module">
    No modules :(
</div>
```

Consider that @each syntax. The first parameter is the name of the view partial. The second is the array or collection to iterate over. The third is the variable name that each item (in this case, each element in the $modules array) will be passed to the view as. And the optional fourth parameter is the view to show if the array or collection is empty (or, optionally, you can pass a string in here that will be used as your template).

View Composers and Service Injection

As we covered in Chapter 3, it's simple to pass data to our views from the route definition (see Example 4-12).

Example 4-12. Reminder on how to pass data to views

```
Route::get('passing-data-to-views', function () {
    return view('dashboard')
        ->with('key', 'value');
});
```

There are times, however, when you will find yourself passing the same data over and over to multiple views. Or, you might find yourself using a header partial or something similar that requires some data; will you now have to pass that data in from every route definition that might ever load that header partial?

Binding Data to Views Using View Composers

Thankfully, there's a simpler way. The solution is called a view composer, and it allows you to define that *any time a particular view loads, it should have certain data passed to it*—without the route definition having to pass that data in explicitly.

Let's say you have a sidebar on every page, which is defined in a partial named `partials.sidebar` (*resources/views/partials/sidebar.blade.php*) and then included on every page. This sidebar shows a list of the last seven posts that were published on your site. If it's on every page, every route definition would normally have to grab that list and pass it in, like in Example 4-13.

Example 4-13. Passing sidebar data in from every route

```
Route::get('home', function () {
    return view('home')
        ->with('posts', Post::recent());
});

Route::get('about', function () {
    return view('about')
        ->with('posts', Post::recent());
});
```

That could get annoying quickly. Instead, we're going to use view composers to "share" that variable with a prescribed set of views. We can do this a few ways, so let's start simple and move up.

Sharing a variable globally

First, the simplest option: just globally "share" a variable with every view in your application like in Example 4-14.

Example 4-14. Sharing a variable globally

```
// Some service provider
public function boot()
{
    ...
    view()->share('posts', Post::recent());
}
```

If you want to use `view()->share()`, the best place would be the `boot()` method of a service provider so that the binding runs on every page load. You can create a custom `ViewComposerServiceProvider` (see Chapter 11 for more about service providers), but for now just put it in `App\Providers\AppServiceProvider` in the `boot()` method.

Using `view()->share()` makes the variable accessible to every view in the entire application, however, so it might be overkill.

Closure-based view composers

The next option is to use a closure-based view composer to share variables with a single view, like in Example 4-15.

Example 4-15. Creating a closure-based view composer

```
view()->composer('partials.sidebar', function ($view) {
    $view->with('posts', Post::recent());
});
```

As you can see, we've defined the name of the view we want it shared with in the first parameter (`partials.sidebar`) and then passed a closure to the second parameter; in the closure, we've used `$view->with()` to share a variable, but now only with a specific view.

View composers for multiple views

Anywhere a view composer is binding to a particular view (like in Example 4-15, which binds to `partials.sidebar`), you can pass an array of view names instead to bind to multiple views.

You can also use an asterisk in the view path, as in `partials.*`, `tasks.*`, or just `*`:

```php
view()->composer(
    ['partials.header', 'partials.footer'],
    function () {
        $view->with('posts', Post::recent());
    }
);

view()->composer('partials.*', function () {
    $view->with('posts', Post::recent());
});
```

Class-based view composers

Finally, the most flexible but also most complex option is to create a dedicated class for your view composer.

First, let's create the view composer class. There's no formally defined place for view composers to live, but the docs recommend `App\Http\ViewComposers`. So, let's create `App\Http\ViewComposers\RecentPostsComposer` like in Example 4-16.

Example 4-16. A view composer

```php
<?php

namespace App\Http\ViewComposers;

use App\Post;
use Illuminate\Contracts\View\View;

class RecentPostsComposer
{
    private $posts;

    public function __construct(Post $posts)
    {
        $this->posts = $posts;
    }

    public function compose(View $view)
    {
        $view->with('posts', $this->posts->recent());
```

```
        }
}
```

As you can see, we're injecting the Post model (typehinted constructor parameters of view composers will be automatically injected; see Chapter 11 for more on the container and dependency injection). Note that we could skip the private $posts and the constructor injection and just use Post::recent() in the compose() method if we wanted. Then, when this composer is called, it runs the compose() method, in which we bind the posts variable to the result of running the recent() method.

Like the other methods of sharing variables, this view composer needs to have a binding somewhere. Again, you'd likely create a custom ViewComposerServiceProvider, but for now, as seen in Example 4-17, we'll just put it in the boot() method of App \Providers\AppServiceProvider.

Example 4-17. Registering a view composer in AppServiceProvider

```
// AppServiceProvider
public function boot()
{
    ...

    view()->composer(
        'partials.sidebar',
        \App\Http\ViewComposers\RecentPostsComposer::class
    );
}
```

Note that this binding is the same as a closure-based view composer, but instead of passing a closure, we're passing the class name of our view composer. Now, every time Blade renders the partials.sidebar view, it'll automatically run our provider and pass the view a posts variable set to the results of the recent() method on our Post model.

Blade Service Injection

There are three primary types of data we're most likely to inject into a view: collections of data to iterate over, single objects that we're displaying on the page, and services that generate data or views.

With a service, the pattern will most likely look like Example 4-18, where we inject an instance of our analytics service into the route definition by typehinting it in the route's method signature, and then pass it into the view.

Example 4-18. Injecting services into a view via the route definition constructor

```
Route::get('backend/sales', function (AnalyticsService $analytics) {
    return view('backend.sales-graphs')
        ->with('analytics', $analytics);
});
```

Just as with view composers, Blade's service injection offers a convenient shortcut to reduce duplication in your route definitions. Normally, the content of a view using our analytics service might look like Example 4-19.

Example 4-19. Using an injected navigation service in a view

```
<div class="finances-display">
    {{ $analytics->getBalance() }} / {{ $analytics->getBudget() }}
</div>
```

Blade service injection makes it easy to inject an instance of a class outside of the container directly from the view, like in Example 4-20.

Example 4-20. Injecting a service directly into a view

```
@inject('analytics', 'App\Services\Analytics')

<div class="finances-display">
    {{ $analytics->getBalance() }} / {{ $analytics->getBudget() }}
</div>
```

As you can see, this `@inject` directive has actually made an `$analytics` variable available, which we're using later in our view.

The first parameter of `@inject` is the name of the variable you're injecting, and the second parameter is the class or interface that you want to inject an instance of. This is resolved just like when you type hint a dependency in a constructor elsewhere in Laravel; if you're unfamiliar with how that works, go to Chapter 11 to learn more.

Just like view composers, Blade service injection makes it easy to make certain data or functionality available to every instance of a view, without having to inject it via the route definition every time.

Custom Blade Directives

All of the built-in syntax of Blade that we've covered so far—`@if`, `@unless`, and so on—are called *directives*. Each Blade directive is a mapping between a pattern (e.g., `@if ($condition)`) and a PHP output (e.g., `<?php if ($condition): ?>`).

Directives aren't just for the core; you can actually create your own. You might think directives are good for making little shortcuts to bigger pieces of code—for example, using @button('buttonName') and having it expand to a larger set of button HTML. This isn't a *terrible* idea, but for simple code expansion like this you might be better off including a view partial.

I've found custom directives to be the most useful when they simplify some form of repeated logic. Say we're tired of having to wrap our code with @if (auth()->guest()) (to check if a user is logged in or not) and we want a custom @ifGuest directive. As with view composers, it might be worth having a custom service provider to register these, but for now let's just put it in the boot() method of App\Providers\AppServiceProvider. Take a look at Example 4-21 to see what this binding will look like.

Example 4-21. Binding a custom Blade directive

```
// AppServiceProvider
public function boot()
{
    Blade::directive('ifGuest', function () {
        return "<?php if (auth()->guest()): ?>";
    });
}
```

We've now registered a custom directive, @ifGuest, which will be replaced with the PHP code <?php if (auth()->guest()): ?>.

This might feel strange. You're writing a *string* that will be returned and then executed as PHP. But what this means is that you can now take the complex, or ugly, or unclear, or repetitive aspects of your PHP templating code and hide them behind clear, simple, and expressive syntax.

Custom directive result caching

You might be tempted to do some logic to make your custom directive faster by performing an operation *in* the binding and then embedding the result within the returned string:

```
Blade::directive('ifGuest', function () {
    // Antipattern! Do not copy.
    $ifGuest = auth()->guest();
    return "<?php if ({$ifGuest}): ?>";
});
```

The problem with this idea is that it assumes this directive will be re-created on every page load. However, Blade caches aggressively, so you're going to find yourself in a bad spot if you try this.

Parameters in Custom Blade Directives

What if you want to check a condition in your custom logic? Check out Example 4-22.

Example 4-22. Creating a Blade directive with parameters

```
// Binding
Blade::directive('newlinesToBr', function ($expression) {
    return "<?php echo nl2br({$expression}); ?>";
});

// In use
<p>@newlinesToBr($message->body)</p>
```

The $expression parameter received by the closure represents whatever's within the parentheses. As you can see, we then generate a valid PHP code snippet and return it.

$expression parameter scoping before Laravel 5.3

Before Laravel 5.3, the $expression parameter also included *the parentheses themselves*. So, in Example 4-22, $expression (which is $message->body in Laravel 5.3 and later) would have instead been ($message->body), and we would've had to write <? php echo nl2br{$expression}; ?>.

If you find yourself constantly writing the same conditional logic over and over, you should consider a Blade directive.

Example: Using Custom Blade Directives for a Multitenant App

So, let's imagine we're building an application that supports *multitenancy*, which means users might be visiting the site from *www.myapp.com*, *client1.myapp.com*, *client2.myapp.com*, or elsewhere.

Suppose we have written a class to encapsulate some of our multitenancy logic and named it Context. This class will capture information and logic about the context of the current visit, such as who the authenticated user is and whether the user is visiting the public website or a client subdomain.

We'll probably frequently resolve that Context class in our views and perform conditionals on it, like in Example 4-23. The app('context') is a shortcut to get an instance of a class from the container, which we'll learn more about in Chapter 11.

Example 4-23. Conditionals on context without a custom Blade directive

```
@if (app('context')->isPublic())
    &copy; Copyright MyApp LLC
@else
    &copy; Copyright {{ app('context')->client->name }}
@endif
```

What if we could simplify `@if (app('context')->isPublic())` to just `@ifPublic`? Let's do it. Check out Example 4-24.

Example 4-24. Conditionals on context with a custom Blade directive

```
// Binding
Blade::directive('ifPublic', function () {
    return "<?php if (app('context')->isPublic()): ?>";
});

// In use
@ifPublic
    &copy; Copyright MyApp LLC
@else
    &copy; Copyright {{ app('context')->client->name }}
@endif
```

Since this resolves to a simple `if` statement, we can still rely on the native `@else` and `@endif` conditionals. But if we wanted, we could also create a custom `@elseIfClient` directive, or a separate `@ifClient` directive, or really whatever else we want.

Testing

The most common method of testing views is through application testing, meaning that you're actually calling the route that displays the views and ensuring the views have certain content (see Example 4-25). You can also click buttons or submit forms and ensure that you are redirected to a certain page, or that you see a certain error. (You'll learn more about testing in Chapter 12.)

Example 4-25. Testing that a view displays certain content

```
// EventsTest.php
public function test_list_page_shows_all_events()
{
    $event1 = factory(Event::class)->create();
    $event2 = factory(Event::class)->create();

    $this->visit('events')
        ->see($event1->title)
```

```
        ->see($event2->title);
}
```

You can also test that a certain view has been passed a particular set of data, which, if it accomplishes your testing goals, is less fragile than checking for certain text on the page. Example 4-26 demonstrates this approach.

Example 4-26. Testing that a view was passed certain content

```
// EventsTest.php
public function test_list_page_shows_all_events()
{
    $event1 = factory(Event::class)->create();
    $event2 = factory(Event::class)->create();

    $this->visit('events');

    $this->assertViewHas('events', Event::all());
    $this->assertViewHasAll([
        'events' => Event::all(),
        'title' => 'Events Page'
    ]);
    $this->assertViewMissing('dogs');
}
```

In 5.3, we gained the ability to pass a closure to $assertViewHas(), meaning we can customize how we want to check more complex data structures. Example 4-27 illustrates how we might use this.

Example 4-27. Passing a closure to assertViewHas()

```
// EventsTest.php
public function test_list_page_shows_all_events()
{
    $event1 = factory(Event::class)->create();

    $this->visit('events/' . $event1->id);

    $this->assertViewHas('event', function ($event) use ($event1) {
        return $event->id === $event1->id;
    });
}
```

TL;DR

Blade is Laravel's templating engine. Its primary focus is a clear, concise, and expressive syntax with powerful inheritance and extensibility. Its "safe echo" brackets are

{{ and }}, its unprotected echo brackets are {!! and !!}, and it has a series of custom tags called directives that all begin with @ (@if and @unless, for example).

You can define a parent template and leave "holes" in it for content using @yield and @section/@show. You can then teach its child views to extend it using @extends('*parent.view.name*'), and define their sections using @section/@endsection. You use @parent to reference the content of the block's parent.

View composers make it easy to define that, every time a particular view or subview loads, it should have certain information available to it. And service injection allows the view itself to request data straight from the application container.

## CHAPTER 5

Frontend Components

Laravel is primarily a PHP framework, but it also has a series of components focused on generating frontend code. Some of these, like pagination and message bags, are PHP helpers that target the frontend, but Laravel also provides a Gulp-based build system called Elixir and some conventions around non-PHP assets.

Since Elixir is at the core of the non-PHP frontend components, let's start there.

Elixir

Elixir (not to be confused with the functional programming language) is a build tool that provides a simple user interface and a series of conventions on top of Gulp (*http://gulpjs.com*). Elixir's core feature is simplifying the most common Gulp tasks by means of a cleaner API and a series of naming and application structure conventions.

A Quick Introduction to Gulp

Gulp is a JavaScript tool designed for compiling static assets and coordinating other steps of your build process.

Gulp is similar to Grunt, Rake, or make—it allows you to define an action (called a "task" in Gulp) or series of actions to take every time you build your application. This will commonly include running a CSS preprocessor like Sass or LESS, copying files, concatenating and minifying JavaScript, and much more.

Gulp, and therefore Elixir, is based on the idea of streams. Most tasks will begin by loading some files into the stream buffer, and then the task will apply transformations to the content—preprocess it, minify it, and then maybe save the content to a new file.

At its core, Elixir is just a tool in your Gulp toolbox. There isn't even such a thing as an Elixir file; you'll define your Elixir tasks in your *gulpfile.js*. But they look a lot different from vanilla Gulp tasks, and you'll have to do a lot less work to get them running out of the box.

Let's look at a common example: running Sass to preprocess your CSS styles. In a normal Gulp environment, that might look a little bit like Example 5-1.

Example 5-1. Compiling a Sass file in Gulp

```
var gulp = require('gulp'),
    sass = require('gulp-ruby-sass'),
    autoprefixer = require('gulp-autoprefixer'),
    rename = require('gulp-rename'),
    notify = require('gulp-notify'),
    livereload = require('gulp-livereload'),
    lr = require('tiny-lr'),
    server = lr();

gulp.task('sass', function() {
    return gulp.src('resources/assets/sass/app.scss')
        .pipe(sass({
            style: 'compressed',
            sourcemap: true
        }))
        .pipe(autoprefixer('last 2 version', 'ie 9', 'ios 6'))
        .pipe(gulp.dest('public/css'))
        .pipe(rename({suffix: '.min'}))
        .pipe(livereload(server))
        .pipe(notify({
            title: "Karani",
            message: "Styles task complete."
        }));
});
```

Now, I've seen worse. It reads well, and it's clear what's going on. But there's a *lot* happening that you'll just pull into every site you ever make. It can get confusing and repetitive.

Let's try that same task in Elixir (Example 5-2).

Example 5-2. Compiling a Sass file in Elixir

```
var elixir = require('laravel-elixir');

elixir(function (mix) {
    mix.sass('app.scss');
});
```

That's it. That covers all the basics—preprocessing, notification, folder structure, autoprefixing, and much more.

ES6 in Elixir 6

Elixir 6, which came out with Laravel 5.3, changed a lot of the syntax to use ES6, the latest version of JavaScript. Here's what Example 5-2 looks like in Elixir 6:

```
const elixir = require('laravel-elixir');

elixir(mix => {
    mix.sass('app.scss')
});
```

Don't worry; this does exactly the same thing.

Elixir Folder Structure

Much of Elixir's simplicity comes from the assumed directory structure. Why make the decision fresh in every new application about where the source and compiled assets live? Just stick with Elixir's convention, and you won't have to think about it ever again.

Every new Laravel app comes with a *resources* folder with an *assets* subfolder, which is where Elixir will expect your frontend assets to live. Your Sass will live in *resources/assets/sass*, or your LESS in *resources/assets/less*, and your JavaScript will live in *resources/assets/js*. These will export to *public/css* and *public/js*.

But if you're interested in changing the structure, you can always change the source and public paths by changing the appropriate properties (`assetsPath` and `public Path`) on the `elixir.config` object.

Running Elixir

Since Elixir runs on Gulp, you'll need to set up a few tools before using it:

1. First, you'll need Node.js installed. Visit the Node website (*http://nodejs.org/*) to learn how to get it running.

2. Next, you'll need to install Gulp globally on your machine. Just run `npm install --global gulp-cli` from the terminal anywhere on your machine.

   Once Node and Gulp are installed, you will never have to run those commands again. Now you're ready to install this project's dependencies.

3. Open the project root in your terminal, and run `npm install` to install the required packages (Laravel ships with an Elixir-ready *package.json* file to direct NPM).

You're now set up! You can run `gulp` to run Gulp/Elixir once, `gulp watch` to listen for relevant file changes and run in response, or `gulp scripts` or `gulp styles` to just run the script or style tasks.

What Does Elixir Provide?

We've already covered that Elixir can preprocess your CSS using Sass or LESS. It can concatenate files, minify them, rename them, and copy them, and it can copy entire directories or individual files.

Elixir can also process ES6/ES2015 JavaScript and run Webpack, Rollup, and/or Autoprefixer on your code. Not only that, but most of the modern coding standards for JavaScript and CSS are covered on every script or style, out of the box.

Elixir can also run your tests. There's a method for PHPUnit and one for PHPSpec; both listen to changes to your test files and rerun your test suite every time you make any changes.

The Elixir documentation (*https://laravel.com/docs/elixir*) covers all of these options and more, but we'll cover a few specific use cases in the following sections.

The --production flag

By default, Elixir doesn't minify all the files it's generating. But if you want to run the build scripts in "production" mode, with all minification enabled, you can just add the `--production` flag:

```
$ gulp --production
```

Passing multiple files

Most of the Elixir methods that normally accept a single file (e.g., `mix.sass('app.scss')`) can also take an array of files, like in Example 5-3.

Example 5-3. Compiling multiple files with Elixir

```
const elixir = require('laravel-elixir');

elixir(mix => {
    mix.sass([
        'app.scss',
        'public.scss'
    ]);
});
```

Source maps

By default, Elixir generates source maps for your files—you'll see them as a *.{file-name}.map* file next to each generated file.

If you're not familiar with source maps, they work with any sort of preprocessor to teach your browser's web inspector which files generated the compiled source you're inspecting.

Without source maps, if you use your browser's development tools to inspect a particular CSS rule or JavaScript action, you'll just see a big mess of compiled code. With source maps, your browser can pinpoint the exact line of the *source file*, whether it be Sass or JavaScript or whatever else, that generated the rule you're inspecting.

If you don't want source maps, you can always change the configuration before your `elixir` block like in Example 5-4.

Example 5-4. Disabling source maps in Elixir

```
const elixir = require('laravel-elixir');

elixir.config.sourcemaps = false;

elixir(mix => {
    mix.sass('app.scss');
});
```

Preprocessorless CSS

If you don't want to deal with a preprocessor, there's a command for that—it will grab all of your CSS files, concatenate them, and output them to the *public/css* directory, just as if they had been run through a preprocessor. If you don't specify an ouput file name, it'll end up in *all.css*. There are a few options, which you can see in Example 5-5.

Example 5-5. Combining stylesheets with Elixir

```
const elixir = require('laravel-elixir');

elixir(mix => {
    // Combines all files from resources/assets/css and subfolders
    mix.styles();

    // Combines files from resources/assets/css
    mix.styles([
        'normalize.css',
        'app.css'
    ]);
```

```
    // Combines all styles from other directory
    mix.stylesIn('resources/some/other/css/directory');

    // Combines given styles from resources/assets/css
    // and outputs to a custom directory
    mix.styles([
        'normalize.css',
        'app.css'
    ], 'public/other/css/output.css');

    // Combines given styles from custom directory
    // and outputs to a custom directory
    mix.styles([
        'normalize.css',
        'app.css'
    ], 'public/other/css/output.css', 'resources/some/other/css/directory');
});
```

Concatenating JavaScript

The options available for working with normal JavaScript files are very similar to those available for normal CSS files. Take a look at Example 5-6. Like with styles(), any commands not provided with an output filename will output to *public/js/all.js*.

Example 5-6. Combining JavaScript files with Elixir

```
const elixir = require('laravel-elixir');

elixir(mix => {
    // Combines files from resources/assets/js
    mix.scripts([
        'jquery.js',
        'app.js'
    ]);

    // Combines all scripts from other directory
    mix.scriptsIn('resources/some/other/js/directory');

    // Combines given scripts from resources/assets/js
    // and outputs to a custom directory
    mix.scripts([
        'jquery.js',
        'app.js'
    ], 'public/other/js/output.js');

    // Combines given scripts from custom directory
    // and outputs to a custom directory
    mix.scripts([
        'jquery.js',
        'app.js'
```

```
    ], 'public/other/js/output.js', 'resources/some/other/js/directory');
});
```

Processing JavaScript

If you want to process your JavaScript—for example, to compile your ES6 code into plain JavaScript—Elixir makes it easy to use either Webpack or Rollup for this purpose (see Example 5-7).

Example 5-7. Processing JavaScript files in Elixir with Webpack or Rollup

```
elixir(function(mix) {
    mix.webpack('app.js');

    // or

    mix.rollup('app.js');
});
```

These scripts look for the provided filename in *resources/assets/js* and output to *public/js/all.js*.

You can use more complicated aspects of Webpack's feature set by creating a *webpack.config.js* file in your project root.

Compiling JavaScript in Elixir 5

 Prior to Laravel 5.3/Elixir 6, you'll want to compile your Java‐Script using `mix.browserify('app.js')`.

Versioning

Most of the tips from Steve Souders' *Even Faster Web Sites* (O'Reilly) have made their way into our everyday development practices. We move scripts to the footer, reduce the number of HTTP requests, and more, often without even realizing where those ideas originated.

One of Steve's tips is still very rarely implemented, though, and that is setting a very long cache life on assets (scripts, styles, and images). Doing this means there will be fewer requests to your server to get the latest version of your assets. But it also means that users are extremely likely to have a cached version of your assets, which will make things get outdated, and therefore break, quickly.

The solution to this is versioning. Append a unique hash to each asset's filename *every time you run your build script*, and then that unique file will be cached indefi‐nitely—or at least until the next build.

What's the problem? Well, first you need to get the unique hashes generated and appended to your filenames. But you also will need to update your views on every build to reference the new filenames.

As you can probably guess, Elixir handles that for you, and it's incredibly simple. There are two components: the versioning task in Elixir, and the `elixir()` PHP helper. First, you can version your assets by running `mix.version()` like in Example 5-8.

Example 5-8. mix.version

```
const elixir = require('laravel-elixir');

elixir(mix => {
    mix.version('public/css/all.css');
});
```

This will generate a version of the specified file with a unique hash appended to it in the *public/build* directory—something like *public/build/css/all-84fa1258.css*.

Next, use the PHP `elixir()` helper in your views to refer to that file like in Example 5-9.

Example 5-9. Using the elixir() helper in views

```
<link rel="stylesheet" href="{{ elixir("css/all.css") }}">

// will output something like:

<link rel="stylesheet" href="/build/css/all-84fa1258.css">
```

How Does Elixir Versioning Work Behind the Scenes?

Elixir uses `gulp-rev`, which takes care of appending the hashes to the filenames, and also generates a file named *public/build/rev-manifest.json*. This stores the information the `elixir()` helper needs to find the generated file. Here's what a sample *rev-manifest.json* looks like:

```
{
    "css/all.css": "css/all-7f592e49.css"
}
```

Tests

With Elixir it's easy to run your PHPUnit or PHPSpec tests every time your test files change.

You have two options, `mix.phpUnit()` and `mix.phpSpec()`, and each will run the respective frameworks directly from the *vendor* folder, so you won't have to do anything to make them work.

If you add one of these methods to your Gulp file, however, you'll find they only run once, even if you're using `gulp watch`. How do you get them to respond to changes in your *tests* folder?

There's a separate Gulp command for that: `gulp tdd`. This grabs just the test commands out of your Gulp file, whether `phpUnit()` or `phpSpec()`, listens to the appropriate folder, and reruns the test suite whenever any files change.

Elixir extensions

Elixir doesn't just provide a simple syntax for its own prebuilt tasks; it also makes it easy to define your own.

Let's say you want to save text to a logfile at certain points. That's a shell command, which is `echo "message" >> file.log`. Normally we'd define this as a Gulp task, using `shell('echo "message" >> file.log')`, like in Example 5-10.

Example 5-10. Using a Gulp task in Elixir

```
// Define the task
gulp.task("log", function () {
    var message = "Something happened";
    gulp.src("").pipe(shell('echo "' + message + '" >> file.log'));
});

elixir(mix => {
    // Use the task in Elixir
    mix.task('log');

    // Bind the task to run every time certain files are changed
    mix.task('log', 'resources/somefiles/to/watch/**/*')
});
```

However, if we want a little more control—for example, if we want to be able to actually pass in the message, which is really sort of vital to make this particular task work—we can create an Elixir *extension* like in Example 5-11.

Example 5-11. Creating an Elixir extension

```
// Either in gulpfile.js, or in an external file and required in gulpfile.js
var gulp = require("gulp"),
    shell = require("gulp-shell"),
    elixir = require("laravel-elixir");
```

```
elixir.extend("log", function (message) {
    new Task('log', function() {
        return gulp.src('').pipe(shell('echo "' + message + '" >> file.log'));
    })
    .watch('./resources/some/files/**/*');
});
```

As with any component, we haven't covered everything there is to learn about Elixir, but hopefully you've learned enough to get you running with it. Want to learn more? Check out the docs (*https://laravel.com/docs/elixir*).

Pagination

For something that is so common across web applications, pagination still can be wildly complicated to implement. Thankfully, Laravel has a built-in concept of pagination, and it's also hooked into Eloquent results *and* the router by default.

A Brief Introduction to Eloquent

We'll be covering Eloquent, database access, and Laravel's query builder in depth in Chapter 8, but there will be a few references between now and then that will make a basic understanding useful.

Eloquent is Laravel's ActiveRecord database object-relational mapper (ORM), which makes it easy to relate a `Post` class (model) to the `posts` database table, and get all records with a call like `Post::all()`.

The query builder is the tool that makes it possible to make calls like `Post::where('active', true)->get()` or even `DB::table('users')->all()`. You're *building* a query by chaining methods one after another.

Paginating Database Results

The most common place you'll see pagination is when you are displaying the results of a database query and there are too many results for a single page. Eloquent and the query builder both read the `page` query parameter from the current page request and use it to provide a `paginate()` method on any result sets; the single parameter you should pass `paginate()` is how many results you want per page. Take a look at Example 5-12 to see how this works.

Example 5-12. Paginating a query builder response

```
// PostsController
    public function index()
    {
```

```
    return view('posts.index', ['posts' => DB::table('posts')->paginate(20)]);
}
```

Example 5-12 defines that this route should return 20 posts per page, and will define which "page" of results the current user is on based on the URL's `page` query parameter, if it has one. Eloquent models all have the same `paginate()` method.

When you display the results in your view, your collection will now have a `links()` method on it (or `render()` for Laravel 5.1) that will output the pagination controls, with bootstrap class names assigned to them by default (see Example 5-13).

Example 5-13. Rendering pagination links in a template

```
// posts/index.blade.php
<table>
@foreach ($posts as $post)
    <tr><td>{{ $post->title }}</td></tr>
@endforeach
</table>

{{ $posts->links() }}

// By defaut, $posts->links() will output something like this:

<ul class="pagination">
    <li class="disabled"><span>&laquo;</span></li>
    <li class="active"><span>1</span></li>
    <li><a href="http://myapp.com/posts?page=2">2</a></li>
    <li><a href="http://myapp.com/posts?page=3">3</a></li>
    <li><a href="http://myapp.com/posts?page=2" rel="next">&raquo;</a></li>
</ul>
```

Manually Creating Paginators

If you're not working with Eloquent or the query builder, *or* if you're working with a complex query (e.g., those using `groupBy`), you might find yourself needing to create a paginator manually. Thankfully, you can do that with the `Illuminate\Pagination\Paginator` or `Illuminate\Pagination\LengthAwarePaginator` classes.

The difference between the two classes is that `Paginator` will only provide previous and next buttons, but no links to each page; `LengthAwarePaginator` needs to know the length of the full result, so that it can generate links for each individual page. You may find yourself wanting to use the `Paginator` on large result sets, so your paginator doesn't have to be aware of a massive count of results that might be costly to run.

Both the `Paginator` and the `LengthAwarePaginator` require you to manually extract the subset of content that you want to pass to the view. Take a look at Example 5-14 for an example.

Example 5-14. Manually creating a paginator in Laravel 5.2 and 5.3

```
use Illuminate\Http\Request;
use Illuminate\Pagination\Paginator;

Route::get('people', function (Request $request) {
    $people = [...]; // huge list of people

    $perPage = 15;
    $offsetPages = $request->input('page', 1) - 1;

    // The Paginator will not slice your array for you
    $people = array_slice(
        $people,
        $offsetPages * $perPage,
        $perPage
    );

    return new Paginator(
        $people,
        $perPage
    );
});
```

The `Paginator` syntax has changed over the last few versions of Laravel, so if you're using 5.1, take a look at the docs to find the correct syntax.

Message Bags

Another common but painful feature in web applications is passing messages between various components of the app, when the end goal is to share them with the user. Your controller, for example, might want to send a validation message: "The email field must be a valid email address." However, that particular message doesn't just need to make it to the view layer; it actually needs to survive a redirect and then end up in the view layer of a different page. How do we structure this messaging logic?

`Illuminate\Support\MessageBag` is a class tasked with storing, categorizing, and returning messages that are intended for the end user. It groups all messages by key, where the keys are likely to be something like `errors` and `messages`, and provides convenience methods for getting all its stored messages or only those for a particular key, and for outputting these messages in various formats.

You can spin up a new instance of `MessageBag` manually like in Example 5-15.

Example 5-15. Manually creating and using MessageBag

```
$messages = [
    'errors' => [
        'Something went wrong with edit 1!'
    ],
    'messages' => [
        'Edit 2 was successful.'
    ]
];
$messagebag = new \Illuminate\Support\MessageBag($messages);

// Check for errors; if there are any, decorate and echo
if ($messagebag->has('errors')) {
    echo '<ul id="errors">';
    foreach ($messagebag->get('errors', '<li><b>:message</b></li>') as $error) {
        echo $error;
    }
    echo '</ul>';
}
```

Message bags are also closely connected to Laravel's validators (learn more in "Valida-tion" on page 103): when validators return errors, they actually return an instance of `MessageBag`, which you can then pass to your view or attach to a redirect using `redirect('route')->withErrors($messagebag)`.

Laravel passes an empty instance of `MessageBag` to every view, assigned to the vari-able `$errors`, and if you've flashed a message bag using `withErrors()` on a redirect, it will get assigned to that `$errors` variable instead. That means every view can always assume it has an `$errors` `MessageBag` it can check in whatever place it does its validation, which leads to Example 5-16 as a common snippet developers place on every page.

Example 5-16. Error bag snippet

```
// partials/errors.blade.php
@if ($errors->any())
    <div class="alert alert-danger">
        <ul>
        @foreach ($errors as $error)
            <li>{{ $error }}</li>
        @endforeach
        </ul>
    </div>
@endif
```

Missing $errors variable

If you have any routes that aren't under the web middleware group, they won't have the session middleware, which means they won't have this $errors variable available.

Named Error Bags

Sometimes you need to differentiate message bags not just by key (notices versus errors) but also by component. Maybe you have a login form and a signup form on the same page; how do you differentiate them?

When you send errors along with a redirect using withErrors(), the second parameter is the name of the bag: redirect('dashboard')->withErrors($validator, 'login'). Then, on the dashboard, you can use $errors->login to call all of the methods we saw before: any(), count(), and more.

String Helpers, Pluralization, and Localization

As developers, we tend to look at blocks of text as big placeholder divs, waiting for the client to put real content into them. Seldom are we involved in any logic inside these blocks.

But there are a few circumstances where you'll be grateful for the tools Laravel provides for string manipulation.

The String Helpers and Pluralization

Laravel has a series of helpers for manipulating strings. They're available as methods on the Str class (e.g., Str::plural()), but most also have a global helper function (e.g., str_plural()).

The Laravel documentation (*https://laravel.com/docs/5.3/helpers*) covers all of the string helpers in detail, but here are a few of the most commonly used helpers:

e

A shortcut for html_entities

starts_with, ends_with, str_contains

Check a string (first parameter) to see if it starts with, ends with, or contains another string (second parameter)

str_is

Checks whether a string (second parameter) matches a particular pattern (first parameter)—for example, foo* will match foobar and foobaz

`str_slug`
    Converts a string to a URL-type slug with hyphens

`str_plural` *(word, num)*, `str_singular`
    Pluralizes a word or singularizes it; English-only (e.g., `str_plural('dog')`
    returns `dogs`)

Localization

Localization allows you to define multiple languages and mark any strings as targets
for translation. You can set a fallback language, and even handle pluralization variations.

In Laravel, you'll need to set an application locale at some point during the page load
so the localization helpers know which bucket of translations to pull from. You'll do
this with `App::setLocale($localeName)`, and you'll likely put it in a service provider. For now you can just put it in the `boot()` method of `AppServiceProvider`, but
you may want to create a `LocaleServiceProvider` if you end up with more than just
this one locale-related binding.

Setting the Locale for Each Request

It can be confusing at first to work out how Laravel "knows" the user's locale, or
provides translations. Most of that work is on you as the developer. Let's look at a
likely scenario.

You'll probably have some functionality allowing the user to choose a locale, or possibly attempting to automatically detect it. Either way, your application will determine
the locale, and then you'll store that in a URL parameter or a session cookie. Then
your service provider—something like a `LocaleServiceProvider`, maybe—will grab
that key and set it as a part of Laravel's bootstrap.

So maybe your user is at *http://myapp.com/es/contacts*. Your `LocaleServiceProvider`
will grab that `es` string, and then run `App::setLocale('es')`. Going forward, every
time you ask for a translation of a string, Laravel will look for the Spanish version of
that string, which you will need to have defined somewhere.

You can define your fallback locale in *config/app.php*, where you should find a `fall
back_locale` key. This allows you to define a default language for your application,
which Laravel will use if it can't find a translation for the requested locale.

Basic localization

So, how do we call for a translated string? There's a helper function, `trans($key)`, that will pull the string for the current locale for the passed key or, if it doesn't exist, grab it from the default locale. Example 5-17 demonstrates how a basic translation works. We'll use the example of a "back to the dashboard" link at the top of a detail page.

Example 5-17. Basic use of trans()

```
// Normal PHP
<?php echo trans('navigation.back'); ?>

// Blade
{{ trans('navigation.back') }}

// Blade directive
@lang('navigation.back')
```

Let's assume we are using the es locale right now. Laravel will look for a file in *resources/lang/es/navigation.php*, which it will expect to return an array. It'll look for a `back` key on that array, and if it exists, it'll return its value. Take a look at Example 5-18 for a sample.

Example 5-18. Using a translation

```
// resources/lang/es/navigation.php
return [
    'back' => 'Volver al panel'
];

// routes/web.php
Route::get('/es/contacts/show/:id', function () {
    // Setting it manually, for this example, instead of in a service provider
    App::setLocale('es');
    return view('contacts.show');
});

// resources/views/contacts/show.blade.php
<a href="/contacts">{{ trans('navigation.back') }}</a>
```

Parameters in localization

The preceding example was relatively simple. Let's dig into some that are more complex. What if we want to define *which* dashboard we're returning to? Take a look at Example 5-19.

Example 5-19. Parameters in translations

```php
// resources/lang/en/navigation.php
return [
    'back' => 'Back to :section dashbaord'
];

// resources/views/contacts/show.blade.php
{{ trans('navigation.back', ['section' => 'contacts']) }}
```

As you can see, prepending a word with a colon (`:section`) marks it as a placeholder that can be replaced. The second, optional, parameter of `trans()` is an array of values to replace the placeholders with.

Pluralization in localization

We already covered pluralization, so now just imagine you're defining your own pluralization rules. There are two ways to do it; we'll start with the simplest, in Example 5-20.

Example 5-20. Defining a simple translation with an option for pluralization

```php
// resources/lang/en/messages.php
return [
    'task-deletion' => 'You have deleted a task|You have successfully deleted tasks'
];

// resources/views/dashboard.blade.php
@if ($numTasksDeleted > 0)
    {{ trans_choice('messages.task-deletion', $numTasksDeleted) }}
@endif
```

As you can see, we have a `trans_choice()` method, which takes the count of items affected as its second parameter; and from this it will determine which string to use.

You can also use any translation definitions that are compatible with Symfony's much more complex `Translation` component; see Example 5-21 for an example.

Example 5-21. Using the Symfony's Translation component

```php
// resources/lang/es/messages.php
return [
    'task-deletion' => "{0} You didn't manage to delete any tasks.|" .
        "[1,4] You deleted a few tasks.|" .
        "[5,Inf] You deleted a whole ton of tasks."
];
```

Testing

In this chapter we focused primarily on Laravel's frontend components. These are less likely the objects of unit tests, but they may at times be used in your integration tests.

Testing with Elixir

You're not going to be writing any tests around your Elixir tasks. However, Elixir provides some functions that will help with your testing, so let's talk about those for a second.

If you add `mix.phpunit()` or `mix.phpspec()` to your *gulpfile.js*, every time you run `gulp` it will run your tests once, inline, as a part of your build script.

And every time you run `gulp watch`, Elixir will listen to any change to your test files or any other core files (like *routes/web.php*) and re-run PHPUnit or PHPSpec every time you make any changes to those files.

Testing Message and Error Bags

There are two primary ways of testing messages passed along with message and error bags. First, you can perform a behavior in your application tests that sets a message that will eventually be displayed somewhere, then redirect to that page and assert that the appropriate message is shown.

Second, for errors (which is the most common use case), you can assert the session has errors with `$this->assertSessionHasErrors($bindings = [])`. Take a look at Example 5-22 to see what this might look like.

Example 5-22. Asserting the session has errors

```
public function test_missing_email_field_errors()
{
    $this->post('person/create', ['name' => 'Japheth']);
    $this->assertSessionHasErrors(['email']);
}
```

Translation and Localization

The simplest way to test localization is with application tests. Set the appropriate context (whether by URL or session), `visit()` the page, and assert that you see the appropriate content.

TL;DR

As a full-stack framework, Laravel provides tools and components for the frontend as well as the backend.

Elixir is a wrapper around common Gulp build tasks that makes it simple to use the most modern build steps. Elixir makes it easy to add CSS preprocessors; JavaScript transpilation, concatenation, and minification; and much more.

Laravel also offers other internal tools that target the frontend, including pagination, message and error bags, and localization.

## CHAPTER 6

Collecting and Handling User Data

Websites that benefit from a framework like Laravel often don't just serve static content. Many deal with complex and mixed data sources, and one of the most common (and most complex) of these sources is user input in its myriad forms: URL paths, query parameters, POST data, and file uploads.

Laravel provides a collection of tools for gathering, validating, normalizing, and filtering user-provided data. We'll look at those here.

Injecting a Request Object

The most common tool for accessing user data in Laravel is injecting an instance of the Illuminate\Http\Request object. It provides easy access to all of the ways users can provide input to your site: POST, posted JSON, GET (query parameters), and URL segments.

Other options for accessing request data

There's also a request() global helper and a Request facade, both of which expose the same methods. Each of these options exposes the entire Illuminate Request object, but for now we're only going to cover the methods that specifically relate to user data.

Since we're planning on injecting a Request object, let's take a quick look at how to get the $request object we'll be calling all these methods on:

```
Route::post('form', function (Illuminate\Http\Request $request) {
    // $request->etc()
});
```

$request->all()

Just like the name suggests, $request->all() gives you an array containing all of the input the user has provided, from every source. Let's say, for some reason, you decided to have a form POST to a URL with a query parameter—e.g., sending a POST to *http://myapp.com/post?utm=12345*. Take a look at Example 6-1 to see what you'd get from $request->all(). (Note that $request->all() also contains information about any files that were uploaded, but we'll cover that later in the chapter.)

Example 6-1. $request->all()

```
<!-- GET route form view at /get-route -->
<form method="post" action="/post-route?utm=12345">
    {{ csrf_field() }}
    <input type="text" name="firstName">
    <input type="submit">
</form>

Route::post('/post-route', function (Request $request) {
    var_dump($request->all());
});

// Outputs:
/**
 * [
 *      '_token' => 'CSRF token here',
 *      'firstName' => 'value',
 *      'utm' => 12345
 * ]
 */
```

$request->except() and $request->only()

$request->except() provides the same output as $request->all, but you can choose one or more fields to exclude—for example, _token. You can pass it either a string or an array of strings.

Example 6-2 shows what it looks like when we use $request->except() on the same form as in Example 6-1.

Example 6-2. $request->except()

```
Route::post('/post-route', function (Request $request) {
    var_dump($request->except('_token'));
});

// Outputs:
/**
 * [
```

```
 *      'firstName' => 'value',
 *      'utm' => 12345
 * ]
 */
```

`$request->only()` is the inverse of `$request->except()`, as you can see in Example 6-3.

Example 6-3. $request->except()

```
Route::post('/post-route', function (Request $request) {
    var_dump($request->only(['firstName', 'utm']));
});

// Outputs:
/**
 * [
 *      'firstName' => 'value',
 *      'utm' => 12345
 * ]
 */
```

$request->has() and $request->exists()

With `$request->has()` you can detect whether a particular piece of user input is available to you. Check out Example 6-4 for an analytics example with our `utm` query string parameter from the previous examples.

Example 6-4. $request->has()

```
// POST route at /post-route
if ($request->has('utm')) {
    // Do some analytics work
}
```

`$request->exists()` and `$request->has()` differ in that they handle empty values differently: `has()` returns FALSE if the key exists and is empty; `exists()` returns TRUE if the key exists, even if it's empty.

$request->input()

Whereas `$request->all()`, `$request->except()`, and `$request->only()` operate on the full array of input provided by the user, `$request->input()` allows you to get the value of just a single field. Example 6-5 provides an example. Note that the second parameter is the default value, so if the user hasn't passed in a value, you can have a sensible (and nonbreaking) fallback.

Example 6-5. $request->input()

```
Route::post('/post-route', function (Request $request) {
    $userName = $request->input('name', '(anonymous)');
});
```

Array Input

Laravel also provides convenience helpers for accessing data from array input. Just use the "dot" notation to indicate the steps of digging into the array structure, like in Example 6-6.

Example 6-6. Dot notation to access array values in user data

```
<!-- GET route form view at /get-route -->
<form method="post" action="/post-route">
    {{ csrf_field() }}
    <input type="text" name="employees[0][firstName]">
    <input type="text" name="employees[0][lastName]">
    <input type="text" name="employees[1][firstName]">
    <input type="text" name="employees[1][lastName]">
    <input type="submit">
</form>

// POST route at /post-route
Route::post('/post-route', function (Request $request) {
    $employeeZeroFirstName = $request->input('employees.0.firstName');
    $allLastNames = $request->input('employees.*.lastName');
    $employeeOne = $request->input('employees.1');
});

// If forms filled out as "Jim" "Smith" "Bob" "Jones":
// $employeeZeroFirstName = 'Jim';
// $allLastNames = ['Smith', 'Jones'];
// $employeeOne = ['firstName' => 'Bob', 'lastName' => 'Jones']
```

JSON Input (and $request->json())

So far we've covered input from query strings (GET) and form submissions (POST). But there's another form of user input that's becoming more common with the advent of JavaScript single-page apps (SPAs): the JSON request. It's essentially just a POST request with the body set to JSON instead of a traditional form POST.

Let's take a look at what it might look like to submit some JSON to a Laravel route, and how to use `$request->input()` to pull out that data (Example 6-7).

Example 6-7. Getting data from JSON with $request->input()

```
POST /post-route HTTP/1.1
Content-Type: application/json

{
    "firstName": "Joe",
    "lastName": "Schmoe",
    "spouse": {
        "firstName": "Jill",
        "lastName":"Schmoe"
    }
}
// post-route
Route::post('post-route', function (Request $request) {
    $firstName = $request->input('firstName');
    $spouseFirstname = $request->input('spouse.firstName');
});
```

Since `$request->input()` is smart enough to pull user data from GET, POST, or JSON, you may wonder why Laravel even offers `$request->json()`. There are two reasons you might prefer `$request->json()`. First, you might want to just be more explicit to other programmers on your project about where you're expecting the data to come from. And second, if the POST doesn't have the correct application/json headers, `$request->input()` won't pick it up as JSON, but `$request->json()` will.

Facade Namespaces, the request() Global Helper, and Injecting $request

Any time you're using facades inside of namespaced classes (e.g., controllers), you'll have to add the full facade path to the import block at the top of your file (e.g., use Illuminate\Support\facades\Request).

Because of this, several of the facades also have a companion global helper function. If these helper functions are run with no parameters, they expose the same syntax as the facade (e.g., `request()->has()` is the same as `Request::has()`). They also have a default behavior for when you pass them a parameter (e.g., `request('firstName')` is a shortcut to `request()->input('firstName')`).

With Request, we've been covering injecting an instance of the Request object, but you could also use the Request facade or the request() global helper. Take a look at Chapter 10 to learn more.

Route Data

It might not be the first thing you think of when you imagine "user data," but the URL is just as much user data as anything else in this chapter.

There are three primary ways you'll get data from the URL: via the Request facade, route parameters, and Request objects. We'll cover Request objects in more detail in Chapter 10.

From Request

Injected Request objects (and the Request facade and the request() helper) have several methods available to represent the state of the current page's URL, but right now let's look primarily at getting information about the URL segments.

If you're not familiar with the idea of URL segments, each group of characters after the domain is called a segment. So, *http://www.myapp.com/users/15/* has two segments: *users* and *15*.

As you can probably guess, we have two methods available to us: $request->segments() returns an array of all segments, and $request->segment($segmentId) allows us to get the value of a single segment. Note that segments are returned on a 1-based index, so in the preceding example, $request->segment(1) would return users.

Request objects, the Request facade, and the request() global helper provide quite a few more methods to help us get data out of the URL. To learn more, check out Chapter 10.

From Route Parameters

The other primary way we get data about the URL is from route parameters, which are injected into the controller method or closure that is serving a current route as shown in Example 6-8.

Example 6-8. Getting URL details from route parameters

```
// routes/web.php
Route::get('users/{id}', function ($id) {
    // If the user visits myapp.com/users/15/, $id will equal 15
});
```

To learn more about routes and route binding, check out Chapter 3.

Uploaded Files

We've talked about different ways to interact with users' text input, but there's also the matter of file uploads to consider. The Request facade provides access to any uploaded files using the `Request::file()` method, which takes the file's input name as a parameter and returns an instance of `Symfony\Component\HttpFoundation\File\UploadedFile`.

Let's walk through an example. First, our form, in Example 6-9.

Example 6-9. A form to upload files

```
<form method="post" enctype="multipart/form-data">
    {{ csrf_field() }}
    <input type="text" name="name">
    <input type="file" name="profile_picture">
    <input type="submit">
</form>
```

Now, let's take a look at what we get from running `$request->all()`, in Example 6-10. Note that `$request->input('profile_picture')` will return `null`; we need to use `$request->file('profile_picture')` instead.

Example 6-10. The output from submitting the form in Example 6-9

```
Route::post('form', function (Request $request) {
    var_dump($request->all());
});

// Output:
// [
//     "_token" => "token here"
//     "name" => "asdf"
//     "profile_picture" => UploadedFile {}
// ]

Route::post('form', function (Request $request) {
    if ($request->hasFile('profile_picture')) {
        var_dump($request->file('profile_picture'));
    }
});

// Output:
// UploadedFile (details)
```

Validating a File Upload

As you can see in Example 6-10, we have access to `$request->hasFile()` to see whether the user uploaded a file. We can also check whether the file upload was successful by using `isValid()` on the file itself:

```
if ($request->file('profile_picture')->isValid()) {
    //
}
```

Because `isValid()` is called on the file itself, it will error if the user didn't upload a file. So, to check for both, you'd need to check for the file's existence first:

```
if (
    $request->hasFile('profile_picture') &&
    $request->file('profile_picture')->isValid()
    ) {
    //
}
```

Symfony's `UploadedFile` class extends PHP's native `SplFileInfo` with methods allowing you to easily inspect and manipulate the file. This list isn't exhaustive, but it gives you a taste of what you can do:

- `guessExtension()`
- `getMimeType()`
- `store($path, $storageDisk = default disk)`
- `storeAs($path, $newName, $storageDisk = default disk)`
- `storePublicly($path, $storageDisk = default disk)`
- `storePubliclyAs($path, $newName, $storageDisk = default disk)`
- `move($directory, $newName = null)`
- `getClientOriginalName()`
- `getClientOriginalExtension()`
- `getClientMimeType()`
- `guessClientExtension()`
- `getClientSize()`
- `getError()`
- `isValid()`

As you can see, most of the methods have to do with getting information about the uploaded file, but there's one that you'll likely use more than all the others: `store()` (new in Laravel 5.3), which takes the file that was uploaded with the request and stores it in a specified directory on your server. Its first parameter is the destination directory, and the optional second parameter will be the storage disk (`s3`, `local`, etc.) to use to store the file.

You can see a common workflow in Example 6-11.

Example 6-11. Common file upload workflow

```
if ($request->hasFile('profile_picture')) {
    $path = $request->profile_picture->store('profiles', 's3');
    auth()->user()->profile_picture = $path;
    auth()->user()->save();
}
```

If you need to specify the filename, you can use `storeAs()` instead of `store()`. The first parameter is still the path; the second is the filename, and the optional third parameter is the storage disk to use.

Proper form encoding for file uploads

If you get `null` when you try to get the contents of a file from your request, you might've forgotten to set the encoding type on your form. Make sure to add the attribute `enctype="multipart/form-data"` on your form:

```
<form method="post" enctype="multipart/form-data">
```

Validation

Laravel has quite a few ways you can validate incoming data. We'll cover form requests in the next section, so that leaves us with two primary options: validating manually or using the `validate()` method in the controller. Let's start with the simpler, and more common, `validate()`.

validate() in the Controller Using ValidatesRequests

Out of the box, all Laravel controllers use the `ValidatesRequests` trait, which provides a convenient `validate()` method. Let's take a look at what it looks like in Example 6-12.

Example 6-12. Basic usage of controller validation

```php
// routes/web.php
Route::get('recipes/create', 'RecipesController@create');
Route::post('recipes', 'RecipesController@store');

// app/Http/Controllers/RecipesController.php
<?php

namespace App\Http\Controllers;

use Illuminate\Http\Request;

class RecipesController extends Controller
{
    public function create()
    {
        return view('recipes.create');
    }

    public function store(Request $request)
    {
        $this->validate($request, [
            'title' => 'required|unique:recipes|max:125',
            'body' => 'required'
        ]);

        // Recipe is valid; proceed to save it
    }
}
```

We only have four lines of code running our validation here, but they're doing a lot.

First, we're explicitly defining the fields we expect and applying rules (here separated by the pipe character, |) to each individually.

Next, the `validate()` method checks the incoming data from the `$request` (which means it can use `$request->all()` or `$request->input()` just like we learned about earlier in the chapter) and determines whether or not it is valid.

If the data is valid, the `validate` method ends and we can move on with your controller method, saving the data or whatever else.

But if the data isn't valid, it throws a `ValidationException`. This contains instructions to the router about how to handle this exception. If the request is Ajax (or if it's requesting JSON as a response), the exception will create a JSON response containing the validation errors. If not, the exception will return a redirect to the previous page, together with all of the user input and the validation errors—perfect for repopulating a failed form and showing some errors.

More on Laravel's Validation Rules

In our examples here (like in the docs) we're using the "pipe" syntax: `'fieldname':` `'rule|otherRule|anotherRule'`. But you can also use the array syntax to do the same thing: `'fieldname': ['rule', 'otherRule', 'anotherRule']`.

Additionally, you can validate nested properties. This matters if you use HTML's array syntax, which allows you to, for example, have multiple "users" on an HTML form, each with an associated name. Here's how you validate that:

```
$this->validate($request, [
    'user.name' => 'required',
    'user.email' => 'required|email',
]);
```

We don't have enough space to cover every possible validation rule here, but here are a few of the most common rules and their functions:

Require the field
> `required`; `required_if:anotherField,equalToThisValue`; `required_unless:anotherField,equalToThisValue`

Field must contain certain types of character
> `alpha`, `alpha_dash`, `alpha_num`, `numeric`, `integer`

Field must contain certain patterns
> `email`, `active_url`, `ip`

Dates
> `after:date`, `before:date` (*date* can be any valid string that `strtotime()` can handle)

Numbers
> `between:min,max`, `min:num`, `max:num`, `size:num` (`size` tests against length for strings, value for integers, `count` for arrays, or size in KB for files)

Image dimensions
> `dimensions:min_width=XXX`; can also use and/or combine with `max_width`, `min_height`, `max_height`, `width`, `height`, and `ratio`

Databases
> `exists:tableName`, `unique:tableName` (expects to look in the same table column as the field name; see the docs (*http://bit.ly/2eMLZDl*) for how to customize)

Manual Validation

If you are not working in a controller, or if for some other reason the previously described flow is not a good fit, you can manually create a `Validator` instance and check for success or failure like in Example 6-13.

Example 6-13. Manual validation

```
Route::get('recipes/create', function () {
    return view('recipes.create');
});

Route::post('recipes', function (Illuminate\Http\Request $request) {
    $validator = Validator::make($request->all(), [
        'title' => 'required|unique:recipes|max:125',
        'body' => 'required'
    ]);

    if ($validator->fails()) {
        return redirect('recipes/create')
            ->withErrors($validator)
            ->withInput();
    }

    // Recipe is valid; proceed to save it
});
```

As you can see, we create an instance of a validator by passing it our input as the first parameter and the validation rules as the second parameter. The validator exposes a `fails()` method that we can check against and can be passed into the `withErrors()` method of the redirect.

Displaying Validation Error Messages

We've already covered much of this in Chapter 5, but here's a quick refresher on how to display errors from validation.

The `validate()` method in controllers (and the `withErrors()` method on redirects that it relies on) flashes any errors to the session. These errors are made available to the view you're being redirected to in the `$errors` variable. And remember that as a part of Laravel's magic, that `$errors` variable will be available every time you load the view, even if it's just empty, so you don't have to check if it exists with `isset()`.

That means you can do something like Example 6-14 on every page.

Example 6-14. Echo validation errors

```
@if ($errors->any())
    <ul id="errors">
        @foreach ($errors->all() as $error)
            <li>{{ $error }}</li>
        @endforeach
    </ul>
@endif
```

Form Requests

As you build out your applications, you might start noticing some patterns in your controller methods. There are certain patterns that are repeated—for example, input validation, user authentication and authorization, and possible redirects. If you find yourself wanting a structure to normalize and extract these common behaviors out of your controller methods, you may be interested in Laravel's form requests.

A form request is a custom request class that is intended to map to the submission of a form, and the request takes the responsibility for validating the request, authorizing the user, and optionally redirecting the user upon a failed validation. Each form request will usually, but not always, explicitly map to a single HTTP request—e.g., "Create Comment."

Creating a Form Request

You can create a new form request using Artisan:

```
php artisan make:request CreateCommentRequest
```

You now have a form request object available at *app/Http/Requests/CreateCommentRequest.php*.

Every form request class provides either one or two public methods. The first is `rules()`, which needs to return an array of validation rules for this request. The second (optional) method is `authorize()`; if this returns `true`, the user is authorized to perform this request, and if `false`, the user is rejected. Take a look at Example 6-15 to see a sample form request.

Example 6-15. Sample form request

```
<?php

namespace App\Http\Requests;

use App\BlogPost;
use App\Http\Requests\Request;
```

```
class CreateCommentRequest extends Request
{
    public function rules()
    {
        return [
            'body' => 'required|max:1000'
        ];
    }

    public function authorize()
    {
        $blogPostId = $this->route('blogPost');

        return auth()->check() && BlogPost::where('id', $blogPostId)
            ->where('user_id', auth()->user()->id)->exists();
    }
}
```

The `rules()` section of Example 6-15 is pretty self-explanatory, but let's look at `authorize()` briefly.

We're grabbing the segment from the route named `blogPost`. That's implying the route definition for this route probably looks a bit like this: `Route::post('blog Posts/{blogPost}', function () { // Do stuff })`. As you can see, we named the route parameter `blogPost`, which makes it accessible in our `Request` using `$this->route('parameter name')`.

We then look at whether the user is logged in and, if so, whether any blog posts exist with that identifier that are owned by the currently logged-in user. We'll cover what implications this has shortly, but the important thing to know is that returning `true` means the user is authorized to perform the specified action (in this case, creating a comment), and `false` means the user is not authorized.

Using a Form Request

Now that we've created a form request object, how do we use it? It's a little bit of Laravel magic. Any route (closure or controller method) that typehints a form request as one of its parameters will benefit from the definitions of that form request.

Let's try it out, in Example 6-16.

Example 6-16. Using a form request

```
Route::post('comments', function (App\Http\Requests\CreateCommentRequest $request) {
    // Store comment
});
```

You might be wondering where we call the form request, but Laravel does it for us. It validates the user input and authorizes the request. If the input is invalid, it'll act just like the in-controller `validate()` method works, redirecting the user to the previous page with their input preserved and with the appropriate error messages passed along. And if the user is not authorized, Laravel will return a 403 Forbidden error and not execute the route code.

Eloquent Model Mass Assignment

Until now, we've been looking at validating at the controller level, which is absolutely the best place to start. But you can also filter the incoming data at the model level.

It's a common pattern to pass the entirety of a form's input directly to a database model. In Laravel, that might look like Example 6-17.

Example 6-17. Passing the entirety of a form to an Eloquent model

```
Route::post('posts', function (Request $request) {
    $newPost = Post::create($request->all());
});
```

We're assuming here that the end user is kind and not malicious, and has kept only the fields we want him to edit—maybe the post `title` or `body`.

But what if our end user can guess, or discern, that we have an `author_id` field on that `posts` table? What if he used his browser tools to add an `author_id` field and set the ID to be someone else's ID, and the other person impersonated the other person by creating fake blog posts attributed to her?

Eloquent has a concept called "mass assignment" that allows you to either whitelist fields that are fillable in this way (using the model's `$fillable` property) or blacklist fields that aren't fillable (using the model's `$guarded` property). Check out Chapter 8 to learn more.

In our example, we might want to fill out the model like Example 6-18 to keep our app safe.

Example 6-18. Guarding an Eloquent model from mischievious mass assignment

```
<?php

namespace App;

use Illuminate\Database\Eloquent\Model;

class Post extends Model
{
```

```
    // Disable mass assignment on the author_id field
    protected $guarded = ['author_id'];
}
```

By setting `author_id` to guarded, we ensure that malicious users will no longer be able to override the value of this field by manually adding it to the contents of a form that they're sending to our app.

Double protection using $request->only()

While it's important to do a good job of protecting our models from mass assignment, it's also worth being careful on the assigning end. Rather than using `$request->all()`, consider `$request->only()` so you can specify which fields you'd like to pass into your model:

```
Route::post('posts', function (Request $request) {
    $newPost = Post::create($request->only([
        'title',
        'body'
    ]));
});
```

{{ Versus {!!

Any time you display content on a web page that was created by a user, you need to guard against malicious input, such as script injection.

Let's say you allow your users to write blog posts on your site. You probably don't want them to be able to inject malicious JavaScript that will run in your unsuspecting visitors' browsers, right? So, you'll want to escape any user input that you show on the page to avoid this.

Thankfully, this is almost entirely covered for you. If you use Laravel's Blade templating engine, the default "echo" syntax ({{ *$stuffToEcho* }}) runs the output through `htmlentities()` (PHP's best way of making user content safe to echo) automatically. You actually have to do *extra* work to avoid escaping the output, by using the {!! *$stuffToEcho* !!} syntax.

Testing

If you're interested in testing your interactions with user input, you're probably most interested in simulating valid and invalid user input and ensuring that if the input is invalid the user is redirected, and if the input is valid, it ends up in the proper place (e.g., the database).

Laravel's end-to-end application testing makes this simple. Let's start with an invalid route that we expect to be rejected, in Example 6-19.

Example 6-19. Testing that invalid input is rejected

```
public function test_input_missing_a_title_is_rejected()
{
    $this->post('posts', ['body' => 'This is the body of my post']);
    $this->assertRedirectedTo('posts/create');
    $this->assertSessionHasErrors();
    $this->assertHasOldInput();
}
```

Here we assert that after invalid input the user is redirected, with errors and with the old input correctly passed back. You can see we're using a few custom PHPUnit assertions that Laravel adds here.

So, how do we test our route's success? Check out Example 6-20.

Example 6-20. Testing that valid input is processed

```
public function test_valid_input_should_create_a_post_in_the_database()
{
    $this->post('posts', ['title' => 'Post Title', 'body' => 'This is the body']);
    $this->seeInDatabase(['title' => 'Post Title']);
}
```

Note that, if you're testing something using the database, you'll need to learn more about database migrations and transactions. More on that in Chapter 12.

TL;DR

There are a lot of ways to get the same data: the `Request` facade, the `request()` global helper, and injecting an instance of `Illuminate\Http\Request`. Each exposes the ability to get all input, some input, or specific pieces of data, and files and JSON input can have some special considerations at times.

URI path segments are also a possible source of user input, and they're also accessible via the request tools.

Validation can be performed manually with `Validator::make()`, or automatically using the `$this->validate()` controller method or form requests. Each automatic tool, upon failed validation, redirects the user to the previous page with all old input stored and errors passed along.

Views and Eloquent models also need to be protected from nefarious user input. Protect Blade views using the double curly brace syntax ({{ }}), which escapes user input, and protect models by only passing specific fields into bulk methods using $request->only() and by defining the mass assignment rules on the model itself.

## CHAPTER 7

Artisan and Tinker

From installation onward, modern PHP frameworks expect many interactions to take place on the command line. Laravel provides three primary tools for command-line interaction: Artisan, a suite of built-in command-line actions with the ability to add more; Tinker, a REPL or interactive shell for your application; and the installer, which we've already covered in Chapter 2.

An Introduction to Artisan

If you've been reading through this book chapter by chapter, you've already learned how to use Artisan commands. They look something like this:

```
php artisan make:controller PostsController
```

If you look in the root folder of your application, you'll see that *artisan* is actually just a PHP file. That's why you're starting your call with `php artisan`; you're passing that file into PHP to be parsed. Everything after that is just passed into Artisan as arguments.

Symfony Console syntax

Artisan is actually a layer on top of the Symfony Console component (*http://bit.ly/2fVqOT8*), so if you're familiar with writing Symfony Console commands you should be right at home.

Since the list of Artisan commands for an application can be changed by a package or by the specific code of the application, it's worth checking every new application you encounter to see what commands are available.

To get a list of all available Artisan commands, you can run `php artisan list` from the project root (although if you just run `php artisan` with no parameters, it will do the same thing).

Basic Artisan Commands

There's not enough space here to cover all of the Artisan commands, but we'll cover many of them. Let's get started with the basic commands:

- `help` provides help for a command; e.g., `php artisan help` *commandName*.
- `clear-compiled` removes Laravel's compiled class file, which is like an internal Laravel cache; run this as a first resort when things are going wrong and you don't know why.
- `down` puts your application in "maintenance mode" in order for you to fix an error, run migrations, or whatever else; `up` restores an application from maintenance mode.
- `env` displays which environment Laravel is running at the moment; it's the equivalent of echoing `app()->environment()` in-app.
- `migrate` runs all database migrations.
- `optimize` optimizes your application for better performance by caching core PHP classes into *bootstrap/cache/compile.php*.
- `serve` spins up a PHP server at `localhost:8000` (you can customize the host and/or port with `--host` and `--port`).
- `tinker` brings up the Tinker REPL, which we'll cover later in this chapter.

Options

Before we cover the rest of the Artisan commands, let's look at a few notable options you can pass any time you run an Artisan command:

- `-q` suppresses all output.
- `-v`, `-vv`, and `-vvv` are the three levels of output verbosity (normal, verbose, and debug).
- `--no-interaction` does not ask any interactive questions, so it won't interrupt automated processes running it.
- `--env` allows you to define which environment the Artisan command should operate in (e.g., `local`, `production`, etc.).

- `--version` shows you which version of Laravel your application is running on.

You've probably guessed from looking at these options that Artisan commands are intended to be used much like basic shell commands: you might run them manually, but they can also function as a part of some automated process at some point.

For example, there are many automated deploy processes that might benefit from certain Artisan commands. You might want to run `php artisan optimize` every time you deploy an application. Flags like `-q` and `--no-interaction` ensure that your deploy scripts, not attended by a human being, can keep running smoothly.

The Grouped Commands

The rest of the commands available out of the box are grouped by context. We won't cover them all here, but we'll cover each context broadly:

app
> This just contains `app:name`, which allows you to replace every instance of the default top-level `App\` namespace with a namespace of your choosing. For example: `php artisan app:name MyApplication`.

auth
> All we have here is `auth:clear-resets`, which flushes all of the expired password reset tokens from the database.

cache
> `cache:clear` clears the caches, and `cache:table` creates a database migration if you plan to use the `database` cache driver.

config
> `config:cache` caches your configuration settings for faster lookup; to clear the cache, use `config:clear`.

db
> `db:seed` seeds your database, if you have configured database seeders.

event
> `event:generate` builds missing event and event listener files based on the definitions in `EventServiceProvider`. We'll learn more about events in Chapter 16.

key
> `key:generate` creates a random application encryption key in your *.env* file.

Rerunning artisan key:generate means losing encryption keys

Only run `php artisan key:generate` once—the first time you set up the application in a new environment—because this key is used to encrypt your data; if you change it after data has been stored, that data will all become inaccessible.

`make`

`make:auth` scaffolds out the views and corresponding routes for a landing page, a user dashboard, and login and register pages.

All the rest of the `make:` actions create a single item, and have parameters that vary accordingly. To learn more about any individual command's parameters, use `help` to read its documentation.

For example, you could run `php artisan help make:migration` and learn that you can pass `--create=`*tableNameHere* to create a migration that already has the create table syntax in the file, as shown here: `php artisan make:migration create_posts_table --create=posts`.

`migrate`

We saw a `migrate` command earlier to run our migrations, but here we can run all the other migration-related commands. Create the migrations table (to keep track of the migrations that are executed) with `migrate:install`, reset your migrations and start from scratch with `migrate:reset`, reset your migrations and run them all again with `migrate:refresh`, roll back just one migration with `migrate:rollback`, or check the status of your migrations with `migrate:status`.

`notifications`

`notifications:table` generates a migration that creates the table for database notifications.

`queue`

We'll cover Laravel's queues in Chapter 16, but the basic idea is that you can push jobs up into remote queues to be executed one after another by a worker. This command group provides all the tools you need to interact with your queues, like `queue:listen` to start listening to a queue, `queue:table` to create a migration for database-backed queues, and `queue:flush` to flush all failed queue jobs. There are quite a few more, which we'll learn about in Chapter 16.

`route`

If you run `route:list`, you'll see the definitions of every route defined in the application, including each route's verb(s), path, name, controller/closure action, and middleware. You can cache the route definitions for faster lookups with `route:cache` and clear your cache with `route:clear`.

schedule

We'll cover Laravel's cron-like scheduler in Chapter 16, but in order for it to work, you need to set the system cron to run `schedule:run` once a minute:

```
* * * * * php /home/myapp.com/artisan schedule:run >> /dev/null 2>&1
```

As you can see, this Artisan command is intended to be run regularly in order to power a core Laravel service.

session

`session:table` creates a migration for applications using database-backed sessions.

storage

`storage:link` creates a symbolic link from *public/storage* to *storage/app/public*. This is a common convention in Laravel apps, to make it easy to put user uploads (or other files that commonly end up in *storage/app*) somewhere where they'll be accessible at a public URL.

vendor

Some Laravel-specific packages need to "publish" some of their assets, either so that they can be served from your *public* directory or so that you can modify them. Either way, these packages register these "publishable assets" with Laravel, and when you run `vendor:publish`, it publishes them to their specified locations.

view

Laravel's view rendering engine automatically caches your views. It usually does a good job of handling its own cache invalidation, but if you ever notice it's gotten stuck, run `view:clear` to clear the cache.

Writing Custom Artisan Commands

Now that we've covered the Artisan commands that come with Laravel out of the box, let's talk about writing your own.

First, you should know: there's an Artisan command for that! Running `php artisan make:command` *YourCommandName* generates a new Artisan command in *app/Console/Commands/{YourCommandName}.php*.

php artisan make:command

5.2 The command signature for make:command has changed a few times. It was originally command:make, but for a while in 5.2 it was console:make and then make:console.

Finally, in 5.3, it's settled: all of the generators are under the make: namespace, and the command to generate new Artisan commands is now make:command.

Your first argument should be the class name of the command, and you can optionally pass a --command parameter to define what the terminal command will be (e.g., appname:action).

So, let's do it:

```
php artisan make:console WelcomeNewUsers --command=email:newusers
```

Take a look at Example 7-1 to see what you'll get.

Example 7-1. The default skeleton of an Artisan command

```php
<?php

namespace App\Console\Commands;

use Illuminate\Console\Command;

class WelcomeNewUsers extends Command
{
    /**
     * The name and signature of the console command.
     *
     * @var string
     */
    protected $signature = 'email:newusers';

    /**
     * The console command description.
     *
     * @var string
     */
    protected $description = 'Command description';

    /**
     * Create a new command instance.
     *
     * @return void
     */
    public function __construct()
    {
```

```
        parent::__construct();
    }

    /**
     * Execute the console command.
     *
     * @return mixed
     */
    public function handle()
    {
        //
    }
}
```

As you can see, it's very easy to define the command signature, the help text it shows in command lists, and the command's behavior on instantiation (__construct()) and on execution (handle()).

Registering Commands

There's one step left to make this new command usable in your application: you need to register it.

Open *app/Console/Kernel.php*. You'll see an array of command class names under the $commands property. To register your new command, add its class to this array. You can write it out, or just use the ::class class name accessor on the class as in Example 7-2.

Example 7-2. Registering a new command in the console kernel

```
class Kernel extends ConsoleKernel
{
    /**
     * The Artisan commands provided by your application.
     *
     * @var array
     */
    protected $commands = [
        \App\Console\Commands\WelcomeNewUsers::class,
    ];
```

Writing closure-based commands

If you'd prefer to keep your command definition process simpler, you can write commands as closures instead of classes by defining them in *routes/console.php*. Everything we discuss in this chapter will apply the same way, but you will just define and register the commands in a single step in that file:

```
// routes/console.php
Artisan::command(
    'password:reset {userId} {--sendEmail}',
    function ($userId, $sendEmail) {
        // do something...
    }
);
```

A Sample Command

We haven't covered mail or Eloquent yet (see Chapter 15 for mail and Chapter 8 for Eloquent), but the sample `handle()` method in Example 7-3 should read pretty clearly.

Example 7-3. A sample Artisan command handle() method

```
...
class WelcomeNewUsers extends Command
{
    public function handle()
    {
        User::signedUpThisWeek()->each(function ($user) {
            Mail::send(
                'emails.welcome',
                ['name' => $user->name],
                function ($m) use ($user) {
                    $m->to($user->email)->subject('Welcome!');
                }
            );
        });
    }
}
```

Now every time you run `php artisan email:newusers`, this command will grab every user that signed up this week and send them the welcome email.

If you would prefer injecting your mail and user dependencies instead of using facades, you can typehint them in the command constructor, and Laravel's container will inject them for you when the command is instantiated.

Take a look at Example 7-4 to see what Example 7-3 might look like using dependency injection and extracting its behavior out to a service class.

Example 7-4. The same command, refactored

```
...
class WelcomeNewUsers extends Command
{
    public function __construct(UserMailer $userMailer)
    {
        parent::__construct();

        $this->userMailer = $userMailer
    }

    public function handle()
    {
        $this->userMailer->welcomeNewUsers();
    }
```

Keep It Simple

It is possible to call Artisan commands from the rest of your code, so you can use them to encapsulate chunks of application logic. This is a very common practice in the Laravel community.

However, the Laravel docs recommend instead packaging the application logic into a service class, and injecting that service into your command. Console commands are seen as being similar to controllers: they're not domain classes, they're traffic cops that just route incoming requests to the correct behavior.

Arguments and Options

The $signature property of the new command looks like it might just contain the command name. But this property is also where you'll define any arguments and options for the command. There's a specific, simple syntax you can use to add arguments and options to your Artisan commands.

Before we dig into that syntax, take a look at an example for some context:

```
protected $signature = 'password:reset {userId} {--sendEmail}';
```

Arguments, required, optional, and/or with defaults

To define a required argument, surround it with braces:

```
password:reset {userId}
```

To make the argument optional, add a question mark:

```
password:reset {userId?}
```

To make it optional and provide a default, use:

```
password:reset {userId=1}
```

Options, required values, value defaults, and shortcuts

Options are similar to arguments, but they're prefixed with -- and can be used with
no value. To add a basic option, surround it with braces:

```
password:reset {userId} {--sendEmail}
```

If your option requires a value, add an = to its signature:

```
password:reset {userId} {--password=}
```

And if you want to pass a default value, add it after the =:

```
password:reset {userId} {--queue=default}
```

Array arguments and array options

Both for arguments and for options, if you want to accept an array as input, use the
* character:

```
password:reset {userIds*}
```

```
password:reset {--ids=*}
```

Using array arguments and parameters looks a bit like Example 7-5.

Example 7-5. Using array syntax with Artisan commands

```
// Argument
php artisan password:reset 1 2 3

// Option
php artisan password:reset --ids=1 --ids=2 --ids=3
```

Array arguments must be the last argument

Since an array argument captures every parameter after its definition and adds them as array items, an array argument has to be the
last argument or option within an Artisan command's signature.

Input descriptions

Remember how the built-in Artisan commands can give us more information about
their parameters if we use `artisan help`? We can provide that same information
about our custom commands. Just add a colon and the description text within the
curly braces, like in Example 7-6.

Example 7-6. Defining description text for Artisan arguments and options

```
protected $signature = 'password:reset
                       {userId : The ID of the user}
                       {--sendEmail : Whether to send user an email}';
```

Using Input

Now that we've prompted for this input, how do we use it in our command's handle() method? We have two options for retrieving the values of arguments and options.

argument()

$this->argument() with no parameters returns an array of all arguments (the first array item will be the command name). With a parameter passed, it'll return the value of the argument specified:

```
// with definition "password:reset {userId}":
php artisan password:reset 5

// $this->argument() returns this array
[
    "command": "password:reset",
    "userId': "5",
]

// $this->argument('userId') returns this string
"5"
```

option()

$this->option() with no parameters returns an array of all options, including some that will by default be false or null. With a parameter, it'll return the value of the option specified:

```
// with definition "password:reset {--userId=}":
php artisan password:reset --userId=5

// $this->option() returns this array
[
    "userId" => "5"
    "help" => false
    "quiet" => false
    "verbose" => false
    "version" => false
    "ansi" => false
    "no-ansi" => false
    "no-interaction" => false
    "env" => null
]
```

```
// $this->option('userId') returns this string
"5"
```

Example 7-7 shows an Artisan command using `argument()` and `option()` in its `handle()` method.

Example 7-7. Getting input from an Artisan command

```php
public function handle()
{
    // All arguments, including the command name
    $arguments = $this->argument();

    // Just the 'userId' argument
    $userid = $this->argument('userId');

    // All options, including some defaults like 'no-interaction' and 'env'
    $options = $this->option();

    // Just the 'sendEmail' option
    $sendEmail = $this->option('sendEmail');
}
```

Prompts

There are a few more ways to get user input from within your `handle()` code, and they all involve prompting the user to enter information during the execution of your command:

`ask()`
> Prompts the user to enter freeform text:
>
> ```php
> $email = $this->ask('What is your email address?');
> ```

`secret()`
> Prompts the user to enter freeform text, but hides the typing with asterisks:
>
> ```php
> $password = $this->ask('What is the DB password?');
> ```

`confirm()`
> Prompts the user for a yes/no answer, and returns a boolean:
>
> ```php
> if ($this->confirm('Do you want to truncate the tables?')) {
>     //
> }
> ```
>
> All answers except y or Y will be treated as a "no."

anticipate()

> Prompts the user to enter freeform text, and provides autocomplete suggestions. Still allows the user to type whatever she wants:

```
$album = $this->anticipate('What is the best album ever?', [
    "The Joshua Tree", "Pet Sounds", "What's Going On"
]);
```

choice()

> Prompts the user to choose one of the provided options. The last parameter is the default if the user doesn't choose:

```
$winner = $this->choice(
    'Who is the best football team?',
    ['Gators', 'Wolverines'],
    0
);
```

> Note that the final parameter, the default, should be the array key. Since we passed a nonassociative array, the key for "Gators" is 0. You could also key your array, if you'd prefer:

```
$winner = $this->choice(
    'Who is the best football team?',
    ['gators' => 'Gators', 'wolverines' => 'Wolverines'],
    'gators'
);
```

Output

During the execution of your command, you might want to write messages to the user. The most basic way to do this is to use $this->info() to output basic green text:

```
$this->info('Your command has run successfully.');
```

You also have available the comment() (orange), question() (highlighted teal), error() (highlighted red), and line() (uncolored) methods to echo to the command line.

Please note that the exact colors may vary from machine to machine, but they try to be in line with the local machine's standards for communicating to the end user.

Table output

The table component makes it simple to create ASCII tables full of your data. Take a look at Example 7-8.

Example 7-8. Outputting tables with Artisan commands

```
$headers = ['Name', 'Email'];

$data = [
    ['Dhriti', 'dhriti@amrit.com'],
    ['Moses', 'moses@gutierez.com']
];

// Or, you could get similar data from the database:
// $data = App\User::all(['name', 'email'])->toArray();

$this->table($headers, $data);
```

Note that Example 7-8 has two sets of data: the headers, and the data itself. Both contain two "cells" per "row"; the first cell in each row is the name, and the second is the email. That way the data from the Eloquent call (which is constrained to pull only name and email) matches up with the headers.

Take a look at Example 7-9 to see what the table output looks like.

Example 7-9. Sample output of an Artisan table

```
+---------+--------------------+
| Name    | Email              |
+---------+--------------------+
| Dhriti  | dhriti@amrit.com   |
| Moses   | moses@gutierez.com |
+---------+--------------------+
```

Progress bars

If you've ever run npm install, you've seen a command-line progress bar before. Let's build one in Example 7-10.

Example 7-10. Sample Artisan progress bar

```
$totalUnits = 10;
$this->output->progressStart($totalUnits);

for ($i = 0; $i < $totalUnits; $i++) {
    sleep(1);

    $this->output->progressAdvance();
}

$this->output->progressFinish();
```

What did we do here? First, we informed the system how many "units" we needed to work through. Maybe a unit is a user, and you have 350 users. The bar will then divide the entire width it has available on your screen by 350, and increment it by 1/350th every time you run `progressAdvance()`. Once you're done, run `progressFinish()` so it knows it's done displaying the progress bar.

Calling Artisan Commands in Normal Code

While Artisan commands are designed to be run from the command line, you can also call them from other code.

The easiest way is to use the `Artisan` facade. You can either call a command using `Artisan::call()` (which will return the command's exit code), or queue a command using `Artisan::queue()`.

Both take two parameters: first, the terminal command (`password:reset`); and second, an array of parameters to pass it. Take a look at Example 7-11 to see how it works with arguments and options.

Example 7-11. Calling Artisan commands from other code

```
Route::get('test-artisan', function () {
    $exitCode = Artisan::call('password:reset', [
        'userId' => 15, '--sendEmail' => true
    ]);
});
```

As you can see, arguments are passed by keying to the argument name, and options with no value can be passed `true` or `false`.

You can also call Artisan commands from other commands, using `$this->call`, (which is the same as `Artisan::call()`, or `$this->callSilent`, which is the same but suppresses all output). See Example 7-12 for an example.

Example 7-12. Calling Artisan commands from other Artisan commands

```
public function handle()
{
    $this->callSilent('password:reset', [
        'userId' => 15
    ]);
}
```

Finally, you can inject an instance of the `Illuminate\Contracts\Console\Kernel` contract, and use its `call()` method.

Tinker

Tinker is a REPL, or read–eval–print loop. If you've ever used IRB in Ruby, you'll be familiar with how a REPL works.

REPLs give you a prompt, similar to the command-line prompt, that mimics a "waiting" state of your application. You type your commands into the REPL, hit Return, and then expect what you typed to be evaluated and the response printed out.

Example 7-13 provides a quick sample to give you a sense of how it works and how it might be useful. We start the REPL with `php artisan tinker` and are then presented with a blank prompt (>>>); every response to our commands is printed on a line prefaced with =>.

Example 7-13. Using Tinker

```
php artisan tinker

>>> $user = new App\User;
=> App\User: {}
>>> $user->email = 'matt@mattstauffer.co';
=> "matt@mattstauffer.co"
>>> $user->password = bcrypt('superSecret');
=> "$2y$10$TWPGBC7e8d1bvJ1q5kv.VDUGfYDnE9gANl4mleuB3htIY2dxcQfQ5"
>>> $user->save();
=> true
```

As you can see, we created a new user, set some data, and saved it to the database. And this is real. If this were a production application, we would've just created a brand new user in our system.

This makes Tinker a great tool for simple database interactions, for trying out new ideas, and for running snippets of code when it'd be a pain to find a place to put them in the application source files.

Tinker is powered by Psy Shell (*http://psysh.org/*), so check that out to see what else you can do with Tinker.

Testing

Since you know how to call Artisan commands from code, it's easy to do that in a test and ensure that whatever behavior you expected to be performed has been performed correctly, as in Example 7-14.

Example 7-14. Calling Artisan commands from a test

```
public function test_empty_log_command_empties_logs_table()
{
    DB::table('logs')->insert(['message' => 'Did something']);
    Artisan::call('logs:empty');
    $this->assertCount(0, DB::table('logs')->get());
}
```

As always, facades are easy to swap out, but if you don't want to do this you can instead inject your dependencies into the constructor of the Artisan command, which will make them easy to swap out at test time.

The Artisan facade provides access to the Illuminate\Contracts\Console\Kernel contract, so if you want to avoid using the facade in your code, you can instead inject an instance of that and use its call() method, as in Example 7-15.

Example 7-15. Injecting the kernel instead of using the Artisan facade

```
use Illuminate\Contracts\Console\Kernel;
...
class NightlyCleanup extends Job
{
    ...
    public function handle(Kernel $kernel)
    {
        // ... do other stuff
        $kernel->call('logs:empty');
    }
```

TL;DR

Artisan commands are Laravel's command-line tools. Laravel comes with quite a few out of the box, but it's also easy to create your own Artisan commands and call them from the command line or your own code.

Tinker is a REPL that makes it simple to get into your application environment and interact with real code and real data.

## CHAPTER 8

Database and Eloquent

Laravel provides a suite of tools for interacting with your application's databases, but the most notable is Eloquent, Laravel's ActiveRecord ORM (object-relational mapper).

Eloquent is one of Laravel's most popular and influential features. It's a great example of how Laravel is different from the majority of PHP frameworks; in a world of Data-Mapper ORMs that are powerful but complex, Eloquent stands out for its simplicity. There's one class per table, which is responsible for retrieving, representing, and persisting data in that table.

Whether or not you choose to use Eloquent, however, you'll still get a ton of benefit from the other database tools Laravel provides. So, before we dig into Eloquent, let's start by covering the basics of Laravel's database functionality: migrations, seeders, and the query builder.

Then we'll cover Eloquent: defining your models; inserting, updating, and deleting; customizing your responses with accessors, mutators, and attribute casting; and finally relationships. There's a lot going on here, and it's easy to get overwhelmed, but just take it one step at a time and we'll make it through.

Configuration

Before we get into how to use Laravel's database tools, let's pause for a second and go over how to configure your database credentials and connections.

The configuration for database access lives in *config/database.php*. Like many other configuration areas in Laravel, you can define multiple "connections" and then decide which the code will use by default.

Database Connections

By default, there's one connection for each of the connection types, as you can see in Example 8-1.

Example 8-1. The default database connections list

```
'connections' => [

    'sqlite' => [
        'driver'   => 'sqlite',
        'database' => database_path('database.sqlite'),
        'prefix'   => '',
    ],

    'mysql' => [
        'driver'    => 'mysql',
        'host'      => env('DB_HOST', 'localhost'),
        'database'  => env('DB_DATABASE', 'forge'),
        'username'  => env('DB_USERNAME', 'forge'),
        'password'  => env('DB_PASSWORD', ''),
        'charset'   => 'utf8',
        'collation' => 'utf8_unicode_ci',
        'prefix'    => '',
        'strict'    => false,
        'engine'    => null,
    ],

    'pgsql' => [
        'driver'   => 'pgsql',
        'host'     => env('DB_HOST', 'localhost'),
        'database' => env('DB_DATABASE', 'forge'),
        'username' => env('DB_USERNAME', 'forge'),
        'password' => env('DB_PASSWORD', ''),
        'charset'  => 'utf8',
        'prefix'   => '',
        'schema'   => 'public',
    ],

    'sqlsrv' => [
        'driver'   => 'sqlsrv',
        'host'     => env('DB_HOST', 'localhost'),
        'database' => env('DB_DATABASE', 'forge'),
        'username' => env('DB_USERNAME', 'forge'),
        'password' => env('DB_PASSWORD', ''),
        'charset'  => 'utf8',
        'prefix'   => '',
    ],

]
```

You could create new named connections, though, and still be able to set the drivers (MySQL, Postgres, etc.) in those new named connections. So, while there's one connection per driver by default, that's not a constraint.

Each connection allows you to define the properties necessary for connecting to and customizing each connection type.

There are a few reasons for the idea of multiple drivers. To start with, the "connections" section as it comes out of the box is a simple template that makes it easy to start apps that use any of the supported database connection types. In many apps, you can pick the database connection you'll be using, fill out its information, and even delete the others if you'd like. I usually just keep them all there, in case I might eventually use them.

But there are also some cases where you might need multiple connections within the same application. For example, you might use different database connections for two different types of data, or you might read from one and write to another. Support for multiple connections makes this possible.

Other Database Configuration Options

The `config.database` configuration section has quite a few other configuration settings. You can configure Redis access, customize the table name used for migrations, determine the default connection, and toggle whether non-Eloquent calls return `stdClass` or array instances.

With any service in Laravel that allows multiple "connections"—sessions can be backed by the database or file storage, the cache can use Redis or Memcached, databases can use MySQL or PostgreSQL—you can define multiple connections and also choose that a particular connection will be the "default," meaning it will be used any time you don't explicitly ask for a particular connection. Here's how you ask for a specific connection, if you want to:

```
$users = DB::connection('secondary')->select('select * from users');
```

Migrations

Modern frameworks like Laravel make it easy to define your database structure with code-driven migrations. Every new table, column, index, and key can be defined in code, and any new environment can be brought from bare database to your app's perfect schema in seconds.

Defining Migrations

A migration is a single file that defines two things: the modifications desired when running this migration *up* and the modifications desired when running this migration *down*.

"Up" and "Down" in Migrations

Migrations are always run in order by date. Every migration file is named something like this: *2014_10_12_000000_create_users_table.php*. When a new system is migrated, the system grabs each migration, starting at the earliest date, and runs its up() method—you're migrating it "up" at this point. But the migration system also allows you to "roll back" your most recent set of migrations. It'll grab each of them and run its down() method, which should undo whatever changes the up migration made.

So, the up() method of a migration should "do" its migration, and the down() method should "undo" it.

Example 8-2 shows what the default "create users table" migration that comes with Laravel looks like.

Example 8-2. Laravel's default "create users table" migration

```php
<?php

use Illuminate\Database\Schema\Blueprint;
use Illuminate\Database\Migrations\Migration;

class CreateUsersTable extends Migration
{
    /**
     * Run the migrations.
     *
     * @return void
     */
    public function up()
    {
        Schema::create('users', function (Blueprint $table) {
            $table->increments('id');
            $table->string('name');
            $table->string('email')->unique();
            $table->string('password', 60);
            $table->rememberToken();
            $table->timestamps();
        });
    }
```

```
/**
 * Reverse the migrations.
 *
 * @return void
 */
public function down()
{
    Schema::drop('users');
}
}
```

As you can see, we have an up() method and a down() method. up() tells the migration to create a new table named users with a few fields, and down() tells it to drop the users table.

Creating a migration

As we saw in Chapter 7, there's an Artisan command for creating a migration file. It's php artisan make:migration, and it has a single parameter, which is the name of the migration. For example, to create the table we just covered, you would run php artisan make:migration create_users_table.

There are two flags you can optionally pass to this command. --create=*table_name* prefills the migration with code designed to create a table named *table_name*, and --table=_table_name_ just prefills the migration for modifications to an existing table. Here are a few examples:

```
php artisan make:migration create_users_table
php artisan make:migration add_votes_to_users_table --table=users
php artisan make:migration create_users_table --create=users
```

Creating tables

We already saw in the default create_users_table migration that our migrations depend on the Schema facade and its methods. Everything we can do in these migrations will rely on the methods of Schema.

To create a new table in a migration, use the create() method—the first parameter is the table name, and the second is a closure that defines its columns:

```
Schema::create('tablename', function (Blueprint $table) {
    // Create columns here
});
```

Creating columns

To create new columns in a table, whether in a create table call or a modify table call, use the instance of Blueprint that's passed into your closure:

```
Schema::create('users', function (Blueprint $table) {
    $table->string('name');
});
```

Let's look at the various methods available on `Blueprint` instances for creating columns. I'll describe how they work in MySQL, but if you're using another database, Laravel will just use the closest equivalent.

The following are the simple field `Blueprint` methods:

`integer(colName)`, `tinyInteger(colName)`, `smallInteger(colName)`, `mediumInteger(colName)`, `bigInteger(colName)`
Adds an `INTEGER` type column, or one of its many variations

`string(colName, OPTIONAL length)`
Adds a `VARCHAR` type column

`binary(colName)`
Adds a `BLOB` type column

`boolean(colName)`
Adds a `BOOLEAN` type column (a `TINYINT(1)` in MySQL)

`char(colName, length)`
Adds a `CHAR` column

`datetime(colName)`
Adds a `DATETIME` column

`decimal(colName, precision, scale)`
Adds a `DECIMAL` column, with precision and scale—e.g., `decimal('amount', 5, 2)` specifies a precision of 5 and a scale of 2

`double(colName, total digits, digits after decimal)`
Adds a `DOUBLE` column—e.g., `double('tolerance', 12, 8)` specifies 12 digits long, with 8 of those digits to the right of the decimal place, as in `7204.05691739`

`enum(colName, [choiceOne, choiceTwo])`
Adds an `ENUM` column, with provided choices

`float(colName)`
Adds a `FLOAT` column (same as double in MySQL)

`json(colName) and jsonb(colName)`
Adds a `JSON` or `JSONB` column (or a `TEXT` column in Laravel 5.1)

`text(colName)`, `mediumText(colName)`, `longText(colName)`
Adds a `TEXT` column (or its various sizes)

time(*colName*)
   Adds a TIME column

timestamp(*colName*)
   Adds a TIMESTAMP column

uuid(*colName*)
   Adds a UUID column (CHAR(36) in MySQL)

And these are the special (joined) Blueprint methods:

increments(*colName*) *and* bigIncrements(*colName*)
   Add an unsigned incrementing INTEGER or BIG INTEGER primary key ID

timestamps() *and* nullableTimestamps()
   Adds created_at and updated_at timestamp columns

rememberToken()
   Adds a remember_token column (VARCHAR(100)) for user "remember me" tokens

softDeletes()
   Adds a deleted_at timestamp for use with soft deletes

morphs(*colName*)
   For a provided +*colName*+, adds an integer colName_id and a string col
   Name_type (e.g., morphs('*tag*') adds integer tag_id and string tag_type); for
   use in polymorphic relationships

Building extra properties fluently

Most of the properties of a field definition—its length, for example—are set as the
second parameter of the field creation method we looked at in the previous section.
But there are a few other properties that we'll set by chaining more method calls after
the creation of the column. For example, this email field is nullable and will be placed
(in MySQL) right after the last_name field:

```
Schema::table('users', function (Blueprint $table) {
    $table->string('email')->nullable()->after('last_name');
});
```

The following methods are used to set additional properties of a field:

nullable()
   Allows NULL values to be inserted into this column

default('*default content*')
   Specifies the default content for this column if no value is provided

```
unsigned()
```
Marks integer columns as unsigned

```
first() (MySQL only)
```
Places the column first in the column order

```
after(colName) (MySQL only)
```
Places the column after another column in the column order

```
unique()
```
Adds a UNIQUE index

```
primary()
```
Adds a primary key index

```
index()
```
Adds a basic index

Note that `unique()`, `primary()`, and `index()` can also be used outside of the fluent column building context, which we'll cover later.

Dropping tables

If you want to drop a table, there's a `drop` method on `Schema` that takes one parameter, the table name:

```
Schema::drop('contacts');
```

Modifying columns

To modify a column, just write the code you would write to create the column as if it were new, and then append a call to the `change()` method after it.

 Required dependency before modifying columns

Before you modify any columns (or drop any columns in SQLite), you'll need to add the `doctrine/dbal` package as a requirement in your *composer.json*, and run `composer update` to bring it in.

So, if we have a string column named `name` that has a length of 255 and we want to change its length to 100, this is how we would write it:

```
Schema::table('users', function ($table) {
    $table->string('name', 100)->change();
});
```

The same is true if we want to adjust any of its properties that aren't defined in the method name. To make a field nullable, we do this:

```
Schema::table('contacts', function ($table) {
    $table->string('deleted_at')->nullable()->change();
});
```

Here's how we rename a column:

```
Schema::table('contacts', function ($table)
{
    $table->renameColumn('promoted', 'is_promoted');
});
```

And this is how we drop a column:

```
Schema::table('contacts', function ($table)
{
    $table->dropColumn('votes');
});
```

Modifying multiple columns at once in SQLite

If you try to drop or modify multiple columns within a single migration closure *and* you are using SQLite, you'll run into errors.

In Chapter 12 I'll recommend that you use SQLite for your testing database, so even if you're using a more traditional database, you may want to consider this a limitation for testing purposes.

However, you don't have to create a new migration for each. Instead, just create multiple calls to Schema::table() within the up() method of your migration:

```
public function up()
{
    Schema::table('contacts', function (Blueprint $table)
    {
        $table->dropColumn('is_promoted');
    });

    Schema::table('contacts', function (Blueprint $table)
    {
        $table->dropColumn('alternate_email');
    });
}
```

Indexes and foreign keys

We've covered how to create, modify, and delete columns. Let's move on to indexing and relating them.

Adding indexes. Check out Example 8-3 for examples of how to add indexes to your column.

Example 8-3. Adding column indexes in migrations

```
// after columns are created...
$table->primary('primary_id'); // Primary key; unnecessary if used increments()
$table->primary(['first_name', 'last_name']); // Composite keys
$table->unique('email'); // Unique index
$table->unique('email', 'optional_custom_index_name'); // Unique index
$table->index('amount'); // Basic index
$table->index('amount', 'optional_custom_index_name'); // Basic index
```

Note that the first example (`primary()`) is not necessary if you're using the `increments()` method to create your index; this will automatically add a primary key index for you.

Removing indexes. We can remove indexes as shown in Example 8-4.

Example 8-4. Removing column indexes in migrations

```
$table->dropPrimary('contacts_id_primary');
$table->dropUnique('contacts_email_unique');
$table->dropIndex('optional_custom_index_name');

// If you pass an array of column names to dropIndex, it will
// guess the index names for you based on the generation rules
$table->dropIndex(['email', 'amount']);
```

Adding and removing foreign keys. To add a foreign key that defines that a particular column references a column on another table, Laravel's syntax is simple and clear:

```
$table->foreign('user_id')->references('id')->on('users');
```

Here we're adding a `foreign` index on the `user_id` column, showing that it references the `id` column on the `users` table. Couldn't get much simpler.

If we want to specify foreign key constraints, we can do that too, with `onDelete()` and `onUpdate()`. For example:

```
$table->foreign('user_id')
    ->references('id')
    ->on('users')
    ->onDelete('cascade');
```

To drop an index, we can either delete it by referencing its index name (which is automatically generated by combining the names of the columns and tables being referenced):

```
$table->dropForeign('contacts_user_id_foreign');
```

or by passing it an array of the fields that it's referencing on the local table:

```
$table->dropForeign(['user_id']);
```

Running Migrations

Once you have your migrations defined, how do you run them? There's an Artisan command for that:

```
php artisan migrate
```

This command runs all "outstanding" migrations. Laravel keeps track of which migrations you have run and which you haven't. Every time you run this command, it checks whether you've run all available migrations, and if you haven't, it'll run any that remain.

There are a few options in this namespace that you can work with. First, you can run your migrations *and* your seeds (which we'll cover next):

```
php artisan migrate --seed
```

You can also run any of the following commands:

- `migrate:install` creates the database table that keeps track of which migrations you have and haven't run; this is run automatically when you run your migrations.
- `migrate:reset` rolls back every database migration you've run on this install.
- `migrate:refresh` rolls back every database migration you've run on this install, and then runs every migration available. It's the same as running `migrate:reset` and then `migrate`, one after the other.
- `migrate:rollback` rolls back *just* the migrations that ran the last time you ran `migrate`, or, with the added option `--step=1`, rolls back the number of migrations you specify.
- `migrate:status` shows a table listing every migration, with a Y or N next to each showing whether or not it has run yet in this environment.

Migrating with Homestead/Vagrant

If you're running migrations on your local machine and your *.env* file points to a database in a Vagrant box, your migrations will fail. You'll need to `ssh` into your Vagrant box and then run the migrations from there. The same is true for seeds and any other Artisan commands that affect or read from the database.

Seeding

Seeding with Laravel is so simple, it has gained widespread adoption as a part of normal development workflows in a way it hasn't in previous PHP frameworks. There's a *database/seeds* folder that comes with a `DatabaseSeeder` class, which has a `run()` method that is called when you call the seeder.

There are two primary ways to run the seeders: along with a migration, or separately.

To run a seeder along with a migration, just add `--seed` to any migration call:

```
php artisan migrate --seed
php artisan migrate:refresh --seed
```

And to run it independently:

```
php artisan db:seed
php artisan db:seed --class=VotesTableSeeder
```

This will run whatever you have defined in the `run()` methods of every seeder class (or just the class you passed to `--class`).

Creating a Seeder

To create a seeder, use the `make:seeder` Artisan command:

```
php artisan make:seeder ContactsTableSeeder
```

You'll now see a `ContactsTableSeeder` class show up in the *database/seeds* directory. Before we edit it, let's add it to the `DatabaseSeeder` class so it will run when we run our seeders:

```
// database/seeds/DatabaseSeeder.php
...
    public function run()
    {
        $this->call(ContactsTableSeeder::class);
    }
```

Now let's edit the seeder itself. The simplest thing we can do there is manually insert a record using the `DB` facade:

```php
<?php

use Illuminate\Database\Seeder;
use Illuminate\Database\Eloquent\Model;

class ContactsTableSeeder extends Seeder
{
    public function run()
    {
        DB::table('contacts')->insert([
            'name' => 'Lupita Smith'
            'email' => 'lupita@gmail.com',
        ]);
    }
}
```

This will get us a single record, which is a good start. But for truly functional seeds, you'll likely want to loop over some sort of random generator and run this `insert()` many times, right?

Model Factories

Model factories define one (or more) patterns for creating fake entries for your database tables. By default they're named after an Eloquent class, but you can also just name them after the table name if you're not going to work with Eloquent. Here's the same table set up both ways:

```
$factory->define(User::class, function (Faker\Generator $faker) {
    return [
        'name' => $faker->name,
    ];
});

$factory->define('users', function (Faker\Generator $faker) {
    return [
        'name' => $faker->name,
    ];
});
```

Theoretially you can name these factories anything you like, but naming the factory after your Eloquent class is the most idiomatic approach.

Creating a model factory

Model factories are defined in *database/factories/ModelFactory.php*. Each factory has a name and a definition of how to create a new instance of the defined class. The `$factory->define()` method takes the factory name as the first parameter and a closure that's run for each generation as the second parameter.

The simplest factory we could define might look something like this:

```
$factory->define(Contact::class, function (Faker\Generator $faker) {
    return [
        'name' => 'Lupita Smith',
        'email' => 'lupita@gmail.com',
    ];
});
```

Now we can use the `factory()` global helper to create an instance of `Contact` in our seeding and testing:

```
// Create one
$contact = factory(Contact::class)->create();

// Create many
factory(Contact::class, 20)->create();
```

However, if we used that factory to create 20 contacts, all 20 would have the same information. That's less useful.

We will get even more benefit from model factories when we take advantage of the instance of `Faker` (*https://github.com/fzaninotto/Faker*) that's passed into the closure; `Faker` makes it easy to randomize the creation of structured fake data. The previous example now turns into this:

```
$factory->define(Contact::class, function (Faker\Generator $faker) {
    return [
        'name' => $faker->name,
        'email' => $faker->email,
    ];
});
```

Now, every time we create a fake contact using this model factory, all of our properties will be unique.

Using a model factory

There are two primary contexts in which we'll use model factories: testing (which we'll cover in Chapter 12) and seeding, which we're talking about here. Let's write a seeder using a model factory; take a look at Example 8-5.

Example 8-5. Using model factories

```
factory(Post::class)->create([
    'title' => 'My greatest post ever'
]);

factory(User::class, 20)->create()->each(function ($u) use ($post) {
    $post->comments()->save(factory(Comment::class)->make([
        'user_id' => $u->id
    ]));
});
```

When we're using a factory, we use the `factory()` global helper, and pass it the name of the factory—which, as we just saw, is the name of the Eloquent class we're generating an instance of. That returns the factory, and then we can run one of two methods on it: `make()` or `create()`.

Both methods generate an instance of this class, using the definition in *modelFactory.php*. The difference is that `make()` creates the instance but doesn't (yet) save it to the database, whereas `create()` saves it to the database instantly.

The second example will make more sense once we cover relationships in Eloquent later in this chapter.

Overriding properties when calling a model factory. If you pass an array to either `make()` or `create()`, you can override specific keys, like we did in Example 8-7 to set the `user_id` on the comment and to manually set the title of our post.

Generating more than one instance with a model factory. If you pass a number as the second parameter to the `factory()` helper, you can specify that you're creating more than one instance. Instead of returning a single instance, it'll return a collection of instances. This means you can treat the result like an array, you can associate each of its instances with another entity, or you can use other entity methods on each instance—like we used `each()` in Example 8-5 to add a comment from each newly created user.

Defining and accessing multiple model factory types

Let's go back to *modelFactory.php* for a second. We have a `Contact` factory defined:

```
$factory->define(Contact::class, function (Faker\Generator $faker) {
    return [
        'name' => $faker->name,
        'email' => $faker->email,
    ];
});
```

But sometimes you need more than one factory for a class of object. What if we need to be able to add some contacts who are very important people (VIPs)? We can define a second factory type for this, as seen in Example 8-6.

Example 8-6. Defining multiple factory types for the same model

```
$factory->define(Contact::class, function (Faker\Generator $faker) {
    return [
        'name' => $faker->name,
        'email' => $faker->email,
    ];
});

$factory->defineAs(Contact::class, 'vip', function (Faker\Generator $faker) {
    return [
        'name' => $faker->name,
        'email' => $faker->email,
        'vip' => true,
    ];
});
```

But that's a lot of duplication, right? Thankfully, we can make any given model factory extend another, and then it can just override one or a few properties. Let's have our "VIP" contact now just extend the previous by using `$factory->raw()`, as shown in Example 8-7.

Example 8-7. Extending a factory type

```
$factory->define(Contact::class, function (Faker\Generator $faker) {
    return [
        'name' => $faker->name,
        'email' => $faker->email,
    ];
});

$factory->defineAs(
    Contact::class,
    'vip',
    function (Faker\Generator $faker) use ($factory) {
        $contact = $factory->raw(Contact::class);

        return array_merge($contact, ['vip' => true]);
    });
```

Now, let's make a specific type:

```
$vip = factory(Contact::class, 'vip')->create();

$vips = factory(Contact::class, 'vip', 3)->create();
```

Query Builder

Now that you're connected and you've migrated and seeded your tables, let's get started with how to use the database tools. At the core of every piece of Laravel's database functionality is the query builder, a fluent interface for interacting with your database.

What Is a Fluent Interface?

A fluent interface is one that primarily uses method chaining to provide a simpler API to the end user. Rather than expecting all of the relevant data to be passed into either a constructor or a method call, fluent call chains can be built gradually, with consecutive calls. Consider this comparison:

```
// Non-fluent:
$users = DB::select(['table' => 'users', 'where' => ['type' => 'donor']]);

// Fluent:
$users = DB::table('users')->where('type', 'donor')->get();
```

Laravel's database architecture can connect to MySQL, Postgres, SQLite, and SQL Server through a single interface, with just the change of a few configuration settings.

If you've ever used a PHP framework, you've likely used a tool that allows you to run "raw" SQL queries with basic escaping for security. The query builder is that, with a lot of convenience layers and helpers on top, so let's start there.

Basic Usage of the DB Facade

Before we get into building complex queries with fluent method chaining, let's take a look at a few sample DB facade commands. The DB facade is used both for query builder chaining and for simpler raw queries, as illustrated in Example 8-8.

Example 8-8. Sample raw SQL and query builder usage

```
// basic statement
DB::statement('drop table users')

// raw select, and parameter binding
DB::select('select * from contacts where validated = ?', [true]);

// select using the fluent builder
$users = DB::table('users')->get();

// joins and other complex calls
DB::table('users')
    ->join('contacts', function ($join) {
        $join->on('users.id', '=', 'contacts.user_id')
            ->where('contacts.type', 'donor');
    })
    ->get();
```

Raw SQL

As we saw in Example 8-1, it's possible to make any raw call to the database using the DB facade and the statement() method: DB::statement('*SQL statement here*').

But there are also specific methods for various common actions: select(), insert(), update(), and delete(). These are still raw calls, but there are differences. First, using update() and delete() will return the number of rows affected, whereas state ment() won't; second, with these methods it's clearer to future developers exactly what sort of statement you're making.

Raw selects

The simplest of the specific DB methods is select(). You can run it without any additional parameters:

```
$users = DB::select('select * from users');
```

This will return a collection of stdClass objects.

Illuminate Collections

Prior to Laravel 5.3, the DB facade returned a stdClass object for methods that return only one row (like first()), and an array for any that return multiple rows (like all()). In Laravel 5.3, the DB facade, like Eloquent, returns a collection for any method that returns (or can return) multiple rows. The DB facade returns an instance of Illuminate\Support\Collection and Eloquent returns an instance of Illuminate \Database\Eloquent\Collection, which extends Illuminate\Support\Collection with a few Eloquent-specific methods.

Collection is like a PHP array with superpowers, allowing you to run map(), filter(), reduce(), each(), and much more on your data. You can learn more about collections in Chapter 17.

Parameter bindings and named bindings

Laravel's database architecture allows for the use of PDO parameter binding, which protects your queries from potential SQL attacks. Passing a parameter to a statement is as simple as replacing the value in your statement with a ?, then adding the value to the second parameter of your call:

```
$usersOfType = DB::select(
    'select * from users where type = ?',
    [$type]
);
```

You can also name those parameters for clarity:

```
$usersOfType = DB::select(
    'select * from users where type = :type',
    ['type' => $userType]
);
```

Raw inserts

From here, the raw commands all look pretty much the same. Raw inserts look like this:

```
DB::insert(
    'insert into contacts (name, email) values (?, ?)',
    ['sally', 'sally@me.com']
);
```

Raw updates

Updates look like this:

```
$countUpdated = DB::update(
    'update contacts set status = ? where id = ?',
    ['donor', $id]
);
```

Raw deletes

And deletes look like this:

```
$countDeleted = DB::delete(
    'delete from contacts where archived = ?',
    [true]
);
```

Chaining with the Query Builder

Up until now, we haven't actually used the query builder, per se. We've just used simple method calls on the DB facade. Let's actually build some queries.

The query builder makes it possible to chain methods together to, you guessed it, *build a query*. At the end of your chain you'll use some method—likely get()—to trigger the actual execution of the query you've just built.

Let's take a look at a quick example:

```
$usersOfType = DB::table('users')
    ->where('type', $type)
    ->get();
```

Here, we built our query—users table, $type type—and then we executed the query and got our result.

Let's take a look at what methods the query builder allows you to chain. The methods can be split up into what I'll call constraining methods, modifying methods, and ending/returning methods.

Constraining methods

These methods take the query as it is and constrain it to return a smaller subset of possible data:

select()
    Allows you to choose which columns you're selecting:

```
$emails = DB::table('contacts')
    ->select('email', 'email2 as second_email')
    ->get();
```

```
// Or
$emails = DB::table('contacts')
    ->select('email')
    ->addSelect('email2 as second_email')
    ->get();
```

where()

Allows you to limit the scope of what's being returned using WHERE. By default, the signature of the where() method is that it takes three parameters—the column, the comparison operator, and the value:

```
$newContacts = DB::table('contact')
    ->where('created_at', '>', Carbon::now()->subDay())
    ->get();
```

However, if your comparison is =, which is the most common comparison, you can drop the second operator: $vipContacts = DB::table('contacts')->where('vip',true)->get();.

If you want to combine where() statements, you can either chain them after each other, or pass an array of arrays:

```
$newVips = DB::table('contacts')
    ->where('vip', true)
    ->where('created_at', '>', Carbon::now()
    ->subDay());
// Or
$newVips = DB::table('contacts')->where([
    ['vip', true],
    ['created_at', '>', Carbon::now()->subDay()],
]);
```

orWhere()

Creates simple OR WHERE statements:

```
$priorityContacts = DB::table('contacts')
    ->where('vip', true)
    ->orWhere('created_at', '>', Carbon::now()->subDay())
    ->get();
```

To create a more complex OR WHERE statement with multiple conditions, pass orWhere() a closure:

```
$contacts = DB::table('contacts')
    ->where('vip', true)
    ->orWhere(function ($query) {
        $query->where('created_at', '>', Carbon::now()->subDay())
            ->where('trial', false);
    })
    ->get();
```

Potential confusion with multiple where and orWhere calls

If you are using orWhere() calls in conjunction with multiple where() calls, you need to be very careful to ensure the query is doing what you think it is. This isn't because of any fault with Laravel, but because a query like the following might not do what you expect:

```
$canEdit = DB::table('users')
    ->where('admin', true)
    ->orWhere('plan', 'premium')
    ->where('is_plan_owner', true)
    ->get();

SELECT * FROM users
    WHERE admin = 1
    OR plan = 'premium'
    AND is_plan_owner = 1;
```

If you want to write SQL that says "if this OR (this and this)," which is clearly the intention in the previous example, you'll want to pass a closure into the orWhere() call:

```
$canEdit = DB::table('users')
    ->where('admin', true)
    ->orWhere(function ($query) {
        $query->where('plan', 'premium')
            ->where('is_plan_owner', true);
    })
    ->get();

SELECT * FROM users
    WHERE admin = 1
    OR (plan = 'premium' AND is_plan_owner = 1);
```

whereBetween(*colName*, [*low, high*])
    Allows you to scope a query to return only rows where a column is between two values (inclusive of the two values):

```
$mediumDrinks = DB::table('drinks')
    ->whereBetween('size', [6, 12])
    ->get();
```

The same works for whereNotBetween(), but it will select the inverse.

whereIn(*colName*, [*1, 2, 3*])
    Allows you to scope a query to return only rows where a column is in an explicitly provided list of options: $closeBy = DB::table('contacts')->whereIn(*state*, [*FL, GA, AL*])->get().

```
$closeBy = DB::table('contacts')->whereIn('state', ['FL', 'GA',
'AL'])->get()
```
The same works for whereNotIn(), but it will select the inverse.

whereNull(*colName*) *and* whereNotNull(*colName*)
Allow you to select only rows where a given column is NULL or is NOT NULL, respectively.

whereRaw()
Allows you to pass in a raw, unescaped string to be added after the WHERE statement: `$goofs = DB::table('contacts')->whereRaw('id = 12345')->get()`.

 Beware of SQL injection!
Any SQL queries passed to whereRaw() will not be escaped. Use this method carefully and infrequently; this is the prime opportunity for SQL injection attacks in your app.

whereExists()
Allows you to select only rows that, when passed into a provided subquery, return at least one row. Imagine you only want to get those users who have left at least one comment:

```
$commenters = DB::table('users')
    ->whereExists(function ($query) {
        $query->select('id')
            ->from('comments')
            ->whereRaw('comments.user_id = users.id');
    })
    ->get();
```

distinct()
Selects only distinct rows. Usually this is paired with select(), because if you use a primary key, there will be no duplicated rows: `$lastNames = DB::table('contacts')->select('last_name')->distinct()->get()`.

Modifying methods

These methods change the way the query's results will be output, rather than just limiting its results:

orderBy(*colName, direction*)
Orders the results. The second parameter may be either asc (the default) or desc:

```
$contacts = DB::table('contacts')
    ->orderBy('last_name', 'asc')
    ->get();
```

---

groupBy() *and* having() *or* havingRaw()

Groups your results by a column. Optionally, having() and havingRaw() allow you to filter your results based on properties of the groups. For example, you could look for only cities with at least 30 people in them:

```
$populousCities = DB::table('contacts')
    ->groupBy('city')
    ->havingRaw('count(contact_id) > 30')
    ->get();
```

skip() *and* take()

Most often used for pagination, these allow you to define how many rows to return and how many to skip before starting the return—like a page number and a page size in a pagination system:

```
$page4 = DB::table('contacts')->skip(30)->take(10)->get();
```

latest(*colName*) *and* oldest(*colName*)

Sort by the passed column (or created_at if no column name is passed) in descending (latest()) or ascending (oldest()) order.

inRandomOrder()

Sorts the result randomly.

Ending/returning methods

These methods stop the query chain and trigger the execution of the SQL query:

get()

Gets all results for the built query:

```
$contacts = DB::table('contacts')->get();
$vipContacts = DB::table('contacts')->where('vip', true)->get();
```

first() *and* firstOrFail()

Get only the first result—like get(), but with a LIMIT 1 added:

```
$newestContact = DB::table('contacts')
    ->orderBy('created_at', 'desc')
    ->first();
```

first()

Fails silently if there are no results, whereas firstOrFail() will throw an exception.

If you pass an array of column names to either method, they'll return the data for just those columns instead of all columns.

find(id) and findOrFail(*id*)
> Like first(), but you pass in an ID value that corresponds to the primary key to look up. find() fails silently if a row with that ID doesn't exist, while findOr Fail() will throw an exception:
>
> ```
> $contactFive = DB::table('contacts')->find(5);
> ```

value()
> Plucks just the value from a single field from the first row. Like first(), but if you only want a single column:
>
> ```
> $newestContactEmail = DB::table('contacts')
>     ->orderBy('created_at', 'desc')
>     ->value('email');
> ```

count()
> Returns an integer count of all of the matching results:
>
> ```
> $countVips = DB::table('contacts')
>     ->where('vip', true)
>     ->count();
> ```

min() *and* max()
> Return the minimum or maximum value of a particular column:
>
> ```
> $highestCost = DB::table('orders')->max('amount');
> ```

sum() *and* avg()
> Return the sum or average of all of the values in a particular column:
>
> ```
> $averageCost = DB::table('orders')
>     ->where('status', 'completed')
>     ->avg('amount');
> ```

Writing raw queries inside query builder methods with DB::raw

We've already seen a few custom methods for raw statements—for example, select() has a selectRaw() counterpart that allows you to pass in a string for the query builder to place after the WHERE statement.

You can also, however, pass in the result of a DB::raw() call to almost any method in the query builder to achieve the same result:

```
$contacts = DB::table('contacts')
    ->select(DB::raw('*, (score * 100) AS integer_score'))
    ->get();
```

Joins

Joins can sometimes be a pain to define, and there's only so much a framework can do to make them simpler, but the query builder does its best. Let's look at a sample:

```
$users = DB::table('users')
    ->join('contacts', 'users.id', '=', 'contacts.user_id')
    ->select('users.*', 'contacts.name', 'contacts.status')
    ->get();
```

The `join()` method creates an inner join. You can also chain together multiple joins one after another, or use `leftJoin()` to get a left join.

Finally, you can create more complex joins by passing a closure into the `join()` method:

```
DB::table('users')
    ->join('contacts', function ($join) {
        $join
            ->on('users.id', '=', 'contacts.user_id')
            ->orOn('users.id', '=', 'contacts.proxy_user_id');
    })
    ->get();
```

Unions

You can union two queries together by creating them first and then using the `union()` or `unionAll()` method to union them:

```
$first = DB::table('contacts')
    ->whereNull('first_name');

$contacts = DB::table('contacts')
    ->whereNull('last_name')
    ->union($first)
    ->get();
```

Inserts

The `insert()` method is pretty simple. Pass it an array to insert a single row or an array of arrays to insert multiple rows, and use `insertGetId()` instead of `insert()` to get the autoincrementing primary key ID back as a return:

```
$id = DB::table('contacts')->insertGetId([
    'name' => 'Abe Thomas',
    'email' => 'athomas1987@gmail.com',
]);

DB::table('contacts')->insert([
    ['name' => 'Tamika Johnson', 'email' => 'tamikaj@gmail.com'],
```

```
        ['name' => 'Jim Patterson', 'email' => 'james.patterson@hotmail.com'],
    ]);
```

Updates

Updates are also simple. Create your update query and, instead of get() or first(), just use update() and pass it an array of parameters:

```
DB::table('contacts')
    ->where('points', '>', 100)
    ->update(['status' => 'vip']);
```

You can also quickly increment and decrement columns using the increment() and decrement() methods. The first parameter of each is the column name, and the second is (optionally) the number to increment/decrement by:

```
DB::table('contacts')->increment('tokens', 5);
DB::table('contacts')->decrement('tokens');
```

Deletes

Deletes are even simpler. Build your query and then end it with delete():

```
DB::table('users')
    ->where('last_login', '<', Carbon::now()->subYear())
    ->delete();
```

You can also truncate the table, which both deletes every row and also resets the auto-incrementing ID:

```
DB::table('contacts')->truncate();
```

JSON operations

If you have JSON columns, you can update or select rows based on aspects of the JSON structure by using the arrow syntax to traverse children:

```
// Select all records where the "isAdmin" property of the "options"
// JSON column is set to true
DB::table('users')->where('options->isAdmin', true)->get();

// Update all records, setting the "verified" property
// of the "options" JSON column to true
DB::table('users')->update(['options->isVerified', true]);
```

 This is a new feature in Laravel 5.3.

Transactions

If you're not familiar with database transactions, they're a tool that allows you to wrap up a series of database queries to be performed in a batch, which you can choose to roll back, undoing the entire series of queries. Transactions are often used to ensure that *all* or *none*, but not *some*, of a series of related queries are performed—if one fails, the ORM will roll back the entire series of queries.

With the Laravel query builder's transaction feature, if any exceptions are thrown at any point within the transaction closure, all the queries in the transaction will be rolled back. If the transaction closure finishes successfully, all the queries will be committed and not rolled back.

Let's take a look at Example 8-9.

Example 8-9. A simple database transaction

```
DB::transaction(function () use ($userId, $numVotes)
{
    // Possibly failing DB query
    DB::table('users')
        ->where('id', $userId)
        ->update(['votes' => $numVotes]);

    // Caching query that we don't want to run if the above query fails
    DB::table('votes')
        ->where('user_id', $userId)
        ->delete();
});
```

We clearly had some previous process that summarized the number of votes from the votes table. We want to cache that number on the users table and then wipe those votes from the votes table. But, of course, we don't want to wipe the votes *until* the update to the users table has run successfully. And we don't want to keep the updated number of votes on the users table if the votes table deletion fails.

If anything goes wrong with either query, the other won't be applied. That's the magic of database transactions.

Note that you can also manually begin and end transactions—and this applies both for query builder queries and for Eloquent queries. Start with DB::beginTransaction(), end with DB::commit(), and abort with DB::rollBack().

Introduction to Eloquent

Eloquent is an ActiveRecord ORM, which means it's a database abstraction layer that provides a single interface to interact with multiple database types. "ActiveRecord" means that a single Eloquent class is responsible for not only providing the ability to interact with the table as a whole (e.g., User::all() gets all users), but also representing an individual table row (e.g., $sharon = new User). Additionally, each instance is capable of managing its own persistence; you can call $sharon->save() or $sharon->delete().

Eloquent has a primary focus on simplicity, and like the rest of the framework, it relies on "convention over configuration" to allow you to build powerful models with minimal code.

For example, you can perform all of the operations in Example 8-11 with the model defined in Example 8-10.

Example 8-10. The simplest Eloquent model

```php
<?php

use Illuminate\Database\Eloquent\Model;

class Contact extends Model {}
```

Example 8-11. Operations achievable with the simplest Eloquent model

```php
public function save(Request $request)
{
    // Create and save a new contact from user input
    $contact = new Contact();
    $contact->first_name = $request->input('first_name');
    $contact->last_name = $request->input('last_name');
    $conatct->email = $request->input('email');
    $contact->save();

    return redirect('contacts');
}

public function show($contactId)
{
    // Return a JSON representation of a Contact based on a URL segment;
    // if the contact doesn't exist, throw an exception
    return Contact::findOrFail($contactId);
}

public function vips()
{
    // Unnecessarily complex example, but still possible with basic Eloquent
    // class; adds a "formalName" property to every VIP entry
    return Contact::where('vip', true)->get()->map(function ($contact) {
        $contact->formalName = "The exalted {$contact->first_name} of the
        {$contact->last_name}s";

        return $contact;
    });
}
```

How? Convention. Eloquent assumes the table name (`Contact` becomes `contacts`), and with that you have a fully functional Eloquent model.

Let's cover how we work with Eloquent models.

Creating and Defining Eloquent Models

First, let's create a model. There's an Artisan command for that:

```
php artisan make:model Contact
```

This is what we'll get, in *app/Contact.php*:

```php
<?php

namespace App;

use Illuminate\Database\Eloquent\Model;

class Contact extends Model
{
    //
}
```

Creating a migration along with your model

If you want to automatically create a migration when you create your model, pass the -m or --migration flag:

```
php artisan make:model Contact --migration
```

Table name

The default behavior for table names is that Laravel "snake cases" and pluralizes your class name, so SecondaryContact would access a table named secondary_contacts. If you'd like to customize the name, set the $table property explicitly on the model:

```
protected $table = 'contacts_secondary';
```

Primary key

Laravel assumes, by default, that each table will have an autoincrementing integer primary key, and it will be named id.

If you want to change the name of your primary key, change the $primaryKey property:

```
protected $primaryKey = 'contact_id';
```

And if you want to set it to be nonincrementing, use:

```
public $incrementing = false;
```

Timestamps

Eloquent expects every table to have `created_at` and `updated_at` timestamp columns. If your table won't have them, disable the `$timestamps` functionality:

```
public $timestamps = false;
```

You can customize the format Eloquent uses to store your timestamps to the database by setting the `$dateFormat` class property to a custom string. The string will be parsed using PHP's `date()` syntax, so the following example will store the date as seconds since the Unix epoch:

```
protected $dateFormat = 'U';
```

Retrieving Data with Eloquent

Most of the time you pull data from your database with Eloquent, you'll use static calls on your Eloquent model.

Let's start by getting everything:

```
$allContacts = Contact::all();
```

That was easy. Let's filter it a bit:

```
$vipContacts = Contact::where('vip', true)->get();
```

We can see that the `Eloquent` facade gives us the ability to chain constraints, and from there the constraints get very familiar:

```
$newestContacts = Contact::orderBy('created_at', 'desc')
    ->take(10)
    ->get();
```

It turns out that once you move past the initial facade name, you're just working with Laravel's query builder. You can do a lot more—we'll cover that soon—but everything you can do with the query builder on the `DB` facade you can do on your Eloquent objects.

Get one

Like we covered earlier in the chapter, you can use `first()` to return only the first record from a query, or `find()` to pull just the record with the provided ID. For either, if you append "orFail" to the method name, it will throw an exception if there are no matching results. This makes `findOrFail()` a common tool in looking up an entity by a URL segment (or throwing an exception if a matching entity doesn't exist) like you can see in Example 8-12.

Example 8-12. Using an Eloquent OrFail() method in a controller method

```
// ContactController
public function show($contactId)
{
    return view('contacts.show')
        ->with('contact', Contact::findOrFail($contactId));
}
```

Any single return (`first()`, `firstOrFail()`, `find()`, or `findOrFail()`) will return an instance of the Eloquent class. So, `Contact::first()` will return an instance of the class `Contact` with the data from row 1 filling it out.

Exceptions

As you can see in Example 8-12, we don't need to catch Eloquent's model not found exception (`Illuminate\Database\Eloquent\Mod elNotFoundException`) in our controllers; Laravel's routing system will catch them and throw a 404 for us.

You could, of course, catch that particular exception and handle it, if you'd like.

Get many

`get()` works with Eloquent just like it does in normal query builder calls—build a query and call `get()` at the end to get the results:

```
$vipContacts = Contact::where('vip', true)->get();
```

However, there is an Eloquent-only method, `all()`, which you'll often see people use when they want to get an unfiltered list of all data in the table:

```
$contacts = Contact::all();
```

Using get() instead of all()

Any time you can use `all()`, you could use `get()`. `Contact::get()` has the same response as `Contact::all()`. However, the moment you start modifying your query—adding a `where()` filter, for example—`all()` will no longer work, but `get()` will continue working.

So, even though `all()` is very common, I'd recommend using `get()` for everything, and ignoring the fact that `all()` even exists.

The other thing that's different about Eloquent's `get()` method is that, prior to Laravel 5.3, it returned an array instead of a collection. In 5.3 and later, they both return collections.

Chunking responses with chunk()

If you've ever needed to process a large amount (thousands or more) of records at a time, you may have run into memory or locking issues. Laravel makes it possible to break your requests into smaller pieces (chunks) and process them in batches, keeping the memory load of your large request smaller. Example 8-13 illustrates the use of chunk().

Example 8-13. Chunking an Eloquent query to limit memory usage

```
Contact::chunk(100, function ($contacts) {
    foreach ($contacts as $contact)  {
        // Do something with $contact
    }
});
```

Aggregates

The aggregates that are available on the query builder are available on Eloquent queries as well. For example:

```
$countVips = Contact::where('vip', true)->count();
$sumVotes = Contact::sum('votes');
$averageSkill = User::avg('skill_level');
```

Inserts and Updates with Eloquent

Inserting and updating values is one of the places where Eloquent starts to diverge from normal query builder syntax.

Inserts

There are two primary ways to insert a new record using Eloquent.

First, you can create a new instance of your Eloquent class, set your properties manually, and call save() on that instance, like in Example 8-14.

Example 8-14. Inserting an Eloquent record by creating a new instance

```
$contact = new Contact;
$contact->name = 'Ken Hirata';
$contact->email = 'ken@hirata.com';
$contact->save();

// or

$contact = new Contact([
    'name' => 'Ken Hirata',
    'email' => 'ken@hirata.com'
```

```
]);
$contact->save();
```

Until you save(), this instance of Contact represents the contact fully—except it has never been saved to the database. That means it doesn't have an id, if the application quits it won't persist, and it doesn't have its created_at and updated_at values set.

You can also pass an array to Model::create() to achieve the same output, as shown in Example 8-15.

Example 8-15. Inserting an Eloquent record by passing an array to create()

```
$contact = Contact::create([
    'name' => 'Keahi Hale',
    'email' => 'halek481@yahoo.com'
]);
```

Also be aware that in any context where you are passing an array (either to new Model(), Model::create(), or Model::update()), every property you set via Model::create() has to be approved for "mass assignment," which we'll cover shortly.

Note that if you're using Model::create(), you don't need to save() the instance—that's handled as a part of the model's create() method.

Updates

Updating records looks very similar to inserting. You can get a specific instance, change its properties, and then save, or you can make a single call and pass an array of updated properties. Example 8-16 illustrates the first approach.

Example 8-16. Updating an Eloquent record by updating an instance and saving

```
$contact = Contact::find(1);
$contact->email = 'natalie@parkfamily.com';
$contact->save();
```

Since this record already exists, it will already have a created_at timestamp and an id, which will stay the same, but the updated_at field will be changed to the current date and time. Example 8-17 illustrates the second approach.

Example 8-17. Updating one or more Eloquent records by passing an array to the update() method

```
Contact::where('created_at', '<', Carbon::now()->subYear())
    ->update(['longevity' => 'ancient']);
```

```
// or
```

```
$contact = Contact::find(1);
$contact->update(['longevity' => 'ancient']);
```

This method expects an array where each key is the column name and each value is the column value.

Mass assignment

We've looked at a few examples of how to pass arrays of values into Eloquent class methods. However, none of these will actually work until you define which fields are "fillable" on the model.

The goal of this is to protect (malicious) user input from accidentally setting new values on fields you don't want changed. Consider the common scenario in Example 8-18.

Example 8-18. Updating an Eloquent model using the entirety of a request's input

```
// ContactController
public function update(Contact $contact, Request $request)
{
    $contact->update($request->all());
}
```

If you're not familiar with the Illuminate `Request` object, Example 8-18 will take every piece of user input and pass it to the `update()` method. That `all()` method includes things like URL parameters and form inputs, so a malicious user could easily add some things in there, like `id` and `owner_id`, that you likely don't want updated.

Thankfully, that won't actually work until you define your model's fillable fields. You can either whitelist the fillable fields, or blacklist the "guarded" fields to determine which fields can or cannot be edited via "mass assignment"—i.e., by passing an array of values into either `create()` or `update()`. Note that nonfillable properties can still be changed by direct assignment (e.g., `$contact\->password = 'abc';`). Example 8-19 shows both approaches.

Example 8-19. Using Eloquent's fillable or guarded properties to define mass-assignable fields

```
class Contact
{
    protected $fillable = ['name', 'email'];

    // or
```

```
    protected $guarded = ['id', 'created_at', 'updated_at', 'owner_id'];
}
```

Using Request::only() with Eloquent mass assignment

In Example 8-18, we needed Eloquent's mass assignment guard because we were using the all() method on the request object to pass the *entirety* of the user input into our Eloquent object.

Eloquent's mass assignment protection is a great tool here, but there's also a helpful trick to keep you from accepting just any input from the user.

The Request class has an only() method that allows you to pluck only a few keys from the user input. So now you can do this:

```
Contact::create($request->only('name', 'email'));
```

firstOrCreate() and firstOrNew()

Sometimes you want to to tell your application, "Get me an instance with these properties, or if it doesn't exist, create it." This is where the firstOr*() methods come in.

The firstOrCreate() and firstOrNew() methods take an array of keys and values as their first parameter:

```
$contact = Contact::firstOrCreate(['email' => 'luis.ramos@myacme.com']);
```

They'll both look for and retrieve the first record matching those parameters, and if there are no matching records, they'll create an instance with those properties; first OrCreate() will persist that instance to the database and then return it, while first OrNew() will return it without saving it.

If you pass an array of values as the second parameter, those values will be added to the created entry (if it's created), but *won't* be used to look up whether the entry exists.

Deleting with Eloquent

Deleting with Eloquent is very similar to updating with Eloquent, but with soft deletes, you can archive your deleted items for later inspection or even recovery.

Normal deletes

The simplest way to delete an instance is to call the delete() method on the instance itself:

```
$contact = Contact::find(5);
$contact->delete();
```

However, if you only have the ID, there's no reason to look up an instance just to delete it; you can pass an ID or an array of IDs to the model's `destroy()` method to delete them directly:

```
Contact::destroy(1);
// or
Contact::destroy([1, 5, 7]);
```

Finally, you can delete all of the results of a query:

```
Contact::where('updated_at', '<', Carbon::now()->subYear())->delete();
```

Soft deletes

Soft deletes mark database rows as deleted without actually deleting them from the database. This gives you the ability to inspect them later; to have records that show more than "no information, deleted" when displaying historic information; and to allow your users (or admins) to restore some or all data.

The hard part about handcoding an application with soft deletes is that *every query* you ever write will need to exclude the soft-deleted data. Thankfully, if you use Eloquent's soft deletes, every query you ever make will be scoped to ignore soft deletes by default, unless you explicitly ask to bring them back.

Eloquent's soft delete functionality requires a `deleted_at` column to be added to the table. Once you enable soft deletes on that Eloquent model, every query you ever write (unless you explicitly include soft-deleted records) will be scoped to ignore soft-deleted rows.

When Should I Use Soft Deletes?

Just because a feature exists, it doesn't mean you should always use it. Many folks in the Laravel community default to using soft deletes on every project just because the feature is there. There are real costs to soft deletes, though. It's pretty likely that, if you view your database directly in a tool like Sequel Pro, you'll forget to check the `deleted_at` column at least once. And if you don't clean up old soft-deleted records, your databases will get larger and larger.

Here's my recommendation: don't use soft deletes by default. Instead, use them when you need them, and when you do, clean out old soft deletes as aggressively as you can. It's a powerful tool, but not worth using unless you need it.

Enabling soft deletes.   You enable soft deletes by doing three things: adding the `deleted_at` column in a migration, importing the `SoftDeletes` trait in the model, and adding the `deleted_at` column to your `$dates` property. There's a `softDe letes()` method available on the query builder to add the `deleted_at` column to a table, as you can see in Example 8-20. And Example 8-21 shows an Eloquent model with soft deletes enabled.

Example 8-20. Migration to add the soft delete column to a table

```
Schema::table('contacts', function (Blueprint $table) {
    $table->softDeletes();
});
```

Example 8-21. An Eloquent model with soft deletes enabled

```php
<?php

use Illuminate\Database\Eloquent\Model;
use Illuminate\Database\Eloquent\SoftDeletes;

class Contact extends Model
{
    use SoftDeletes; // use the trait

    protected $dates = ['deleted_at']; // mark this column as a date
}
```

Once you make these changes, every `delete()` and `destroy()` call will now set the deleted_at column on your row to be the current date and time instead of deleting that row. And all future queries will exclude that row as a result.

Querying with soft deletes. So, how do we get soft-deleted items?

First, you can add soft-deleted items to a query:

```
$allHistoricContacts = Contact::withTrashed()->get();
```

Next, you can use the `trashed()` method to see if a particular instance has been soft deleted:

```
if ($contact->trashed()) {
    // do something
}
```

Finally, you can get *only* soft-deleted items:

```
$deletedContacts = Contact::onlyTrashed()->get();
```

Restoring soft-deleted entities. If you want to restore a soft-deleted item, you can run `restore()` on an instance or a query:

```
$contact->restore();

// or
```

```
Contact::onlyTrashed()->where('vip', true)->restore();
```

Force-deleting soft-deleted entities.   You can delete a soft-deleted entity by calling `forceDelete()` on an entity or query:

```
$contact->forceDelete();

// or

Contact::onlyTrashed()->forceDelete();
```

Scopes

We've covered "filtered" queries, meaning any query where we're not just returning every result for a table. But every time we've written them so far in this chapter, it's been a manual process using the query builder.

Local and global scopes in Eloquent allow you to define prebuilt "scopes" (filters) that you can use either every time a model is queried ("global") or every time you query it with a particular method chain ("local").

Local scopes

Local scopes are the simplest to understand. Let's take this example:

```
$activeVips = Contact::where('vip', true)->where('trial', false)->get();
```

First of all, if we write this combination of query methods over and over, it will get tedious. But additionally, the *knowledge* of how to define someone being an "active VIP" is now spread around our application. We want to centralize that knowledge. What if we could just write this?

```
$activeVips = Contact::activeVips()->get();
```

We can—it's called a local scope. And it's easy to define on the `Contact` class:

```
class Contact
{
    public function scopeActiveVips($query)
    {
        return $query->where('vip', true)->where('trial', false);
    }
}
```

To define a local scope, we add a method to the Eloquent class that begins with "scope" and then contains the title-cased version of the scope name. This method is passed a query builder and needs to return a query builder, but of course you can modify the query before returning—that's the whole point.

You can also define scopes that accept parameters:

```
class Contact
{
    public function scopeStatus($query, $status)
    {
        return $query->where('status', $status);
    }
```

And you use them in the same way, just passing the parameter to the scope:

```
$friends = Contact::status('friend')->get();
```

Global scopes

Remember how we talked about soft deletes only working if you scope *every query* on the model to ignore the soft-deleted items? That's a global scope. And we can define our own global scopes, which will be applied on every query made from a given model.

There are two ways to define a global scope: using a closure or using an entire class. In each, you'll register the defined scope in the model's `boot()` method. Let's start with the closure method, illustrated in Example 8-22.

Example 8-22. Adding a global scope using a closure

```
...
class Contact extends Model
{
    protected static function boot()
    {
        parent::boot();

        static::addGlobalScope('active', function (Builder $builder) {
            $builder->where('active', true);
        });
    }
}
```

That's it. We just added a global scope, named `active`, and every query on this model will be scoped to only rows with `active` set to `true`.

Next, let's try the longer way, as shown in Example 8-23. Create a class that implements `Illuminate\Database\Eloquent\Scope`, which means it will have an `apply()` method that takes an instance of a query builder and an instance of the model.

Example 8-23. Creating a global scope class

```
<?php

namespace App\Scopes;
```

```php
use Illuminate\Database\Eloquent\Scope;
use Illuminate\Database\Eloquent\Model;
use Illuminate\Database\Eloquent\Builder;

class ActiveScope implements Scope
{
    public function apply(Builder $builder, Model $model)
    {
        return $builder->where('active', true);
    }
}
```

To apply this scope to a model, once again override the parent's boot() method and call addGlobalScope() on the class using static, as shown in Example 8-24.

Example 8-24. Applying a class-based global scope

```php
<?php

use App\Scopes\ActiveScope;
use Illuminate\Database\Eloquent\Model;

class Contact extends Model
{
    protected static function boot()
    {
        parent::boot();

        static::addGlobalScope(new ActiveScope);
    }
}
```

Contact with no namespace

You may have noticed that several of these examples have used the class Contact, with no namespace. This is abnormal, and I've only done this to save space in the book. Normally even your top-level models would live at something like App\Contact.

Removing global scopes.   There are three ways to remove a global scope, and all three use the withoutGlobalScope() or withoutGlobalScopes() methods. If you're removing a closure-based scope, the first parameter of that scope's addGlobalScope() registration will be the key you used to enable it:

```php
$allContacts = Contact::withoutGlobalScope('active')->get();
```

If you're removing a single class-based global scope, you can pass the class name to withoutGlobalScope() or withoutGlobalScopes():

```
Contact::withoutGlobalScope(ActiveScope::class)->get();

Contact::withoutGlobalScopes([ActiveScope::class, VipScope::class])->get();
```

Or, you can just disable all global scopes for a query:

```
Contact::withoutGlobalScopes()->get();
```

Customizing Field Interactions with Accessors, Mutators, and Attribute Casting

Now that we've covered how to get records into and out of the database with Eloquent, let's talk about decorating and manipulating the individual attributes on your Eloquent models.

Accessors, mutators, and attribute casting all allow you to customize the way individual attributes of Eloquent instances are input or output. Without using any of these, each attribute of your Eloquent instance is treated like a string, and you can't have any attributes on your models that don't exist on the database. But we can change that.

Accessors

Accessors allow you to define custom attributes on your Eloquent models for when you are *reading* data from the model instance. This may be because you want to change how a particular column is output, or because you want to create a custom attribute that doesn't exist in the database table at all.

You define an accessor by writing a method on your model with the following structure: get{PascalCasedPropertyName}Attribute. So, if your property name is first_name, the accessor method would be named getFirstNameAttribute.

Let's try it out. First, we'll decorate a preexisting column (Example 8-25).

Example 8-25. Decorating a preexisting column with Eloquent accessors

```
// Model definition:
class Contact extends Model
{
    public function getNameAttribute($value)
    {
        return $value ?: '(No name provided)';
    }
}

// Accessor usage:
$name = $contact->name;
```

But we can also use accessors to define attributes that never existed in the database, as seen in Example 8-26.

Example 8-26. Defining an attribute with no backing column using Eloquent accessors

```
// Model definition:
class Contact extends Model
{
    public function getFullNameAttribute()
    {
        return $this->first_name . ' ' . $this->last_name;
    }
}

// Accessor usage:
$fullName = $contact->full_name;
```

Mutators

Mutators work the same way as accessors, except they're for determining how to process *setting* the data instead of *getting* it. Just like with accessors, you can use it to modify the process of writing data to existing columns, or to allow for setting columns that don't exist in the database.

You define a mutator by writing a method on your model with the following structure: `set{PascalCasedPropertyName}Attribute`. So, if your property name is `first_name`, the mutator method would be named `setFirstNameAttribute`.

Let's try it out. First, we'll add a constraint to updating a preexisting column (Example 8-27).

Example 8-27. Decorating setting the value of an attribute with Eloquent mutators

```
// Defining the mutator
class Order extends Model
{
    public function setAmountAttribute($value)
    {
        $this->attributes['amount'] = $value > 0 ? $value : 0;
    }
}

// Using the mutator
$order->amount = '15';
```

This reveals that the way mutators are expected to "set" data on the model is by setting it in `$this->attributes` with the column name as the key.

Now, let's add a proxy column for setting, as shown in Example 8-28.

Example 8-28. Allowing for setting the value of a nonexistent attribute with Eloquent mutators

```
// Defining the mutator
class Order extends Model
{
    public function setWorkgroupNameAttribute($workgroupName)
    {
        $this->attributes['email'] = "{$workgroupName}@ourcompany.com";
    }
}

// Using the mutator
$order->workgroup_name = 'jstott';
```

As you can probably guess, it's relatively uncommon to create a mutator for a non-existent column, because it can be confusing to set one property and have it change a different column—but it is possible.

Attribute casting

You can probably imagine writing accessors to cast all of your integer-type fields as integers, encode and decode JSON to store in TEXT column, or convert TINYINT 0 and 1 to and from boolean values.

Thankfully, there's a system for that in Eloquent already. It's called attribute casting, and it allows you to define that any of your columns should always be treated, both on read and on write, as if they are of a particular data type. The options are listed in Table 8-1.

Table 8-1. Possible attribute casting column types

Type	Description
int|integer	Casts with PHP (int)
real|float|double	Casts with PHP (float)
string	Casts with PHP (string)
bool|boolean	Casts with PHP (bool)
object	Parses to/from JSON, as a stdClass object
array	Parses to/from JSON, as an array
collection	Parses to/from JSON, as a collection
date|datetime	Parses from database DATETIME to Carbon, and back
timestamp	Parses from database TIMESTAMP to Carbon, and back

Example 8-29 shows how you use attribute casting in your model.

Example 8-29. Using attribute casting on an Eloquent model

```
class Contact
{
    protected $casts = [
        'vip' => 'boolean',
        'children_names' => 'array',
        'birthday' => 'date',
    ];
}
```

Date mutators

You can choose for particular columns to be mutated as `timestamp` columns by adding them to the `dates` array, as seen in Example 8-30.

Example 8-30. Defining columns to be mutated as timestamps

```
class Contact
{
    protected $dates = [
        'met_at'
    ];
}
```

By default, this array contains `created_at` and `updated_at`, so adding entries to `dates` just adds them to the list.

 However, there's no difference between adding columns to this list and adding them to `$this->casts` as `timestamp`, so this is becoming a bit of an unnecessary feature now that attribute casting can cast timestamps (new in Laravel 5.2).

Eloquent Collections

When you make any query call in Eloquent that has the potential to return multiple rows, instead of an array they'll come packaged in an Eloquent collection, which is a specialized type of collection. Let's take a look at collections and Eloquent collections, and what makes them better than plain arrays.

Introducing the base collection

Laravel's `Collection` objects (`Illuminate\Support\Collection`) are a little bit like arrays on steroids. The methods they expose on array-like objects are so helpful that, once you've been using them for a while, you'll likely want to pull Illuminate into even non-Laravel projects just for collections—which you can, with the Tightenco/ Collect (*https://github.com/tightenco/collect*) package.

You can create a collection by passing an array into its constructor, or by creating an empty collection and pushing entries onto it. Laravel also has a `collect()` helper, which is the simplest way to create a collection. Let's try it:

```
$collection = collect([1, 2, 3]);
```

Now let's say we want to filter out any even numbers:

```
$odds = $collection->reject(function ($item) {
    return $item % 2 === 0;
});
```

Or what if we want to get a version of the array where each item is multiplied by 10? We can do that as follows:

```
$multiplied = $collection->map(function ($item) {
    return $item * 10;
});
```

We can even get only the evens, multiply them all by 10, and reduce them to a single number by sum:

```
$sum = $collection
    ->filter(function ($item) {
        return $item % 2 == 0;
    })->map(function ($item) {
        return $item * 10;
    })->sum();
```

As you can see, collections provide a series of methods, which can optionally be chained, to perform functional operations on your arrays. They provide the same functionality as native PHP methods like `array_map()` and `array_reduce()`, but you don't have to memorize PHP's unpredictable parameter order, and the method chaining syntax is endlessly more readable.

There are more than 60 methods available on the `Collection` class, including methods like `max()` and `whereIn()`, `flatten()`, and `flip()`, and there's not enough space to cover them all here. We'll cover more in "Collections" on page 398, or you can check out the Laravel docs on Collections (*https://laravel.com/docs/master/collections*) to see all of the methods.

 Collections in the place of arrays

Collections can also be used in any context (except typehinting) where you can use arrays; they allow for iteration, so you can pass them to `foreach`, and they allow for array access, so if they're keyed you can try `$a = $collection['a']`.

What Eloquent collections add

Each Eloquent collection is a normal collection, but extended for the particular needs of a collection of Eloquent results.

Once again, there's not enough room here to cover all of the additions, but they're centered around the unique aspects of interacting with a collection not just of generic objects, but objects meant to represent database rows.

For example, every Eloquent collection has a method called modelKeys() that returns an array of the primary keys of every instance in the collection. find($id) looks for an instance that has the primary key of $id.

One additional feature available here is the ability to define that any given model should return its results wrapped in a specific class of collection. So, if you want to add specific methods to any collection of objects of the Order class—possibly related to summarizing the financial details of your orders—you could create a custom Order Collection that extends the Illuminate\Database\Eloquent\Collection class, and then register it in your model, as shown in Example 8-31.

Example 8-31. Custom Collection classes for Eloquent models

```
...
class OrderCollection extends Collection
{
    public function sumBillableAmount()
    {
        return $this->reduce(function ($carry, $order) {
            return $carry + ($order->billable ? $order->amount : 0);
        }, 0);
    }
}

...
class Order extends Model
{
    public function newCollection(array $models = [])
    {
        return new OrderCollection($models);
    }
}
```

Now, any time you get back a collection of Orders (e.g., from Order::all()) it'll actually be an instance of the OrderCollection class:

```
$orders = Order::all();
$billableAmount = $orders->sumBillableAmount();
```

Eloquent Serialization

Serialization is what happens when you take something complex—an array, or an object—and convert it to a string. In a web-based context, that string is often JSON, but it could take other forms as well.

Serializing complex database records can be, well, complex, and this is one of the places many ORMs fall short. Thankfully, you get two powerful methods for free with Eloquent: `toArray()` and `toJson()`. Collections also have `toArray()` and `toJson()`, so all of these are valid:

```
$contactArray = Contact::first()->toArray();
$contactJson = Contact::first()->toJson();
$contactsArray = Contact::all()->toArray();
$contactsJson = Contact::all()->toJson();
```

You can also cast an Eloquent instance or collection to a string (`$string = (string) $contact;`), but both models and collections will just run `toJson()` and return the result.

Returning models directly from route methods

Laravel's router eventually converts everything routes return to a string, so there's a clever trick you can use. If you return the result of an Eloquent call in a controller, it will be automatically cast to a string, and therefore returned as JSON. That means a JSON-returning route can be as simple as either of the ones in Example 8-32.

Example 8-32. Returning JSON from routes directly

```
// routes/web.php
Route::get('api/contacts', function () {
    return Contact::all();
});

Route::get('api/contacts/{id}', function ($id) {
    return Contact::findOrFail($id);
});
```

Hiding attributes from JSON

It's very common to use JSON returns in APIs, and it's very common to want to hide certain attributes in these contexts, so Eloquent makes it easy to hide any attributes every time you cast to JSON.

You can either blacklist attributes, hiding the ones you list:

```
class Contact extends Model
{
    public $hidden = ['password', 'remember_token'];
```

or whitelist attributes, showing only the ones you list:

```
class Contact extends Model
{
    public $visible = ['name', 'email', 'status'];
```

This also works for relationships:

```
class User extends Model
{
    public $hidden = ['contacts'];

    public function contacts()
    {
        return $this->hasMany(Contact::class);
    }
```

Loading the contents of a relationship

By default, the contents of a relationship are not loaded when you get a database record, so it doesn't matter whether you hide them or not. But, as we'll learn shortly, it's possible to get a record *with* its related items, and in this context, those items will not be included in a serialized copy of that record if you choose to hide that relationship.

In case you're curious now, you can get a User with all contacts—assuming you've set up the relationship correctly—with the following call:

```
$user = User::with('contacts')->first();
```

There might be times when you want to make an attribute visible just for a single call. That's possible, with the Eloquent method makeVisible():

```
$array = $user->makeVisible('remember_token')->toArray();
```

Adding a generated column to array and JSON output

If you have created an accessor for a column that doesn't exist—for example, our `full_name` column from Example 8-26—add it to the `$appends` array on the model to add it to the array and JSON output:

```
class Contact extends Model
{
    protected $appends = ['full_name'];

    public function getFullNameAttribute()
    {
        return "{$this->first_name} {$this->last_name}";
```

Eloquent Relationships

In a relational database model, it's expected that you will have tables that are *related* to each other—hence the name. Eloquent provides simple and powerful tools to make the process of relating your database tables easier than ever before.

Many of our examples in this chapter have been centered around a *user* who has many *contacts*, a relatively common situation.

In an ORM like Eloquent, you would call this a *one-to-many* relationship: the one user *has many* contacts.

If it was a CRM where a contact could be assigned to many users, then this would be a *many-to-many* relationship: many users can be related to one contact, and each user can be related to many contacts. A user *has and belongs to many* contacts.

If each contact can have many phone numbers, and a user wanted a database of every phone number for their CRM, you would say the user *has many* phone numbers *through* contacts—that is, a user *has many* contacts, and the contact *has many* phone numbers, so the contact is sort of an intermediary.

And what if each contact has an address, but you're only interested in tracking one address? You could have all the address fields on the `Contact`, but you might also create an `Address` model—meaning the contact *has one* address.

Finally, what if you want to be able to star (favorite) contacts, but also events? This would be a *polymorphic* relationship, where a user *has many* stars, but some may be contacts and some may be events.

So, let's dig into how to define and access these relationships.

One to one

Let's start simple: a `Contact` *has one* `PhoneNumber`. This relationship is defined in Example 8-33.

Example 8-33. Defining a one-to-one relationship

```
class Contact extends Model
{
    public function phoneNumber()
    {
        return $this->hasOne(PhoneNumber::class);
    }
}
```

As you can tell, the methods defining relationships are on the Eloquent model itself (`$this->hasOne()`) and take, at least in this instance, the fully qualified class name of the class that you're relating them to.

How should this be defined in your database? Since we've defined that the `Contact` has one `PhoneNumber`, Eloquent expects that the table supporting the `PhoneNumber` class (likely `phone_numbers`) has a `contact_id` column on it. If you named it something different (for instance, `owner_id`), you'll need to change your definition:

```
return $this->hasOne(PhoneNumber::class, 'owner_id');
```

Here's how we access the phone number on a contact:

```
$contact = Contact::first();
$contactPhone = $contact->phoneNumber;
```

Notice that we define the method in Example 8-33 with `phoneNumber()`, but we access it with `->phoneNumber`. That's the magic. You could also access it with `->phone_number`. This will return a full Eloquent instance of the related `PhoneNumber` record.

But what if we want to access the `Contact` from the `PhoneNumber`? There's a method for that, too (see Example 8-34).

Example 8-34. Defining a one-to-one relationship's inverse

```
class PhoneNumber extends Model
{
    public function contact()
    {
        return $this->belongsTo(Contact::class);
    }
}
```

Then we access it the same way:

```
$contact = $phoneNumber->contact;
```

Inserting related items

Each relationship type has its own quirks for how to relate models, but here's the core of how it works: pass an instance to save(), or an array of instances to saveMany(). You can also pass properties to create() and it'll make a new instance for you:

```
$contact = Contact::first();

$phoneNumber = new PhoneNumber;
$phoneNumber->number = 8008675309;
$contact->phoneNumbers()->save($phoneNumber);

// or

$contact->phoneNumbers()->saveMany([
    PhoneNumber::find(1),
    PhoneNumber::find(2),
]);

// or

$contact->phoneNumbers()->create([
    'number' => '+13138675309'
]);
```

One to many

The one-to-many relationship is by far the most common. Let's take a look at how to define that our User *has many* Contacts (Example 8-35).

Example 8-35. Defining a one-to-many relationship

```
class User extends Model
{
    public function contacts()
    {
        return $this->hasMany(Contact::class);
    }
}
```

Once again, this expects that the Contact model's backing table (likely contacts) has a user_id column on it. If it doesn't, override it by passing the correct column name as the second parameter of hasMany().

We can get a user's contacts as follows:

```
$user = User::first();
$usersContacts = $user->contacts;
```

Just like with one to one, we use the name of the relationship method and call it as if it were a property instead of a method. However, this method returns a collection instead of a model instance. And this is a normal Eloquent collection, so you can have all sorts of fun with it:

```
$donors = $user->contacts->filter(function ($contact) {
    return $contact->status == 'donor';
});

$lifetimeValue = $contact->orders->reduce(function ($carry, $order) {
    return $carry + $order->amount;
}, 0);
```

Just like with one to one, we can also define the inverse (Example 8-36).

Example 8-36. Defining a one-to-many relationship's inverse

```
class Contact extends Model
{
    public function user()
    {
        return $this->belongsTo(User::class);
    }
}
```

And just like one to one, we can access the User from the Contact:

```
$userName = $contact->user->name;
```

 Attaching and detaching related items from the attached item

Most of the time we attach related items by running save() on the parent and passing in the related item, as in $user->contacts()->save($contact). But if you want to perform the behaviors on the attached ("child") item, you can use associate() and dissociate() on the method that returns the belongsTo():

```
$contact = Contact::first();

$contact->user()->associate(User::first());
$contact->save();

// and later

$contact->user()->dissociate();
$contact->save();
```

Using relationships as query builders.   Until now, we've taken the method name (e.g., contacts()) and called it as if were a property (e.g., $user->contacts). What happens if we call it as a method? Instead of processing the relationship, it will return a prescoped query builder.

So if you have User 1, and you call its contacts() method, you will now have a query builder prescoped to "all contacts that have a field user_id with the value of 1." You can then build out a functional query from there:

```
$donors = $user->contacts()->where('status', 'donor')->get();
```

Selecting only records that have a related item. You can also choose to select only records that meet particular criteria with regard to their related items using has():

```
$postsWithComments = Post::has('comments')->get();
```

You can also adjust the criteria further:

```
$postsWithManyComments = Post::has('comments', '>=', 5)->get();
```

You can nest the criteria:

```
$usersWithPhoneBooks = User::has('contacts.phoneNumbers')->get();
```

And finally, you can write custom queries on the related items:

```
// Gets all contacts with a phone number containing the string "867-5309"
$jennyIGotYourNumber = Contact::whereHas('phoneNumbers', function ($query) {
    $query->where('number', 'like', '%867-5309%');
});
```

Has many through

"Has many through" is really a convenience method for pulling in relationships of a relationship. This is the example I gave earlier where a User has many Contacts and each Contact has many PhoneNumbers. What if you want to get a user's list of contact phone numbers? That's has many through.

This structure assumes that your contacts table has a user_id to relate the contacts to the users, and the phone_numbers table has a contact_id to relate it to the contacts. Then, we define the relationship on the User as in Example 8-37.

Example 8-37. Defining a has-many-through relationship

```
class User extends Model
{
    public function phoneNumbers()
    {
        return $this->hasManyThrough(PhoneNumber::class, Contact::class);
    }
}
```

You'd access this relationship using $user->phone_numbers, and as always you can customize the relationship key on the intermediate model (with the third parameter of hasmanyThrough()) and the relationship key on the distant model (with the fourth parameter).

Many to many

This is where things start to get complex. Let's take our example of a CRM that allows a User to have many Contacts, and each Contact to be related to multiple users.

First, we define the relationship on the User as in Example 8-38.

Example 8-38. Defining a many-to-many relationship

```
class User extends Model
{
    public function contacts()
    {
        return $this->belongsToMany(Contact::class);
    }
}
```

And since this is many to many, the inverse looks exactly the same (Example 8-39).

Example 8-39. Defining a many-to-many relationship's inverse

```
class Contact extends Model
{
    public function users()
    {
        return $this->belongsToMany(User::class);
    }
}
```

Since a single Contact can't have a user_id column and a single User can't have a contact_id column, many-to-many relationships rely on a pivot table that connects the two. The conventional naming of this table is done by placing the two singular table names together, ordered alphabetically, and separating them by an underscore.

So, since we're linking users and contacts, our pivot table should be named contacts_users (if you'd like to customize the table name, pass it as the second parameter to the belongsToMany() methods). It needs two columns: contact_id and user_id.

Just like with hasMany(), we get access to a collection of the related items, but this time it's from both sides (Example 8-40).

Example 8-40. Accessing the related items from both sides of a many-to-many relationship

```
$user = User::first();

$user->contacts->each(function ($contact) {
    // do something
```

```
});

$contact = Contact::first();

$contact->users->each(function ($user) {
    // do something
});

$donors = $user->contacts()->where('status', 'donor')->get();
```

Unique Aspects of Attaching and Detaching Many-to-Many Related Items

Since your pivot table can have its own properties, you need to be able to set those properties when you're attaching a many-to-many related item. You can do that by passing an array as the second parameter to save():

```
$user = User::first();
$contact = Contact::first();
$user->contacts()->save($contact, ['status' => 'donor']);
```

Additionally, you can use attach() and detach() and, instead of passing in an instance of a related item, you can just pass an ID. They work just the same as save(), but can also accept an array of IDs without you needing to rename the method to something like attachMany():

```
$user = User::first();
$user->contacts()->attach(1);
$user->contacts()->attach(2, ['status' => 'donor']);
$user->contacts()->attach([1, 2, 3]);
$user->contacts()->attach([
    1 => ['status' => 'donor'],
    2,
    3
]);

$user->contacts()->detach(1);
$user->contacts()->detach([1, 2]);
$user->contacts()->detach(); // Detaches all contacts
```

You can also use updateExistingPivot() to make changes just to the pivot record:

```
$user->contacts()->updateExistingPivot($contactId, [
    'status' => 'inactive'
]);
```

And if you'd like to replace the current relationships, effectively detaching all previous relationships and attaching new ones, you can pass an array to sync():

```
$user->contacts()->sync([1, 2, 3]);
$user->contacts()->sync([
    1 => ['status' => 'donor'],
```

```
            2,
            3
    ]);
```

Getting data from the pivot table. One thing that's unique about many to many is that it's our first relationship that has a pivot table. The less data you have on a pivot table, the better, but there are some cases where it's valuable to store information on your pivot table—for example, you might want to store a `created_at` field to see when this relationship was created.

In order to store these fields, you have to add them to the relationship definition, like in Example 8-41. You can define specific fields using `withPivot()` or add `created_at` and `updated_at` timestamps using `withTimestamps()`.

Example 8-41. Adding fields to a pivot record

```
public function contacts()
{
    return $this->belongsToMany(Contact::class)
        ->withTimestamps()
        ->withPivot('status', 'preferred_greeting');
}
```

When you get a model instance through a relationship, it will have a `pivot` property on it, which will represent its place in the pivot table you just pulled it from. So, you can do something like Example 8-42.

Example 8-42. Getting data from a related item's pivot entry

```
$user = User::first();

$user->contacts->each(function ($contact) {
    echo sprintf(
        'Contact associated with this user at: %s',
        $contact->pivot->created_at
    );
});
```

Polymorphic

Remember, our polymorphic relationship is where we have multiple Eloquent classes corresponding to the same relationship. We're going to use `Stars` (like favorites) right now. A user can star both `Contacts` and `Events`, and that's where the name polymorphic comes from: a single interface to objects of multiple types.

So, we'll need three tables, and three models: Star, Contact, and Event (and, of course, User, but we'll get there in a second). The contacts and events tables will just be as they normally are, and the stars table will contain an id field, a starrable_id, and a starrable_type. For each Star, you'll be defining which "type" (e.g., Contact or Event) and which ID of that type (e.g., 1) it is.

Let's create our models, as seen in Example 8-43.

Example 8-43. Creating the models for a polymorphic starring system

```
class Star extends Model
{
    public function starrable()
    {
        return $this->morphsTo();
    }
}

class Contact extends Model
{
    public function stars()
    {
        return $this->morphMany(Star::class, 'starrable');
    }
}

class Event extends Model
{
    public function stars()
    {
        return $this->morphMany(Star::class, 'starrable');
    }
}
```

So, how do we create a Star?

```
$contact = Contact::first();
$contact->stars()->create();
```

It's that easy. The Contact is now starred.

In order to find all of the Stars on a given Contact, we call the stars() method like in Example 8-44.

Example 8-44. Retrieving the instances of a polymorphic relationship

```
$contact = Contact::first();

$contact->stars->each(function ($star) {
```

```
    // Do stuff
});
```

If we have an instance of Star, we can get its target by calling the method we used to define its morphTo(), which in this context is starrable(). Take a look at Example 8-45.

Example 8-45. Retrieving the target of polymorphic instance

```
$stars = Star::all();

$stars->each(function ($star) {
    var_dump($star->starrable); // An instance of Contact or Event
});
```

Finally, you might be wondering, "What if I care who starred this contact?" That's a great question; of course you do. It's as simple as adding user_id to your stars table, and then setting up that a User *has many* Stars and a Star belongs to_ one User—a one-to-many relationship (Example 8-46). The stars table becomes almost a pivot table between your User and your Contacts and Events.

Example 8-46. Extending a polymorphic system to differentiate by user

```
class Star extends Model
{
    public function starrable()
    {
        return $this->morphsTo;
    }

    public function user()
    {
        return $this->belongsTo(User::class);
    }
}

class User extends Model
{
    public function stars()
    {
        return $this->hasMany(Star::class);
    }
}
```

That's it! You can now run $star->user or $user->stars to find a list of a User's Stars or to find the starring User from a Star. Also, when you create a new Star, you'll now want to pass the User:

```
$user = User::first();
$event = Event::first();
$event->stars()->create(['user_id' => $user->id]);
```

Many to many polymorphic

The most complex and least common of the relationship types, many-to-many polymorphic relationships are like polymorphic relationships, except instead of being one
to many they're many to many.

The most common example for this relationship type is the tag, so I'll keep it safe and
use that as our example. Let's imagine you want to be able to tag Contacts and
Events. The uniqueness of many-to-many polymorphism is that it's many to many:
each tag may be applied to multiple items, and each tagged item might have multiple
tags. And to add to that, it's polymorphic: tags can be related to items of several different types. For the database, we'll start with the normal structure of the polymorphic relationship but also add a pivot table.

This means we'll need a contacts table, an events table, and a tags table, all shaped
like normal with an ID and whatever properties you want, *and* a new taggables
table, which will have a tag_id, a taggable_id, and a taggable_type. Each entry
into the taggables table will relate a tag with one of the taggable content types.

Now let's define this relationship on our models, as seen in Example 8-47.

Example 8-47. Defining a polymorphic many-to-many relationship

```
class Contact extends Model
{
    public function tags()
    {
        return $this->morphToMany(Tag::class, 'taggable');
    }
}

class Event extends Model
{
    public function tags()
    {
        return $this->morphToMany(Tag::class, 'taggable');
    }
}

class Tag extends Model
{
    public function contacts()
    {
        return $this->morphedByMany(Contact::class, 'taggable');
    }
```

```
    public function events()
    {
        return $this->morphedByMany(Event::class, 'taggable');
    }
}
```

Here's how to create your first tag:

```
$tag = Tag::firstOrCreate(['name' => 'likes-cheese']);
$contact = Contact::first();
$contact->tags()->attach($tag->id);
```

We get the results of this relationship like normal, as seen in Example 8-48.

Example 8-48. Accessing the related items from both sides of a many-to-many polymorphic relationship

```
$contact = Contact::first();

$contact->tags->each(function ($tag) {
    // Do stuff
});

$tag = Tag::first();

$tag->contacts->each(function ($contact) {
    // Do stuff
});
```

Child Records Updating Parent Record Timestamps

Remember, any Eloquent models by default will have created_at and updated_at timestamps. Eloquent will set the updated_at timestamp automatically any time you make any changes to a record.

When a related item either belongsTo() or belongsToMany() another item, it might be valuable to mark the other item as updated any time the related item is updated. For example, if a PhoneNumber is updated, the Contact it's connected to should be marked as having been updated as well.

We can accomplish this by adding the method name for that relationship to a $touches array property on the child class, as in Example 8-49.

Example 8-49. Updating a parent record any time the child record is updated

```
class PhoneNumber extends Model
{
    protected $touches = ['contact'];
```

```
public function contact()
{
    return $this->belongsTo(Contact::class);
}
```

Eager loading

By default, Eloquent loads relationships using "lazy loading." This means when you first load a model instance, its related models will not be loaded along with it. Rather, they'll only be loaded if you make a separate call to pull them in; they're "lazy" and don't do any work until called upon.

This can become a problem if you're iterating over a list of model instances and each has a related item (or items) that you're working on. The problem with lazy loading is that it can introduce significant database load (often the $N+1$ problem, if you're familiar with the term; if not, just ignore this parenthetical remark). For instance, every time the loop in Example 8-50 runs, it executes a new database query to look up the PhoneNumber for that Contact.

Example 8-50.

```
$contacts = Contact::all();

foreach ($contacts as $contact) {
    foreach ($contact->phone_numbers as $phone_number) {
        echo $phone_number->number;
    }
}
```

If you are loading a model instance and you know you'll be working with its relationships, you can instead choose to "eager-load" one or many of its sets of related items:

```
$contacts = Contact::with('phoneNumbers')->get();
```

Using the with() method with a retrieval gets all of the items related to the pulled item(s), and as you can see in this example, you pass it the name of the method the relationship is defined by.

When we use eager loading, instead of pulling the related items one at a time when they're requested (selecting one phone number each time a foreach loop runs), we have a single query to pull the initial items (selecting all contacts) and a second query to pull all their related items (selecting all phone numbers owned by the contacts we just pulled).

You can eager-load multiple relationships by passing multiple parameters to the with() call:

```
$contacts = Contact::with('phoneNumbers', 'addresses')->get();
```

And you can nest eager loading to eager-load the relationships of relationships:

```
$authors = Author::with('posts.comments')->get();
```

Constraining eager loads. If you want to eager-load a relationship, but not all of the items, you can pass a closure to `with()` to define exactly which related items to eager-load:

```
$contacts = Contact::with(['addresses' => function ($query) {
    $query->where('mailable', true);
}])->get();
```

Lazy eager loading. I know it sounds crazy, because we just defined eager loading as sort of the opposite of lazy loading, but sometimes you don't know you want to perform an eager-load query until after the initial instances have been pulled. You can still perform an eager load after the fact, with lazy eager loading:

```
$contacts = Contact::all();

if ($showPhoneNumbers) {
    $contacts->load('phoneNumbers');
}
```

Eager loading only the count

If you want to eager-load relationships but only so you can have access to the count of items in each relationship, you can try `withCount()`:

```
$authors = Author::withCount('posts')->get();

// adds a "posts_count" integer to each Author with a count of that
// Author's number of related posts
```

Eloquent Events

Eloquent models fire events out into the void of your application every time certain actions happen, regardless of whether you're listening. If you're familiar with pub/sub, it's this same model (and you can learn more about Laravel's entire event system in Chapter 16).

Here's a quick rundown of binding a listener to when a new `Contact` is created. We're going to bind it in the `boot()` method of `AppServiceProvider`, and let's imagine we're notifying a third-party service every time we create a new `Contact`.

Example 8-51. Binding a listener to an Eloquent event

```
class AppServiceProvider extends ServiceProvider
{
    public function boot()
```

```
{
    $thirdPartyService = new SomeThirdPartyService;

    Contact::creating(function ($contact) use ($thirdPartyService) {
        try {
            $thirdPartyService->addContact($contact);
        } catch (Exception $e) {
            Log::error('Failed adding contact to ThirdPartyService; cancelled.');

            return false;
        }
    });
}
```

We can see a few things in Example 8-51. First, we use *Modelname::eventName()* as the method, and pass it a closure. The closure gets access to the model instance that is being operated on. Second, we're going to need to define this listener in a service provider somewhere. And third, if we return `false`, the operation will cancel and the `save()` or `update()` will be cancelled.

Here are the events that every Eloquent model fires:

- `creating`
- `created`
- `updating`
- `updated`
- `saving`
- `saved`
- `deleting`
- `deleted`
- `restoring`
- `restored`

Most of these should be pretty clear, except possibly `restoring` and `restored`, which fire when you're restoring a soft-deleted row. Also, `saving` is fired for both `creating` and `updating` and `saved` is fired for both `created` and `updated`.

Testing

Laravel's entire application testing framework makes it easy to test your database—not by writing unit tests against Eloquent, but by just being willing to test your entire application.

Take this scenario. You want to test to ensure that a particular page shows one contact but not another. Some of that logic has to do with the interplay between the URL and the controller and the database, so the best way to test it is an application test. You might be thinking about mocking Eloquent calls and trying to avoid the system hitting the database. *Don't do it.* Try Example 8-52 instead.

Example 8-52. Testing database interactions with simple application tests

```
public function test_active_page_shows_active_and_not_inactive_contacts()
{
    $activeContact = factory(Contact::class, 'active')->create();
    $inactiveContact = factory(Contact::class, 'inactive')->create();

    $this->visit('active-contacts')
        ->see($activeContact->name)
        ->dontSee($inactiveContact->name);
}
```

As you can see, model factories and Laravel's application testing features are great for testing database calls.

Alternatively, you can look for that record directly in the database, as in Example 8-53.

Example 8-53. Using seeInDatabase() to check for certain records in the database

```
public function test_contact_creation_works()
{
    $this->post('contacts', [
        'email' => 'jim@bo.com'
    ]);

    $this->seeInDatabase('contacts', [
        'email' => 'jim@bo.com'
    ]);
}
```

Eloquent and Laravel's database framework are tested extensively. *You don't need to test them.* You don't need to mock them. If you really want to avoid hitting the database, you can use a repository and then return unsaved instances of your Eloquent models. But the most important message is, test the way your application uses your database logic.

If you have custom accessors, mutators, scopes, or whatever else, you can also test them directly, as in Example 8-54.

Example 8-54. Testing accessors, mutators, and scopes

```
public function test_full_name_accessor_works()
{
    $contact = factory(Contact::class)->make([
        'first_name' => 'Alphonse',
        'last_name' => 'Cumberbund'
    ]);

    $this->assertEquals('Alphonse Cumberbund', $contact->fullName);
}

public function test_vip_scope_filters_out_non_vips()
{
    $vip = factory(Contact::class, 'vip')->create();
    $nonVip = factory(Contact::class)->create();

    $vips = Contact::vips()->get();
    $this->assertTrue($vips->contains(['id' => $vip->id]));
    $this->assertFalse($vips->contains(['id' => $nonVip->id]));
}
```

Just avoid writing tests that leave you creating complex "Demeter chains" to assert that a particular fluent stack was called on some database mock. If your testing starts to get overwhelming and complex around the database layer, it's because you're allowing preconceived notions to force you into unnecessarily complex systems. Keep it simple.

TL;DR

Laravel comes with a suite of powerful database tools, including migrations, seeding, an elegant query builder, and Eloquent, a powerful ActiveRecord ORM. Laravel's database tools don't require you to use Eloquent at all—you can access and manipulate the database with a thin layer of convenience without having to write SQL directly. But adding an ORM, whether it's Eloquent or Doctrine or whatever else, is easy and can work neatly with Laravel's core database tools.

Eloquent follows the Active Record pattern, which makes it simple to define a class of database-backed objects, including which table they're stored in, the shape of their columns, accessors and mutators, and much more. Eloquent can handle every sort of normal SQL action and also complex relationships, up to and including polymorphic many-to-many relationships.

Laravel also has a robust system for testing databases, including model factories.

## CHAPTER 9

User Authentication and Authorization

Setting up a basic user authentication system—including registration, login, sessions, password resets, and access permissions—can often be one of the more time-consuming pieces of creating the foundation of an application. It's a prime candidate for extracting functionality out to a library, and there are quite a few such libraries.

But because of how much authentication needs vary across projects, most authentication systems grow bulky and unusable quickly. Thankfully, Laravel has found a way to make an authentication system that's easy to use and understand, but flexible enough to fit in a variety of settings.

Every new install of Laravel has a `create_users_table` migration and a `User` model built in out of the box. Laravel offers an Artisan `make:auth` command that seeds a collection of authentication-related views and routes. And every install comes with a `RegisterController`, a `LoginController`, a `ForgotPasswordController`, and a `ResetPasswordController`. The APIs are clean and clear, and the conventions all work together to provide a simple—and seamless—authentication and authorization system.

Differences in auth structure in Laravel 5.3

Note that in Laravel 5.1 and 5.2, most of this functionality lived in the `AuthController`; in 5.3, this functionality has been split out into multiple controllers. Many of the specifics we'll cover here about how to customize redirect routes, auth guards, and such are different in 5.1 and 5.2 (though all the core functionality is the same). So, if you're on 5.1 or 5.2 and want to change some of the default authentication behaviors, you'll likely need to dig a bit into your `AuthController` to see how exactly you should customize it.

The User Model and Migration

When you create a new Laravel application, the first migration and model you'll see are the `create_users_table` migration and the `App\User` model. Example 9-1 shows, straight from the migration, the fields you'll get in your `users` table.

Example 9-1. Laravel's default user migration

```
Schema::create('users', function (Blueprint $table) {
    $table->increments('id');
    $table->string('name');
    $table->string('email')->unique();
    $table->string('password');
    $table->rememberToken();
    $table->timestamps();
});
```

We have an autoincrementing primary key ID, a name, a unique email, a password, a "remember me" token, and created and modified timestamps. This covers everything you need to handle basic user authentication in most apps.

The difference between authentication and authorization

Authentication means verifying who someone is, and allowing them to act as that person in your system. This includes the login and logout processes, and any tools that allow the users to identify themselves during their time using the application.

Authorization means determining whether the authenticated user is *allowed* (authorized) to perform a specific behavior. For example, an authorization system allows us to forbid any nonadministrators from viewing the site's earnings.

The `User` model is a bit more complex, as you can see in Example 9-2. The `App\User` class itself is simple, but it extends the `Illuminate\Foundation\Auth\User` class, which pulls in several traits.

Example 9-2. Laravel's default User model

```
<?php
// App\User

namespace App;

use Illuminate\Notifications\Notifiable;
use Illuminate\Foundation\Auth\User as Authenticatable;
```

```php
class User extends Authenticatable
{
    use Notifiable;

    /**
     * The attributes that are mass assignable.
     *
     * @var array
     */
    protected $fillable = [
        'name', 'email', 'password',
    ];

    /**
     * The attributes excluded from the model's JSON form.
     *
     * @var array
     */
    protected $hidden = [
        'password', 'remember_token',
    ];
}
<?php
// Illuminate\Foundation\Auth\User

namespace Illuminate\Foundation\Auth;

use Illuminate\Auth\Authenticatable;
use Illuminate\Database\Eloquent\Model;
use Illuminate\Auth\Passwords\CanResetPassword;
use Illuminate\Foundation\Auth\Access\Authorizable;
use Illuminate\Contracts\Auth\Authenticatable as AuthenticatableContract;
use Illuminate\Contracts\Auth\Access\Authorizable as AuthorizableContract;
use Illuminate\Contracts\Auth\CanResetPassword as CanResetPasswordContract;

class User extends Model implements
    AuthenticatableContract,
    AuthorizableContract,
    CanResetPasswordContract
{
    use Authenticatable, Authorizable, CanResetPassword;
}
```

Eloquent model refresher

If this is entirely unfamiliar, consider reading Chapter 8 before continuing to learn how Eloquent models work.

So, what can we learn from this model? First, users live in the `users` table; Laravel will infer this from the class name. We are able to fill out the `name`, `email`, and `password` properties when creating a new user, and the `password` and `remember_token` properties are excluded when outputting the user as JSON. Looking good so far.

We also can see from the contracts and the traits in the `Illuminate\Foundation\Auth` verison of `User` that there are some features in the framework (the ability to authenticate, to authorize, and to reset passwords) that theoretically could be applied to other models, not just the `User` model, and that could be applied individually or together.

Contracts and Interfaces

You may have noticed that sometimes I write the word "contract" and sometimes "interface," and that almost all of the interfaces in Laravel are under the `Contracts` namespace.

A PHP interface is essentially an agreement between two classes that one of the classes will "behave" a certain way. It's a bit like a contract between them, and thinking about it as a contract gives a bit more inherent meaning to the name than calling it an interface does.

In the end, though, they're the same thing: an agreement that a class will provide certain methods with a certain signature.

On a related note, the `Illuminate\Contracts` namespace contains a group of interfaces that Laravel components implement and typehint. This makes it easy to develop similar components that implement the same interfaces and swap them into your application in place of the stock `Illuminate` components. When the Laravel core and components typehint a mailer, for example, they don't typehint the `Mailer` class. Instead, they typehint the `Mailer` contract (interface), making it easy to provide your own mailer. To learn more about how to do this, take a look at Chapter 11.

The `Authenticatable` contract requires methods (`getAuthIdentifier()`, etc.) that allow the framework to authenticate instances of this model to the auth system; the `Authenticatable` trait includes the methods necessary to satisfy that contract with an average Eloquent model.

The `Authorizable` contract requires methods (`can()`, `cannot()`) that allow the framework to authorize instances of this model for their access permissions in different contexts. Unsurprisingly, the `Authorizable` trait provides methods that will satisfy the `Authorizable` contract for an average Eloquent model.

And finally, the `CanResetPassword` contract requires one method (`getEmailForPass wordReset()`) that allows the framework to, you guessed it, reset the password of any entity that satisfies this contract. The trait provides that method for an average Eloquent model.

At this point, we have the ability to easily represent an individual user in the database (with the migration), and to pull them out with a model instance that can be authenticated (logged in and out), authorized (checked for access permissions to a particular resource), and sent a password reset email.

Using the auth() Global Helper and the Auth Facade

The auth() global helper is the easiest way to interact with the status of the authenticated user throughout your app. You can also inject an instance of Illuminate\Auth \AuthManager and get the same functionality, or use the Auth facade.

The most common usages are to check whether a user is logged in (auth()->check() returns true if the current user is logged in; auth()->guest() returns true if the user is not logged in) and to get the currently logged-in user (use auth()->user(), or auth()->id() for just the ID; both return null if no user is logged in).

Take a look at Example 9-3 for a sample usage of the global helper in a controller.

Example 9-3. Sample usage of the auth() global helper in a controller

```
public function dashboard()
{
    if (auth()->guest()) {
        return redirect('sign-up');
    }

    return view('dashboard')
        ->with('user', auth()->user());
}
```

The Auth Controllers

So, how do we actually log users in? And how do we trigger those password resets?

It all happens in the Auth-namespaced controllers: RegisterController, LoginController, ResetPasswordController, and ForgotPasswordController.

RegisterController

The RegisterController, in combination with the RegistersUsers trait, contains sensible defaults for how to show new users a registration form, how to validate their input, how to create new users once their input is validated, and where to redirect them afterward.

The controller itself just contains a few hooks that the traits will call at given points. That makes it easy to customize a few common behaviors without having to dig deeply into the code that makes it all work.

The $redirectTo property defines where users will be redirected after registration. The validator() method defines how to validate registrations. And the create() method defines how to create a new user based on an incoming registration. Take a look at Example 9-4 to see the default RegisterController.

Example 9-4. Laravel's default RegisterController

```
...
class RegisterController extends Controller
{
    use RegistersUsers;

    protected $redirectTo = '/home';

    ...

    protected function validator(array $data)
    {
        return Validator::make($data, [
            'name' => 'required|max:255',
            'email' => 'required|email|max:255|unique:users',
            'password' => 'required|min:6|confirmed',
        ]);
    }

    protected function create(array $data)
    {
        return User::create([
            'name' => $data['name'],
            'email' => $data['email'],
            'password' => bcrypt($data['password']),
        ]);
    }
}
```

RegistersUsers trait

The RegistersUsers trait, which the RegisterController imports, handles a few primary functions for the registration process. First, it shows users the registration form view, with the showRegistrationForm() method. If you want new users to register with a view other than auth.register you can override the showRegistration Form() method in your RegisterController.

Next, it handles the POST of the registration form with the register() method. This method passes the user's registration input to the validator from the validator() method of your RegisterController, and then on to the create() method.

And finally, the redirectPath() method (pulled in via the RedirectsUsers trait) defines where users should be redirected after a successful registration. You can define this URI with the redirectTo property on your controller, or you can override the redirectPath() method and return whatever you want.

If you want this trait to use a different auth guard than the default (you'll learn more about guards in "Guards" on page 209), you can override the auth() method and have it return whichever guard you'd like.

LoginController

The LoginController, unsurprisingly, allows the user to log in. It brings in the AuthenticatesUsers trait, which brings in the RedirectsUsers and ThrottlesLogins traits.

Like the RegistrationController, the LoginController has a $redirectTo property that allows you to customize the path the user will be redirected to after a successful login. Everything else lives behind the AuthenticatesUsers trait.

AuthenticatesUsers trait

The AuthenticatesUsers trait is responsible for showing users the login form, validating their logins, throttling failed logins, handling logouts, and redirecting users after a successful login.

The showLoginForm() method defaults to showing the user the auth.login view, but you can override it if you'd like it to use a different view.

The login() method accepts the POST from the login form. It validates the request using the validateLogin() method, which you can override if you'd like to customize the validation. It then hooks into the functionality of the ThrottlesLogins trait, which we'll cover shortly, to reject users with too many failed logins. And finally, it redirects the user, either to her intended path (if the user was redirected to the login page when attempting to visit a page within the app) or to the path defined by the redirectPath() method, which returns your $redirectTo property.

The trait calls the empty authenticated() method after a successful login, so if you'd like to perform any sort of behavior in response to a successful login, just override this method in your LoginController.

There's a `username()` method that defines which of your `users` columns is the "username"; this defaults to `email` but you can change that by overwriting the `username()` method in your controller to return the name of your username column.

And, like in the `RegistersUsers` trait, you can override the `guard()` method to define which auth guard (more on that in "Guards" on page 209) this controller should use.

ThrottlesLogins trait

The `ThrottlesLogins` trait is an interface to Laravel's `Illuminate\Cache\RateLimiter` class, which is a utility to rate-limit any event using the cache. This trait applies rate limiting to user logins, limiting users from using the login form if they've had too many failed logins within a certain amount of time. This functionality does not exist in Laravel 5.1.

If you import the `ThrottlesLogins` trait, all of its methods are protected, which means they can't actually be accessed as routes. Instead, the `AuthenticatesUsers` trait looks to see whether you've imported the `ThrottlesLogins` trait, and if so, it'll attach its functionality to your logins without any work on your part. Since the default `LoginController` imports both, you'll get this functionality for free if you use the auth scaffold.

`ThrottlesLogins` limits any given combination of username and IP address to 5 attempts per 60 seconds. Using the cache, it increments the "failed login" count of a given username/IP address combination, and if any user reaches 5 failed login attempts within 60 seconds, it redirects that user back to the login page with an appropriate error until the 60 seconds is over.

ResetPasswordController

The `ResetPasswordController` simply pulls in the `ResetsPasswords` trait. This trait provides validation and access to basic password reset views, and then uses an instance of Laravel's `PasswordBroker` class (or anything else implementing the `PasswordBroker` interface, if you choose to write your own) to handle sending password reset emails and actually resetting the passwords.

Just like the other traits we've covered, it handles showing the reset password view (`showResetForm()` shows the `auth.passwords.reset` view), and the POST request that is sent from that view (`reset()` validates and sends the appropriate response). The `resetPassword()` method actually resets the password, and you can customize the broker with `broker()` and the auth guard with `guard()`.

If you're interested in customizing any of this behavior, just override the specific method you want to customize in your controller.

ForgotPasswordController

The `ForgotPasswordController` simply pulls in the `SendsPasswordResetEmails` trait. It shows the `auth.passwords.email` form with the `showLinkRequestForm()` method, and handles the `POST` of that form with the `sendResetLinkEmail()` method. You can customize the broker with the `broker()` method.

Auth::routes()

Now that we have the auth controllers providing some methods for a series of predefined routes, we'll want our users to actually be able to *hit* those routes. We could add all these routes manually to *routes/web.php*, but there's already a convenience tool for that, called `Auth::routes()`:

```
// routes/web.php
Auth::routes();
```

As you can probably guess, `Auth::routes()` brings in a bundle of predefined routes to your routes file. In Example 9-5 you can see the routes that are actually being defined there.

Example 9-5. The routes provided by Auth::routes()

```
// Authentication Routes
$this->get('login', 'Auth\LoginController@showLoginForm');
$this->post('login', 'Auth\LoginController@login');
$this->get('logout', 'Auth\LoginController@logout');

// Registration Routes
$this->get('register', 'Auth\RegisterController@showRegistrationForm');
$this->post('register', 'Auth\RegisterController@register');

// Password Reset Routes
$this->get('password/reset', 'Auth\ForgotPasswordController@showLinkRequestForm');
$this->post('password/email', 'Auth\ForgotPasswordController@sendResetLinkEmail');
$this->get('password/reset/{token}', 'Auth\ResetPasswordController@showResetForm');
$this->post('password/reset', 'Auth\ResetPasswordController@reset');
```

Basically, `Auth::routes()` includes the routes for authentication, registration, and password resets.

The Auth Scaffold

At this point you have a migration, a model, controllers, and routes for your authentication system. But what about your views?

Laravel handles that by providing an auth scaffold (new in Laravel 5.2), which is intended to be run on a new application and provide you with even more skeleton code to get your auth system running quickly.

The auth scaffold takes care of adding `Auth::routes()` to your routes file, adds a view for each route, and creates a `HomeController` to serve as the landing page for logged-in users; it also routes to the `index()` method of `HomeController` at the */home* URI.

Just run `php artisan make:auth`, and the following files will be made available to you:

```
app/Http/Controllers/HomeController.php
resources/views/auth/login.blade.php
resources/views/auth/register.blade.php
resources/views/auth/passwords/email.blade.php
resources/views/auth/passwords/reset.blade.php
resources/views/layouts/app.blade.php
resources/views/home.blade.php
```

At this point, you have / returning the `welcome` view, */home* returning the `home` view, and a series of auth routes for login, logout, registration, and password reset pointing to the auth controllers. Each of the seeded views has Bootstrap-based layouts and form fields for all necessary fields for login, registration, and password reset, and they already point to the correct routes.

At this point, you have all of the pieces in place for every step of the normal user registration and authentication flow. You can tweak all you want, but you're entirely ready to register and authenticate users.

Let's review quickly the steps from new site to full authentication system:

```
laravel new MyApp
cd MyApp
```

```
php artisan make:auth
php artisan migrate
```

That's it. Run those commands, and you will have a landing page and a bootstrap-based user registration, login, logout, and password reset system, with a basic landing page for all authenticated users.

"Remember Me"

The auth scaffold has this implemented out of the box, but it's still worth learning how it works and how to use it on your own. If you want to implement a "remember me"–style long-lived access token, make sure you have a `remember_token` column on your `users` table (which you will if you used the default migration).

When you're normally logging in a user (and this is how the `LoginController` does it, with the `AuthenticatesUsers` trait), you'll "attempt" an authentication with the user-provided information, like in Example 9-6.

Example 9-6. Attempting a user authentication

```
if (auth()->attempt([
    'email' => request()->input('email'),
    'password' => request()->input('password')
    ])) {
    // Handle the successful login
}
```

This provides you with a user login that lasts as long as the user's session. If you want Laravel to extend the login indefinitely using cookies (as long as the user is on the same computer and doesn't log out), you can pass a boolean `true` as the second parameter of the `auth()->attempt()` method. Take a look at Example 9-7 to see what that request looks like.

Example 9-7. Attempting a user authentication with a "remember me" checkbox check

```
if (auth()->attempt([
    'email' => request()->input('email'),
    'password' => request()->input('password')
    ]), request()->has('remember')) {
    // Handle the successful login
}
```

You can see that we checked whether the input has a `remember` property, which will return a boolean. This allows our users to decide if they want to be remembered with a checkbox in the login form.

And later, if you need to manually check whether the current user was authenticated by a remember token, there's a method for that: `auth()->viaRemember()` returns a boolean indicating whether or not the current user authenticated via a remember token. This will allow you to prevent certain higher-sensitivity features from being accessible by remember token, and you can require users to reenter their passwords.

Manually Authenticating Users

The most common case for user authentication is that you'll allow the users to provide their credentials, and then use `auth()->attempt()` to see whether the provided credentials match any real users. If so, you log them in.

But sometimes there are contexts where it's valuable for you to be able to choose to log a user in on your own. For example, you may want to allow admin users to switch users.

There are two methods that make this possible. First, you can just pass a user ID:

```
auth()->loginUsingId(5);
```

Second, you can pass a `User` object (or any other object that implements the `Illuminate\Contracts\Auth\Authenticatable` contract):

```
auth()->login($user);
```

Auth Middleware

In Example 9-3, we saw how to check whether visitors are logged in and redirect them if not. You could perform these sorts of checks on every route in your application, but it would very quickly get tedious. It turns out that route middleware (see Chapter 10 to learn more about how they work) are a perfect fit for restricting certain routes to guests or to authenticated users.

Once again, Laravel comes with the middleware we need to do this out of the box. You can see which route middleware you have defined in `App\Http\Kernel`:

```
protected $routeMiddleware = [
    'auth' => \Illuminate\Auth\Middleware\Authenticate::class,
    'auth.basic' => \Illuminate\Auth\Middleware\AuthenticateWithBasicAuth::class,
    'bindings' => \Illuminate\Routing\Middleware\SubstituteBindings::class,
    'can' => \Illuminate\Auth\Middleware\Authorize::class,
    'guest' => \App\Http\Middleware\RedirectIfAuthenticated::class,
    'throttle' => \Illuminate\Routing\Middleware\ThrottleRequests::class,
];
```

Three of the default route middleware are authentication-related: `auth` restricts route access to authenticated users, `auth.basic` restricts access to authenticated users using HTTP Basic Authentication, and `guest` restricts access to unauthenticated users. `can` is used for authorizing user access to given routes.

It's most common to use `auth` for your authenticated-user-only sections and `guest` for any routes you don't want authenticated users to see (like the login form). `auth.basic` is a much less commonly used middleware for authenticating via request headers.

Example 9-8 shows a few sample routes protected by the `auth` middleware.

Example 9-8. Sample routes protected by auth middleware

```
Route::group(['middleware' => 'auth'], function () {
    Route::get('account', 'AccountController@dashboard');
});

Route::get('login', 'Auth\LoginController@getLogin')->middleware('guest');
```

Guards

Every aspect of Laravel's authentication system is routed through something called a *guard*. Each guard is a combination of two pieces: a *driver* that defines how it persists and retrieves the authentication state (for example, *session*), and a *provider* that allows you to get a user by certain criteria (for example, *users*).

Out of the box Laravel has two guards: `web` and `api`. `web` is the more traditional authentication style, using the session driver and the basic user provider. `api` also uses the same user provider, but it uses the token driver instead of the session to authenticate each request.

You'd change drivers if you wanted to handle the identification and persistence of a user's identity differently (for example, changing from a long-running session to a provided-every-page-load token), and you'd change providers if you wanted to change the storage type or retrieval methods for your users (for example, moving to storing your users in Mongo instead of MySQL).

Changing the Default Guard

The guards are defined in *config/auth.php*, and you can change them, add new guards, and also define which guard will be the default there.

The default guard will be that which is used any time you use any auth features. `auth()->user()` will pull the currently authenticated user using the default guard.

You can change this guard by changing the `auth.defaults.guard` setting in *config/auth.php*:

```
'defaults' => [
    'guard' => 'web', // Change the default here
    'passwords' => 'users',
],
```

If you're using Laravel 5.1, you'll notice that the structure of the authentication information is a little different from this. Don't worry; the features all still work the same, they're just structured differently.

Configuration conventions

You may have noticed that I refer to configuration sections with references like `auth.defaults.guard`. What that translates to is: in *config/auth.php*, in the array section keyed `defaults`, there should be a property keyed `guard`. That one is `auth.defaults.guard`.

Using Other Guards Without Changing the Default

If you want to use another guard, but *not* change the default, you can start your `Auth` calls with `guard()`:

```
$apiUser = auth()->guard('api')->user();
```

This will, just for this call, get the current user using the `api` guard.

Adding a New Guard

You can add a new guard at any time in *config/auth.php*, in the `auth.guards` setting:

```
'guards' => [
    'trainees' => [
        'driver' => 'session',
        'provider' => 'trainees',
    ],
],
```

As you can see here, we've created a new guard (in addition to `web` and `api`) named `trainees`. Let's imagine, for the rest of this section, that we're building an app where our users are physical trainers and they each have their *own* users—trainees—who can log in to their subdomains. So, we need a separate guard for them.

The only two options for `driver` are `token` and `session`. Out of the box, the only option for `provider` is `users`, but you can create your own provider easily.

Creating a Custom User Provider

Just below where the guards are defined in *config/auth.php*, there's an auth.provid ers section that defines the available providers. Let's create a new provider named trainees:

```
'providers' => [
    'users' => [
        'driver' => 'eloquent',
        'model' => App\User::class,
    ],

    'trainees' => [
        'driver' => 'eloquent',
        'model' => App\Trainee::class,
    ],
],
```

The two options for driver are eloquent and database; if you use eloquent, you'll need a model property that contains an Eloquent class name (the model to use for your User class), and if you use database, you'll need a table property to define which table it should authenticate against.

In our example, you can see that this application has a User and a Trainee, and they need to be authenticated separately. This way, the code can differentiate between auth()->guard(users) and auth()->guard(trainees).

One last note: the auth route middleware can take a parameter that is the guard name. So, you can guard certain routes with a specific guard:

```
Route::group(['middleware' => 'auth:trainees'], function () {
    // Trainee-only routes here
});
```

Custom User Providers for Nonrelational Databases

The user provider creation flow just described still relies on the same UserProvider class, which means it's expecting to pull the identifying information out of a relational database. But if you're using Mongo or Riak or something similar, you'll actually need to create your own class.

To do this, create a new class that implements the Illuminate\Contracts\Auth\User Provider interface, and then bind it in AuthServiceProvider@boot:

```
auth()->provider('riak', function ($app, array $config) {
    // Return an instance of Illuminate\Contracts\Auth\UserProvider...
    return new RiakUserProvider($app['riak.connection']);
});
```

Auth Events

We'll talk more about events in Chapter 16, but Laravel's event system is a basic pub/sub framework. There are system- and user-generated events that are broadcast, and the user has the ability to create event listeners that do certain things in response to certain events.

So, what if you wanted to send a ping to a particular security service every time a user was locked out after too many failed login attempts? Maybe this service watches out for a certain number of failed logins from certain geographic regions, or something else. You could, of course, inject a call in the appropriate controller. But with events, you can just create an event listener that listens to the "user locked out" event, and register that.

Take a look at Example 9-9 to see all of the events that the authentication system emits.

Example 9-9. Authentication events generated by the framework

```
protected $listen = [
    'Illuminate\Auth\Events\Attempting' => [],
    'Illuminate\Auth\Events\Login' => [],
    'Illuminate\Auth\Events\Logout' => [],
    'Illuminate\Auth\Events\Lockout' => [],
];
```

As you can see, there are listeners for "user attempting login," "successful login," "logout," and "lockout." To learn more about how to build event listeners for these events, check out Chapter 16.

Authorization (ACL) and Roles

Finally, let's cover Laravel's authorization system. It enables you to determine whether a user is *authorized* to do a particular thing, which you'll check using a few primary verbs: can, cannot, allows, and denies. The access control list (ACL) system is new in Laravel 5.2.

Most of this authorization control will be performed using the Gate facade, but there are also convenience helpers in your controllers, on the User model, as middleware, and available as Blade directives. Take a look at this example to get a taste of what we'll be able to do:

```
if (Gate::denies('edit', $contact)) {
    abort(403);
}

if (! Gate::check('create', Contact::class)) {
```

```
    abort(403);
}
```

Defining Authorization Rules

The default place to define authorization rules is the `boot()` method of the `AuthServi ceProvider`. It should already have an instance of `Illuminate\Contracts\Auth \Access\Gate` (aliased as `GateContract`) typehinted and injected as `$gate`.

An authorization rule is called an *ability*, and is comprised of two things: a string key (e.g., `update-contact`) and a closure that returns a boolean. Example 9-10 shows an ability for updating a contact.

Example 9-10. Sample ability for updating a contact

```
class AuthServiceProvider extends ServiceProvider
{
    public function boot(GateContract $gate)
    {
        $this->registerPolicies($gate);

        $gate->define('update-contact', function ($user, $contact) {
            return $user->id === $contact->user_id;
        });
    }
}
```

Let's walk through the steps for defining an ability.

First, you want to define a key. In naming this key, you should consider what string makes sense in your code's flow to refer to the ability you're providing the user. You can see the code sample uses the convention `{verb}-{modelName}`: `create-contact`, `update-contact`, etc.

Second, you define the closure. The first parameter will be the currently authenticated user, and all parameters after that will be the object(s) you're checking for access to— in this instance, the contact.

So, given those two objects, we can check whether the user is authorized to update this contact. You can write this logic however you want, but in the app we're looking at at the moment, authorization depends on being the creator of the contact row. The closure will return `true` (authorized) if the current user created the contact, and `false` (unauthorized) if not.

Just like with route definitions, you could also use a class and method instead of a closure to resolve this definition:

```
$gate->define('update-contact', 'ContactACLChecker@updateContact');
```

The Gate Facade (and Injecting Gate)

Now that you've defined an ability, it's time to test against it. The simplest way is to use the Gate facade, as in Example 9-11 (or you can inject an instance of Illuminate \Contracts\Auth\Access\Gate).

Example 9-11. Basic Gate facade usage

```
if (Gate::allows('update-contact', $contact)) {
    // Update contact
}

// or...
if (Gate::denies('update-contact', $contact)) {
    abort(403);
}
```

You might also define an ability with multiple parameters—maybe a contact can be in groups, and you want to authorize whether the user has access to add a contact to a group. Example 9-12 shows how to do this.

Example 9-12. Abilities with multiple parameters

```
// Definition
$gate->define('add-contact-to-group', function ($user, $contact, $group) {
    return $user->id === $contact->user_id && $user->id === $group->user_id;
});

// Usage
if (Gate::denies('add-contact-to-group', [$contact, $group])) {
    abort(403);
}
```

And if you need to check authorization for a user other than the currently authenticated user, try forUser(), like in Example 9-13.

Example 9-13. Specifying the user for Gate

```
if (Gate::forUser($user)->denies('create-contact')) {
    abort(403);
}
```

The Authorize Middleware

If you want to authorize entire routes, you can use the Authorize middleware (which has a shortcut of can), like in Example 9-14.

Example 9-14. Using the Authorize middleware

```
Route::get('people/create', function () {
    // Create person...
})->middleware('can:create-person');

Route::get('people/{person}/edit', function () {
    // Create person...
})->middleware('can:create,person');
```

Here, the `{person}` parameter (whether it's defined as a string or as a bound route model) will be passed to the ability method as an additional parameter.

Controller Authorization

The parent `App\Http\Controllers\Controller` class in Laravel imports the `Authori zesRequests` trait, which provides three methods for authorization: `authorize()`, `authorizeForUser()`, and `authorizeResource()`.

`authorize()` takes an ability key and an object (or array of objects) as parameters, and if the authorization fails, it'll quit the application with a 403 (Unauthorized) status code. That means this feature can turn three lines of authorization code into just one, as you can see in Example 9-15.

Example 9-15. Simplifying controller authorization with authorize()

```
// From this:
public function show($contactId)
{
    $contact = Contact::findOrFail($contactId);

    if (Gate::cannot('update-contact', $contact)) {
        abort(403);
    }
}

// To this:
public function show($contactId)
{
    $contact = Contact::findOrFail($contactId);

    $this->authorize('update-contact', $contact);
}
```

`authorizeForUser()` is the same, but allows you to pass in a `User` object instead of defaulting to the currently authenticated user:

```
$this->authorizeForUser($user, 'update-contact', $contact);
```

authorizeResource(), called once in the controller constructor, maps a predefined set of authorization rules to each of the RESTful controller methods in that controller —something like Example 9-16.

Example 9-16. The authorization-to-method mappings of authorizeResource()

```
...
class ContactsController extends Controller
{
    public function __construct()
    {
        // This call does everything you see in the methods below.
        // If you put this here, you can remove all authorize
        // calls in the individual resource methods here.
        $this->authorizeResource(Contact::class);
    }

    public function index()
    {
        $this->authorize('view', Contact::class);
    }

    public function create()
    {
        $this->authorize('create', Contact::class);
    }

    public function store(Request $request)
    {
        $this->authorize('create', Contact::class);
    }

    public function show(Contact $contact)
    {
        $this->authorize('view', $contact);
    }

    public function edit(Contact $contact)
    {
        $this->authorize('update', $contact);
    }

    public function update(Request $request, Contact $contact)
    {
        $this->authorize('update', $contact);
    }

    public function destroy(Contact $contact)
    {
        $this->authorize('delete', $contact);
```

```
        }
}
```

Checking on the User Instance

If you're not in a controller, you're more likely to be checking the capabilities of a specific user than the currently authenticated user. That's already possible with the Gate facade using the forUser() method, but sometimes the syntax can feel a little off.

Thankfully, the Authorizable trait on the User class provides three methods to make a more readable authorization feature: $user->can(), $user->cant(), and $user->cannot(). As you can probably guess, cant() and cannot() do the same thing, and can() is their exact inverse.

That means you can do something like Example 9-17.

Example 9-17. Checking authorization on a user instance

```
$user = User::find(1);

if ($user->can('create-contact')) {
    // do something
}
```

Behind the scenes, these methods are just passing your params to Gate; in the preceding example, Gate::forUser($user)->can('create-contact').

Blade Checks

Blade also has a little convenience helper: a @can directive. Example 9-18 illustrates its usage.

Example 9-18. Using Blade's @can directive

```
<nav>
    <a href="/">Home</a>
    @can('edit-contact', $contact)
        <a href="{{ route('contacts.edit', [$contact->id]) }}">Edit This Contact</a>
    @endcan
</nav>
```

You can also use @else in between @can and @endcan, and you can use @cannot and @endcannot as in Example 9-19.

Example 9-19. Using Blade's @cannot directive

```
<h1>{{ $contact->name }}</h1>
@cannot('edit-contact', $contact)
    LOCKED
@endcannot
```

Intercepting Checks

If you've ever built an app with an admin user class, you've probably looked at all of the simple authorization closures so far in this chapter and thought about how you could add a superuser class that overrides these checks in every case. Thankfully, there's already a tool for that.

In `AuthServiceProvider`, where you're already defining your abilities, you can also add a `before()` check that runs before all the others and can optionally override them, like in Example 9-20.

Example 9-20. Overriding Gate checks with before()

```
$gate->before(function ($user, $ability) {
    if ($user->isOwner()) {
        return true;
    }
});
```

Note that the string name for the ability is also passed in, so you can differentiate your `before` hooks based on your ability naming scheme.

Policies

Up until this point, all of the access controls have required you to manually associate Eloquent models with the ability names. You could have created an ability named something like `visit-dashboard` that's not related to a specific Eloquent model, but you'll probably have noticed that most of our examples have had to do with *doing something to something*—and in most of these cases, the *something* that's the recipient of the action is an Eloquent model.

Authorization policies are organizational structures that help you group your authorization logic based on the resource you're controlling access to. They make it easy to manage defining authorization rules for behavior toward a particular Eloquent model (or other PHP class), all together in a single location.

Generating policies

Policies are PHP classes, which can be generated with an Artisan command:

```
php artisan make:policy ContactPolicy
```

Once they're generated, they need to be registered. The `AuthServiceProvider` has a `$policies` property, which is an array. The key of each item is the class name of the protected resource (usually, but not always, an Eloquent class), and the value is the policy class name:

```
class AuthServiceProvider extends ServiceProvider
{
    protected $policies = [
        Contact::class => ContactPolicy::class,
    ]
```

A policy class that's generated by Artisan doesn't have any special properties or methods. But every method that you add is now mapped as an ability key for this object.

Let's define an `update()` method to take a look at how it works (Example 9-21).

Example 9-21. A sample update() policy method

```
<?php

namespace App\Policies;

class ContactPolicy
{
    public function update($user, $contact)
    {
        return $user->id === $contact->user_id;
    }
}
```

Notice that the contents of this method look exactly like they would in a `Gate` definition.

Policy methods that don't take an instance, before 5.3

In Laravel 5.2, if you want to define a policy method that relates to the class but not a specific instance—for example, "can this user create contacts at all?" rather than just "can this user view this specific contact?"—create that method and add "Any" at the end of its name:

```
...
class ContactPolicy
{
    public function createAny($user)
    {
        return $user->canCreateContacts();
    }
}
```

In Laravel 5.3, you can drop the Any suffix and treat this just like a normal method.

Checking policies

If there's a policy defined for a resource type, the `Gate` will use the first parameter to figure out which method to check on your policy. If you run `Gate::allows('update', $contact)`, it will check the `ContactPolicy@update` method for authorization.

This also works for the `Authorize` middleware and for `User` model checking and Blade checking, as seen in Example 9-22.

Example 9-22. Checking authorization against a policy

```
// Gate
if (Gate::denies('update', $contact)) {
    abort(403);
}

// Gate if you don't have an explicit instance
if (! Gate::check('create', Contact::class)) {
    abort(403);
}

// User
if ($user->can('update', $contact)) {
    // Do stuff
}

// Blade
@can('update', $contact)
    <!-- show stuff -->
@endcan
```

Additionally, there's a `policy()` helper that allows you to retrieve a policy class and run its methods:

```
if (policy($contact)->update($user, $contact)) {
    // Do stuff
}
```

Overriding policies

Just like with normal ability definitions, policies can define a `before()` method that allows you to override any call before it's even processed (see Example 9-23).

Example 9-23. Overriding policies with the before() method

```
public function before($user, $ability)
{
    if ($user->isAdmin()) {
        return true;
```

```
    }
}
```

Passport and OAuth

There's a Laravel package called Passport that makes it easy to set up your own OAuth server as a part of your Laravel app. Take a look at "API Authentication with Laravel Passport" on page 297 to learn more about how it works.

Testing

Application tests often need to perform a particular behavior on behalf of a particular user. We therefore need to be able to authenticate as a user in application tests, and we need to test authorization rules and authentication routes.

Of course, it's possible to write an application test that manually visits the login page and then fills out the form and submits it, but that's not necessary. Instead, the simplest option is to use the ->be() method to simulate being logged in as a user. Take a look at Example 9-24.

Example 9-24. Authenticating as a user in application tests

```
public function test_it_creates_a_new_contact()
{
    $user = factory(User::class)->create();
    $this->be($user);

    $this->post('contacts', [
        'email' => 'my@email.com'
    ]);

    $this->seeInDatabase('contacts', [
        'email' => 'my@email.com',
        'user_id' => $user->id,
    ]);
}
```

We can also test authorization like in Example 9-25.

Example 9-25. Testing authorization rules

```
public function test_non_admins_cant_create_users()
{
    $user = factory(User::class)->create([
        'admin' => false
    ]);
    $this->be($user);
```

```
$this->post('users', ['email' => 'my@email.com']);

$this->dontSeeInDatabase('users', [
    'email' => 'my@email.com'
]);
}
```

Or we can test for a 403 response like in Example 9-26.

Example 9-26. Testing authorization rules by checking status code

```
public function test_non_admins_cant_create_users()
{
    $user = factory(User::class)->create([
        'admin' => false
    ]);
    $this->be($user);

    $this->post('users', ['email' => 'my@email.com']);

    $this->assertResponseStatus(403);
}
```

We need to test that our authentication (sign up and sign in) routes work too, as illustrated in Example 9-27.

Example 9-27. Testing authentication routes

```
public function test_users_can_register()
{
    $this->post('register', [
        'name' => 'Sal Leibowitz',
        'email' => 'sal@leibs.net',
        'password' => 'abcdefg123',
        'password_confirmation' => 'abcdefg123',
    ]);

    $this->followRedirects()->assertResponseOk();

    $this->seeInDatabase('users', [
        'name' => 'Sal Leibowitz',
        'email' => 'sal@leibs.net',
    ]);
}

public function test_users_can_log_in()
{
    $user = factory(User::class)->create([
        'password' => bcrypt('abcdefg123')
    ]);
```

```
    $this->post('login', [
        'email' => $user->email,
        'password' => 'abcdefg123',
    ]);

    $this->followRedirects()->assertResponseOk();

    $this->assertTrue(auth()->check());
}
```

You could also use the integration test features to direct the test to "click" your authentication fields and "submit" the fields to test the entire flow.

TL;DR

Between the default User model, the create_users_table migration, the auth controllers, and the auth scaffold, Laravel comes with a full user authentication system out of the box. The RegisterController handles user registration, the LoginControl ler handles user authentication, and the ResetPasswordController and the Forgot PasswordController handle password resets. Each has certain properties and methods that can be used to override some of the default behavior.

The Auth facade and the auth() global helper provide access to the current user (auth()->user()) and makes it easy to check whether a user is logged in (auth()->check() and auth()->guest()).

Laravel also has an authorization system built in that allows you to define specific abilities (create-contact, visit-secret-page) or define policies for user interaction with entire models.

You can check for authorization with the Gate facade, the ->can() and ->cannot() methods on the User class, the @can and @cannot directives in Blade, the ->authorize() methods on the controller, or the can middleware.

## CHAPTER 10

Requests and Responses

We've already covered the Illuminate `Request` object a bit—how you can typehint it in constructors to get an instance, and then use that to get information about the user's input. In Chapter 3, for example, we saw how you can typehint it in constructors to get an instance, and in Chapter 6 we looked at how you can use it to get information about the user's input.

In this chapter, we'll learn more about what that `Request` object is, how it's generated and what it represents, and what part it plays in your application's lifecycle. We'll also talk about the `Response` object and Laravel's implementation of the middleware pattern.

Laravel's Request Lifecycle

Every request coming into a Laravel application, whether generated by an HTTP request or a command-line interaction, is immediately converted into an Illuminate `Request` object, which then crosses many layers and ends up being parsed by the application itself. The application then generates an Illuminate `Response` object, which is sent back out across those layers and finally returned to the end user.

This request/response lifecycle is illustrated in Figure 10-1.

Let's take a look at what it takes to make each of these steps happen, from the first line of code to the last.

Every Laravel application has some form of configuration set up at the web server level, in an *.htaccess* file or an Nginx configuration setting or something similar, that captures every web request regardless of URL and routes it to *public/index.php* in the Laravel application directory (*app*).

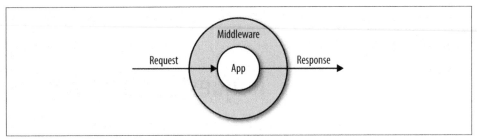

Figure 10-1. Request/response lifecycle

Bootstrapping the Application

index.php doesn't actually have that much code in it. It has three primary functions.

First, it loads Composer's autoload file and Laravel's compiled application cache, which lives at *bootstrap/cache/compiled.php*. This file is what's generated when you run php artisan optimize, and it preloads all of the most commonly used classes for faster loading.

Composer and Laravel

Laravel's core functionality is separated into a series of components under the Illuminate namespace, which are all pulled into each Laravel app using Composer. Laravel also pulls in quite a few packages from Symfony and several other community-developed packages. In this way, Laravel is just as much an opinionated collection of components as it is a framework.

Next, it kicks off Laravel's bootstrap, creating the application container (you'll learn more about the container in Chapter 11) and registering a few core services (including the kernel, which we'll talk about in just a bit).

Finally, it creates an instance of the kernel, creates a request representing the current user's web request, and passes the request to the kernel to handle. The kernel responds with an Illuminate Response object, which *index.php* then returns to the end user, and terminates the page request.

Laravel's kernel

The kernel is the core router of every Laravel application, responsible for taking in a user request, processing it through middleware and handling exceptions and passing it to the page router, and then returning the final response. There are actually two kernels, but only one is used for each page request. One of the routers handles web requests (the HTTP kernel) and the other handles console, cron, and Artisan requests (the console kernel). Each has a `handle()` method that's responsible for taking in an Illuminate `Request` object and returning an Illuminate `Response` object.

The kernel runs all of the bootstraps that need to run before every request, including determining which environment the current request is running in (staging, local, production, etc.) and running all of the service providers. The HTTP kernel additionally defines the list of middleware that will wrap each request, including the core middleware responsible for sessions and CSRF protection.

Service Providers

While there's a bit of procedural code in these bootstraps, almost all of Laravel's bootstrap code is separated into something Laravel calls *service providers*. A service provider is a class that encapsulates logic that various parts of your application need to run in order to bootstrap their core functionality.

For example, there's an `AuthServiceProvider` that bootstraps all of the registrations necessary for Laravel's authentication system and a `RouteServiceProvider` that bootstraps the routing system.

The concept of service providers can be a little hard to understand at first, so think about it this way: many components of your application have bootstrap code that needs to run when the application initializes. Service providers are a tool for grouping that bootstrap code into related classes. If you have any code that needs to run *in preparation* for your application code to work, it's a strong candidate for a service provider.

For example, if you ever find that the feature you're working on requires some classes registered in the container (we'll learn more about this in Chapter 11), you would create a service provider just for that piece of functionality. You might have a `GitHubServiceProvider` or a `MailerServiceProvider`.

Service providers have two important methods: `boot()` and `register()`. There's also a `$defer` property that you might choose to use. Here's how they work.

First, all of the service providers' `register()` methods are called. This is where we want to bind classes and aliases to the container. You don't want to do anything in `register()` that relies on the entire application being bootstrapped.

Second, all of the service providers' `boot()` methods are called. You can now do any other bootstrapping here, like binding event listeners or defining routes—anything that may rely on the entire Laravel application having been bootstrapped.

If your service provider is only going to register bindings in the container (i.e., teach the container how to resolve a given class or interface), but not perform any other bootstrapping, you can "defer" its registrations, which means they won't run unless one of their bindings is explicitly requested from the container. This can speed up your application's average time to bootstrap.

If you want to defer your service provider's registrations, first give it a `protected` `$defer` property and set it to `true`, and then give it a `provides()` method that returns a list of bindings the provider provides, as shown in Example 10-1.

Example 10-1. Deferring the registration of a service provider

```
...
class GitHubServiceProvider extends ServiceProvider
{
    protected $defer = true;

    public function provides()
    {
        return [
            GitHubClient::class
        ];
    }
}
```

More uses for service providers

Service providers also have a suite of methods and configuration options that can provide advanced functionality to the end user when the provider is published as part of a Composer package. Take a look at the service provider definition in the Laravel source (*http://bit.ly/2eQtW0s*) to learn more about how this can work.

Now that we've covered the application bootstrap, let's take a look at the `Request` object, the most important output of the bootstrap.

The Request Object

The Illuminate `Request` class is a Laravel-specific extension of Symfony's `HttpFounda` `tion\Request` object.

Symfony HttpFoundation

If you're not familiar with it, Symfony's `HttpFoundation` suite of classes powers almost every PHP framework in existence at this point; this is the most popular and powerful set of abstractions available in PHP for representing HTTP requests, responses, headers, cookies, and more.

Each Request object is intended to represent every relevant piece of information you could care to know about a user's HTTP request.

In native PHP code, you might find yourself looking to $_SERVER, $_GET, $_POST, and other combinations of globals and processing logic to get information about the current user's request. What files has the user uploaded? What's his IP address? What fields did he post? All of this is sprinkled around the language—and your code—in a way that's hard to understand and harder to mock.

Symfony's Request object instead collects all of the information necessary to represent a single HTTP request into a single object, and then tacks on convenience methods to make it easy to get useful information from it. The Illuminate Request object adds even more convenience methods to get information about the request it's representing.

Capturing a request

You'll very likely never need to do this in a Laravel app, but if you ever need to capture your own Illuminate Request directly from PHP's globals, you can use the capture() method:

```
$request = Illuminate\Http\Request::capture();
```

Getting a Request Object in Laravel

Realistically, you're not going to be capturing your own requests. Laravel does this for you in its bootstrap, and there are a few ways you can get access to it.

First—and again, we'll cover this more in Chapter 11—you can typehint the class in any constructor or method that's resolved by the container. That means you can typehint it in a controller method or a service provider, as seen in Example 10-2.

Example 10-2. Typehinting in a container-resolved method to receive a Request object

```
...
use Illuminate\Http\Request;

class PeopleController extends Controller
{
    public function index(Request $request)
    {
        $allInput = $request->all();
    }
```

You can also use the `request()` global helper, which allows you to call methods on it (e.g., `request()->input()`) and also allows you to call it on its own to get an instance of `$request`:

```
$request = request();
$allInput = request()->all();
```

And you can also use the `app()` global method to get an instance of `Request`. You can pass either the fully qualified class name or the shortcut, `request`:

```
$request = app(Illuminate\Http\Request::class);
$request = app('request');
```

Getting Basic Information About a Request

Now that we know how to get an instance of `Request`, what can we do with it? The primary purpose of the `Request` object is to represent the current HTTP request, so the primary functionality the `Request` class offers is to make it easy to get useful information about the current request.

I've categorized the methods described here, but note that there's certainly overlap between the categories, and the categories are a bit arbitrary—for example, query parameters could just as easily be in "User and request state" as they are in "Basic user input." Hopefully these categories will make it easy for you to learn, and then you can throw away the categories.

Also, be aware that there are many more methods available on the `Request` object; these are just the most commonly used methods.

Basic user input

The basic user input methods make it simple to get information that the users themselves explicitly provide—likely through submitting a form or an Ajax component. When I reference "user-provided input" here, I'm talking about input from query strings (`GET`), form submissions (`POST`), or JSON:

- `all()` returns an array of all user-provided input.
- `input(fieldName)` returns the value of a single user-provided input field.
- `only(fieldName|[array,of,field,names])` returns an array of all user-provided input for the specified field name(s).
- `except(fieldName|[array,of,field,names])` returns an array of all user-provided input except for the specified field name(s).
- `exists(fieldName)` returns a boolean of whether or not the field exists in the input.

- has(*fieldName*) returns a boolean of whether the field exists in the input *and* is not empty (has a value).
- json() returns a ParameterBag if the page had JSON sent to it.
- json(*keyName*) returns the value of the given key from JSON sent to the page.

ParameterBag

Sometimes in Laravel you'll run into a ParameterBag. This class is sort of like an associative array. You can get a particular key using get():

```
echo $bag->get('name');
```

You can also use has() to check for the existence of a key, all() to get an array of all keys and values, count() to count the number of items, and keys() to get an array of just the keys.

Example 10-3 gives a few quick examples of how to use the user-provided information methods from a request.

Example 10-3. Getting basic user-provided information from the request

```
// form
<form method="POST" action="/form">
    {{ csrf_field() }}
    <input name="name"> Name<br>
    <input type="submit">
</form>

// route receiving the form
Route::post('form', function (Request $request) {
    echo 'name is ' . $request->input('name');
    echo 'all input is ' . print_r($request->all());
    echo 'user provided email address: ' . $request->has('email') ? 'true' : 'false';
});
```

User and request state

The user and request state methods include input that wasn't explicitly provided by the user through a form:

- method() returns the method (GET, POST, PATCH, etc.) used to access this route.
- path() returns the path (without the domain) used to access this page; e.g., for *http://www.myapp.com/abc/def* it would return abc/def.

- `url()` returns the URL (with the domain) used to access this page; e.g., for *http://www.myapp.com/abc* it would return `http://www.myapp.com/abc`.

- `is()` returns a boolean of whether or not the current page request fuzzy-matches a provided string (e.g., /a/b/c would be matched by `$request->is('*b*')`, where * stands for any characters). It uses a custom regex parser found in `Str::is`.

- `ip()` returns the user's IP address.

- `header()` returns an array of headers (e.g., `['accept-language' => ['en-US,en;q=0.8']]`), or, if passed a header name as a parameter, returns just that header.

- `server()` returns an array of the variables traditionally stored in `$_SERVER` (e.g., `REMOTE_ADDR`), or, if passed a `$_SERVER` variable name, returns just that value.

- `secure()` returns a boolean of whether this page was loaded using HTTPS.

- `pjax()` returns a boolean of whether this page request was loaded using Pjax.

- `wantsJson()` returns a boolean of whether this request has any /json content types in its `Accept` headers.

- `isJson()` returns a boolean of whether this page request has any /json content types in its `Content-Type` header.

- `accepts()` returns a boolean of whether this page request accepts a given content type.

Files

So far, all of the input we've covered is either explicit (retrieved by methods like `all()`, `input()`, etc.) or defined by the browser or referring site (retrieved by methods like `pjax()`). File inputs are similar to explicit user input, but they're handled much differently:

- `file()` returns an array of all uploaded files, or, if a key is passed (the file upload field name), returns just the one file.

- `hasFile()` returns a boolean of whether a file was uploaded at the specified key.

Every file that's uploaded will be an instance of `Symfony\Component\HttpFoundation\File\UploadedFile`, which provides a suite of tools for validating, processing, and storing uploaded files.

Take a look at Chapter 14 for more examples of how to handle uploaded files.

Persistence

The request can also provide functionality for interacting with the session. Most session functionality lives elsewhere, but there are a few methods that are particularly relevant to the current page request:

- `flash()` flashes the current request's user input to the session to be retrieved later.
- `flashOnly()` flashes the current request's user input for any keys in the provided array.
- `flashExcept()` flashes the current requests's user input, except for any keys in the provided array.
- `old()` returns an array of all previously flashed user input, or, if passed a key, returns the value for that key if it was previously flashed.
- `flush()` wipes all previously flashed user input.
- `cookie()` retrieves all cookies from the request, or, if a key is provided, retrieves just that cookie.
- `hasCookie()` returns a boolean of whether the request has a cookie for the given key.

The `flash*()` and `old()` methods are used for storing user input and retrieving it later, often after the input is validated and rejected.

The Response Object

Similar to the `Request` object, there's an Illuminate `Response` object that represents the response your application is sending to the end user, complete with headers, cookies, content, and anything else used for sending the end user's browser instructions on rendering a page.

Just like `Request`, the `Illuminate\Http\Response` object extends a Symfony class: `Symfony\Component\HttpFoundation\Response`. This is a base class with a series of properties and methods that make it possible to represent and render a response; Illuminate's `Response` class decorates it with a few helpful shortcuts.

Using and Creating Response Objects in Controllers

Before we talk about how you can customize your response objects, let's step back and see how we most commonly work with response objects.

In the end, any response object returned from a route definition will be converted into an HTTP response. It may define specific headers or specific content, set cookies, or whatever else, but eventually it will be converted into a response your users' browsers can parse.

Let's take a look at the simplest possible response, in Example 10-4.

Example 10-4. Simplest possible HTTP response

```
Route::get('route', function () {
    return new Illuminate\Http\Response('Hello!');
});

// Same, using global function:
Route::get('route', function () {
    return response('Hello!');
});
```

We create a response, give it some core data, and then return it. We can also customize the HTTP status, headers, cookies, and more, like in Example 10-5.

Example 10-5. Simple HTTP response with customized status and headers

```
Route::get('route', function () {
    return response('Error!', 400)
        ->header('X-Header-Name', 'header-value')
        ->cookie('cookie-name', 'cookie-value');
});
```

Setting headers

We define a header on a response by using the `header()` fluent method, like in Example 10-5. The first parameter is the header name and the second is the header value.

Adding cookies

We can also set cookies directly on the response object if we'd like. We'll cover Laravel's cookie handling a bit more in Chapter 14, but take a look at Example 10-6 for a simple use case for attaching cookies to a response.

Example 10-6. Attaching a cookie to a response

```
    return response($content)
        ->cookie('signup_dismissed', true);
```

Specialized Response Types

There are also a few special response types for views, downloads, files, and JSON. Each is a predefined macro that makes it easy to reuse particular templates for headers or content structure.

View responses

In Chapter 4, I used the global `view()` helper to show how to return a template—for example, `view(view.name.here)` or something similar. But if you need to customize headers, HTTP status, or anything else when returning a view, you can use the `view()` response type as shown in Example 10-7.

Example 10-7. Using the view() response type

```
Route::get('/', function (XmlGetterService $xml) {
    $data = $xml->get();
    return response()
        ->view('xml-structure', $data)
        ->header('Content-Type', 'text/xml');
});
```

Download responses

Sometimes you want your application to force the user's browser to download a file, whether you're creating the file in Laravel or serving it from a database or a protected location. The `download()` response type makes this simple.

The required first parameter is the path for the file you want the browser to download. If it's a generated file, you'll need to save it somewhere temporarily.

The optional second parameter is the filename for the downloaded file (e.g., *export.csv*). If you don't pass a string here, it will be automatically generated. The optional third parameter allows you to pass an array of headers. Example 10-8 illustrates the use of the `download()` response type.

Example 10-8. Using the download() response type

```
public function export()
{
    return response()
        ->download('file.csv', 'export.csv', ['header' => 'value']);
}

public function otherExport()
{
    return response()->download('file.pdf');
}
```

File responses

The file response is similar to the download response, except it allows the browser to display the file instead of forcing a download. This is most common with images and PDFs.

The required first parameter is the filename, and the optional second parameter can be an array of headers (see Example 10-9).

Example 10-9. Using the file() response type

```
public function invoice($id)
{
    return response()->file("./invoices/{$id}.pdf", ['header' => 'value']);
}
```

JSON responses

JSON responses are so common that, even though they're not really particularly complex to program, there's a custom response for them as well.

JSON responses convert the passed data to JSON (with `json_encode()`) and set the `Content-Type` to `application/json`. You can also optionally use the `setCallback()` method to create a JSONP response instead of JSON, as seen in Example 10-10.

Example 10-10. Using the json() response type

```
public function contacts()
{
    return response()->json(Contact::all());
}

public function jsonpContacts(Request $request)
{
    return response()
        ->json(Contact::all())
        ->setCallback($request->input('callback'));
}

public function nonEloquentContacts()
{
    return response()->json(['Tom', 'Jerry']);
}
```

Redirect responses

Redirects aren't commonly called on the `response()` helper, so they're a bit different from the other custom response types we discussed already, but they're still just a different sort of response. Redirects, returned from a Laravel route, send the user a redirect (often a 301) to another page or back to the previous page.

You technically *can* call a redirect from `response()`, as in `return response()->redirectTo('/')`. But more commonly you'll use the redirect-specific global helpers.

There is a global `redirect()` function that can be used to create redirect responses, and a global `back()` function that is a shortcut to `redirect()->back()`.

Just like most global helpers, the `redirect()` global function can either be passed parameters or can be used to get an instance of its class that you then chain method calls onto. If you don't chain, but just pass parameters, `redirect()` performs the same as `redirect()->to()`; it takes a string and redirects to that string URL. Example 10-11 shows some examples of its use.

Example 10-11. Examples of using the redirect() global helper

```
return redirect('account/payment');
return redirect()->to('account/payment');
return redirect()->route('account.payment');
return redirect()->action('AccountController@showPayment');

// If named route or controller needs parameters:
return redirect()->route('contacts.edit', ['id' => 15]);
return redirect()->action('ContactsController@edit', ['id' => 15]);
```

You can also redirect "back" to the previous page, which is especially useful when handling and validating user input. Example 10-12 shows a common pattern in validation contexts.

Example 10-12. Redirect back with input

```
public function store()
{
    // If validation fails...
    return back()->withInput();
}
```

Finally, you can redirect and flash data to the session at the same time. This is common with error and success messages, like in Example 10-13.

Example 10-13. Redirect with flashed data

```
Route::post('contacts', function () {
    // store the contact...

    return redirect('dashboard')->with('message', 'Contact created!');
```

```
});

Route::get('dashboard', function () {
    // Get the flashed data from session--usually handled in Blade template
    echo session('message');
});
```

Custom response macros

You can also create your own custom response types using "macros". This allows you to define a series of modifications to make to the response and its provided content.

Let's re-create the `json()` custom response type, just to see how it works. As always, you should probably create a custom service provider for these sorts of bindings, but for now we'll just put it in `AppServiceProvider`, as seen in Example 10-14.

Example 10-14. Creating a custom response macro

```
...
class AppServiceProvider
{
    public function boot()
    {
        Response::macro('myJson', function ($content) {
            return response(json_encode($content))
                ->headers(['Content-Type' => 'application/json']);
        });
    }
```

Then, we can use it just like we would use the predefined `json` macro:

```
return response()->myJson(['name' => 'Sangeetha']);
```

This will return a response with the body of that array encoded for JSON, with the JSON-appropriate `Content-Type` header.

Laravel and Middleware

Take a look back at Figure 10-1, at the start of this chapter.

We've covered the requests and responses, but we haven't actually looked into what middleware is. You may already be familiar with middleware; it's not unique to Laravel, but rather a widely used architecture pattern.

An Introduction to Middleware

The idea of middleware is that there is a series of layers wrapping around your application, like a multilayer cake or an onion. Just as shown in Example 10-1, every request passes through every middleware layer on its way into the application, and then the resulting response passes back through the middleware layers on its way out to the end user.

Middleware is most often considered separate from your application logic, and usually is constructed in a way that should theoretically be applicable to any application, not just the one you're working on at the moment.

Middleware can inspect a request and decorate it, or reject it, based on what it finds. That means middleware is great for something like rate limiting: it can inspect the IP address, check how many times it's accessed this resource in the last minute, and send back a 429 (Too Many Requests) status if a threshold is passed.

Because middleware also gets access to the response on its way out of the application, it's great for decorating responses. For example, Laravel uses a middleware to add all of the queued cookies from a given request/response cycle to the response right before it is sent to the end user.

But some of the most powerful uses of middleware come from the fact that it can be nearly the *first* and the *last* thing to interact with the request/response cycle. That makes it perfect for something like enabling sessions—PHP needs you to open the session very early and close it very late, and middleware is great for this.

Creating Custom Middleware

Let's imagine we want to have a middleware that rejects every request that uses the DELETE HTTP method, and also sends a cookie back for every request.

There's an Artisan command to create custom middleware. Let's try it out:

```
php artisan make:middleware BanDeleteMethod
```

You can now open up the file at *app/Http/Middleware/BanDeleteMethod.php*. The default contents are shown in Example 10-15.

Example 10-15. Default middleware contents

```
...
class BanDeleteMethod
{
    public function handle($request, Closure $next)
    {
        return $next($request);
    }
}
```

How this `handle()` method represents the processing of both the incoming request *and* the outgoing response is the most difficult thing to understand about middleware, so let's walk through it.

Understanding middleware's handle() method

First, remember that middleware are layered one on top of another, and then finally on top of the app. The first middleware that's registered gets *first* access to a request when it comes in, then that request is passed to every other middleware in turn, then to the app; then the resulting response is passed outward through the middleware, and finally this first middleware gets *last* access to the response when it goes out.

Let's imagine we've registered `BanDeleteMethod` as the first middleware to run. That means the `$request` coming into it is the raw request, unadulterated by any other middleware. Now what?

Passing that request to `$next()` means handing it off to the rest of the middleware. The `$next()` closure just takes that `$request` and passes it to the `handle()` method of the next middleware in the stack. It then gets passed on down the line until there are no more middleware to hand it to, and it finally ends up at the application.

Next, how does the response come out? This is where it might be hard to follow. The application returns a response, which is passed back up the chain of middleware—because each middleware returns its response. So, within that same `handle()` method, the middleware can decorate a `$request` and pass it to the `$next()` closure, and can then choose to do something with the output it receives before finally returning that output to the end user. Let's look at some pseudocode to make this clearer (Example 10-16).

Example 10-16. Pseudocode explaining the middleware call process

```
...
class BanDeleteMethod
{
    public function handle($request, Closure $next)
    {
        // At this point, $request is the raw request from the user.
        // Let's do something with it, just for fun.
        if ($request->ip() === '192.168.1.1') {
            return response('BANNED IP ADDRESS!', 403);
        }

        // Now we've decided to accept it. Let's pass it on to the next
        // middleware in the stack. We pass it to $next(), and what is
        // returned is the response after the $request has been passed
        // down the stack of middleware to the application and the
        // application's response has been passed back up the stack.
        $response = $next($request);
```

```
        // At this point, we can once again interact with the response
        // just before it is returned to the user
        $response->cookie('visited-our-site', true);

        // Finally, we can release this response to the end user
        return $response;
    }
}
```

Finally, let's make the middleware do what we actually promised (Example 10-17).

Example 10-17. Sample middleware banning the delete method

```
...
class BanDeleteMethod
{
    public function handle($request, Closure $next)
    {
        // Test for the DELETE method
        if ($request->method() === 'DELETE') {
            return response(
                "Get out of here with that delete method",
                405
            );
        }

        $response = $next($request);

        // Assign cookie
        $response->cookie('visited-our-site', true);

        // Return response
        return $response;
    }
}
```

Binding Middleware

We're not quite done yet. We need to register this middleware in one of two ways: globally or for specific routes.

Global middleware are applied to every route; route middleware are applied on a route-by-route basis.

Binding global middleware

Both bindings happen in *app/Http/Kernel.php*. To add a middleware as global, add its class name to the $middleware property, as in Example 10-18.

Example 10-18. Binding global middleware

```
// app/Http/Kernel.php
protected $middleware = [
    \Illuminate\Foundation\Http\Middleware\CheckForMaintenanceMode::class,
    \App\Http\Middleware\BanDeleteMethod::class,
];
```

Binding route middleware

Middleware intended for specific routes can be added as a route middleware or as part of a middleware group. Let's start with the former.

Route middleware are added to the $routeMiddleware array in *app/Http/Kernel.php*. It's similar to adding them to $middleware, except we have to give one a key that will be used when applying this middleware to a particular route, as seen in Example 10-19.

Example 10-19. Binding route middleware

```
// app/Http/Kernel.php
protected $routeMiddleware = [
    'auth' => \App\Http\Middleware\Authenticate::class,
    ...
    'nodelete' => \App\Http\Middleware\BanDeleteMethod::class,
];
```

We can now use this middleware in our route definitions, like in Example 10-20.

Example 10-20. Applying route middleware in route definitions

```
// Doesn't make much sense for our current example...
Route::get('contacts', [
    'middleware' => 'nodelete',
    'uses' => 'ContactsController@index'
]);

// Makes more sense for our current example...
Route::group(['prefix' => 'api', 'middleware' => 'nodelete', function () {
    // All routes related to an API
}]);
```

Using middleware groups

Laravel 5.2 introduced the concept of middleware groups. They're essentially pre-packaged bundles of middleware that make sense to be together in specific contexts.

Middleware groups in 5.2

The default routes file in earlier releases of 5.2, *routes.php*, had three distinct sections: the root route (/) wasn't under any middleware group, and then there was a web middleware group and an api middleware group. It was a bit confusing for new users, and that meant the root route didn't have access to the session or anything else that's kicked off in the middleware.

In later versions of 5.2 everything's simplified: every route in *routes.php* is in the web middleware group. In 5.3, you get a *routes/ web.php* file for web routes and a *routes/api.php* file for API routes. If you want to add routes in other groups, read on.

Out of the box there are two groups: web and api. web has all the middleware that will be useful on almost every Laravel page request, including middleware for cookies, sessions, CSRF protection, and more. api has none of those—it has a throttle middleware and a route model binding middleware, and that's it. These are all defined in *app/Http/Kernel.php*.

You can apply middleware groups to routes just like you apply route middleware to routes, with the middleware() fluent method:

```
Route::get('/', 'HomeController@index')->middleware('web');
```

You can also create your own middleware groups and add and remove route middleware to and from preexisting middleware groups. It works just like adding route middleware normally, but you're instead adding them to keyed groups in the $middlewareGroups array.

You might be wondering how these middleware groups match up with the two default routes files. Unsurprisingly, the *routes/web.php* file is wrapped with the web middleware group, and the *routes/api.php* file is wrapped with the api middleware group.

The *routes/** files are loaded in the RouteServiceProvider. Take a look at the map() method there (Example 10-21) and you'll find a mapWebRoutes() and a mapApi Routes() method, each of which loads its respective files already wrapped in the appropriate middleware group.

Example 10-21. Default route service provider in Laravel 5.3

```
// App\Providers\RouteServiceProvider
    public function map()
    {
        $this->mapApiRoutes();
        $this->mapWebRoutes();
    }
```

```
protected function mapApiRoutes()
{
    Route::group([
        'middleware' => 'api',
        'namespace' => $this->namespace,
        'prefix' => 'api',
    ], function ($router) {
        require base_path('routes/api.php');
    });
}

protected function mapWebRoutes()
{
    Route::group([
        'middleware' => 'web',
        'namespace' => $this->namespace,
    ], function ($router) {
        require base_path('routes/web.php');
    });
}
```

As you can see in Example 10-21, we're using the router to load a route group under the default namespace (App\Http\Controllers) and with the web middleware group, and another under the api middleware group.

Passing Parameters to Middleware

It's not common, but there are times when you need to pass parameters to a route middleware. For example, you might have an authentication middleware that will act differently depending on whether you're guarding for the member user type or the owner user type:

```
Route::get('company', function () {
    return view('company.admin');
})->middleware('auth:owner');
```

To make this work, you'll need to add one or more parameters to the middleware's handle() method, and update that method's logic accordingly:

```
public function handle($request, $next, $role)
{
    if (auth()->check() && auth()->user()->hasRole($role)) {
        return $next($request);
    }

    return redirect('login');
}
```

Note that you can also add more than one parameter to the `handle()` method, and pass multiple parameters to the route definition by separating them with commas:

```
Route::get('company', function () {
    return view('company.admin');
})->middleware('auth:owner,view');
```

Form Request Objects

In this chapter we covered how to inject an Illuminate `Request` object, which is the base—and most common—request object.

However, you can also extend the `Request` object and inject that instead. You'll learn more about how to bind and inject custom classes in Chapter 11, but there's one special type, called the form request, that has its own set of behaviors.

See "Form Requests" on page 107 to learn more about creating and using form requests.

Testing

Outside of the context of you as a developer using requests, responses, and middleware in your own testing, Laravel itself actually uses each quite a bit.

When you're doing application testing—calls like `$this->visit('/')`, clicks, and whatever else—you're instructing Laravel's application testing framework to generate request objects that represent the interactions that you're describing. Then those request objects are passed to your application as if it were an actual visit. That's why the application tests are so accurate: your application doesn't actually "know" that it's not a real user that's interacting with it.

In this context, many of the assertions you're making—say, `assertResponseOk()`—are assertions against the response object generated by the application testing framework. The `assertResponseOk()` method just looks at the response object and asserts that its `isOk()` method returns `true`—which is just checking that its status code is 200. In the end, *everything* in application testing is acting as if this were a real page request.

Find yourself in a context where you need a request to work with in your tests? You can always pull one from the container with `$request = request()`. Or you could create your own—the constructor parameters for the `Request` class, all optional, are as follows:

```
$request = new Illuminate\Http\Request(
    $query,      // GET array
    $request,    // POST array
```

```
    $attributes, // "attributes" array; empty is fine
    $cookies,    // cookies array
    $files,      // files array
    $server,     // servers array
    $content     // raw body data
);
```

If you're really interested in an example, check out the method Symfony uses to create a new Request from the globals PHP provides: Symfony\Component\HttpFoundation \Request@createFromGlobals().

Responses are even simpler to create manually, if you need to. Here are the (optional) parameters:

```
$response = new Illuminate\Http\Response(
    $content, // response content
    $status,  // HTTP status, default 200
    $headers  // array headers array
);
```

Finally, if you need to disable your middleware during an application test, import the WithoutMiddleware trait into that test.

TL;DR

Every request coming into a Laravel application is converted into an Illuminate Request object, which then passes through all middleware, and is processed by the application. The application generates a response object, which is then passed back through all of the middleware (in reverse order) and returned to the end user.

Request and response objects are responsible for encapsulating and representing every relevant piece of information about the incoming user request and the outgoing server response.

Service providers collect together related behavior for binding and registering classes for use by the application.

Middleware wrap the application and can reject or decorate any request and response.

## CHAPTER 11

The Container

Laravel's service container, or dependency injection container, sits at the core of almost every other feature. The container is a simple tool you can use to bind and resolve concrete instances of classes and interfaces, and at the same time it's a powerful and nuanced manager of a network of interrelated dependencies. In this chapter, we'll learn more about what it is, how it works, and how you can use it.

Naming and the container

You'll notice in this book, in the documentation, and in other educational sources that there are quite a few names folks use for the container. These include:

- Application container
- IoC (inversion of control) container
- Service container
- DI (dependency injection) container

All are useful and valid, but just know they're all talking about the same thing. They're all referring to the service container.

A Quick Introduction to Dependency Injection

Dependency injection means that, rather than being instantiated ("newed up") within a class, each class's dependencies will be *injected* in from the outside. This most commonly occurs with *constructor injection*, which means an object's dependencies are injected when it's created. But there's also *setter injection*, where the class exposes a method specifically for injecting a given dependency, and *method injection*, where one or more methods expect their dependencies to be injected when they're called.

Take a look at Example 11-1 for a quick example of constructor injection, the most common type of dependency injection.

Example 11-1. Basic dependency injection

```php
<?php

class UserMailer
{
    protected $mailer;

    public function __construct(Mailer $mailer)
    {
        $this->mailer = $mailer;
    }

    public function welcome($user)
    {
        return $this->mailer->mail($user->email, 'Welcome!');
    }
}
```

As you can see, this `UserMailer` class expects an object of type `Mailer` to be injected when it's instantiated, and its methods then refer to that instance.

The primary benefits of dependency injection are that it gives us the freedom to change what we're injecting, mock dependencies for testing, and instantiate shared dependencies just once for shared use.

Inversion of Control

You may have heard the phrase "inversion of control" used in conjunction with "dependency injection," and sometimes Laravel's container is called the IoC container.

The two concepts are very similar. Inversion of control references the idea that, in traditional programming, the lowest-level code—specific classes, instances, and procedural code—"controls" which instance of a particular pattern or interface to use. For example, if you're instantiating your mailer in each class that needs it, each class gets to decide whether to use Mailgun or Mandrill or Sendgrid.

The idea of inversion of control refers to flipping that "control" to live at the opposite end of your application. Now the definition of which mailer to use lives at the highest, most abstract level of your application, often in configuration. Every instance, every piece of low-level code, looks up to the high-level configuration to essentially "ask": "Can you give me a mailer?" They don't "know" which mailer they're getting, just that they're getting one.

Dependency injection and especially DI containers provide a great opportunity for inversion of control, because you can define once which concrete instance of the `Mailer` interface, for example, to provide when injecting mailers into any class that needs them.

Dependency Injection and Laravel

As we saw in Example 11-1, the most common pattern for dependency injection is constructor injection, or injecting the dependencies of an object when it's instantiated ("constructed").

Let's take our `UserMailer` class from Example 11-1. Example 11-2 shows what it might look like to create and use an instance of it.

Example 11-2. Simple manual dependency injection

```
$mailer = new MailgunMailer($mailgunKey, $mailgunSecret, $mailgunOptions);
$userMailer = new UserMailer($mailer);

$userMailer->welcome($user);
```

Now let's imagine we want our `UserMailer` class to be able to log messages, as well as sending a notification to a Slack channel every time it sends a message. Example 11-3 shows what this would look like. As you can see, it would start to get pretty unwieldy if we had to do all this work every time we wanted to create a new instance—especially when you consider that we'll have to get all these parameters from somewhere.

Example 11-3. More complex manual dependency injection

```
$mailer = new MailgunMailer($mailgunKey, $mailgunSecret, $mailgunOptions);
$logger = new Logger($logPath, $minimumLogLevel);
$slack = new Slack($slackKey, $slackSecret, $channelName, $channelIcon);
$userMailer = new UserMailer($mailer, $logger, $slack);

$userMailer->welcome($user);
```

Imagine having to write that code every time you wanted a `UserMailer`. Dependency injection is great, but this is a mess.

The app() Global Helper

Before we go too far into how the container actually works, let's take a quick look at the simplest way to get an object out of the container: the `app()` helper.

Pass any string to that helper, whether it's a fully qualified class name (FQCN) or a Laravel shortcut (we'll talk about those more in a second), and it'll return an instance of that class:

```
$logger = app(Logger::class);
```

This is the absolute simplest way to interact with the container. It creates an instance of this class and returns it for you. Nice and easy.

Different Syntaxes for Making a Concrete Instance

The simplest way to "make" a concrete instance is to use the global helper and pass the class or interface name directly to the helper, using app('*FQCN*').

However, if you have an instance of the container—whether it was injected somewhere, or if you're in a service provider and using $this->app, or (a lesser-known trick) if you get one by just running $container = app()—there are a few ways to make an instance from there.

The most common way is to run the make() method. $app->make('*FQCN*') works well. However, you may also see other developers and the documentation use this syntax sometimes: $app['*FQCN*']. Don't worry. That's doing the same thing; it's just a different way of writing it.

Creating the Logger instance as shown here seems simple enough, but you might've noticed that our $logger class in Example 11-3 has two parameters: $logPath and $minimumLogLevel. How does the container know what to pass here?

Short answer: it doesn't. You can use the app() global helper to create an instance of a class that has no parameters in its constructor, but at that point you could've just run new Logger yourself. The container shines when there's some complexity in the constructor, and that's when we need to look at how exactly the container can figure out how to construct classes with constructor parameters.

How the Container Is Wired

Before we dig further into the Logger class, take a look at Example 11-4.

Example 11-4. Laravel autowiring

```
class Bar
{
    public function __construct() {}
}
```

```
class Baz
{
    public function __construct() {}
}

class Foo
{
    public function __construct(Bar $bar, Baz $baz) {}
}

$foo = app(Foo::class);
```

This looks similar to our mailer example in Example 11-3. What's different is that these dependencies (Bar and Baz) are both so simple that the container can resolve them without any further information. The container reads the typehints in the constructor, resolves an instance of each, and then injects them into the new Foo instance when it's creating it. This is called autowiring: resolving instances based on type-hints without the developer needing to explicitly bind those classes in the container.

 Typehints in PHP

"Typehinting" in PHP means putting the name of a class or interface in front of a variable in a method signature:

```
public function __construct(Logger $logger) {}
```

This typehint is telling PHP that whatever is passed into the method *must* be of type Logger, which could be either an interface or a class.

Autowiring means that, if a class has not been explicitly bound to the container (like Foo, Bar, or Baz in this context) but the container can figure out how to resolve it anyway, the container will resolve it. This means any class with no constructor dependencies (like Bar and Baz) and any class with constructor dependencies that the container can resolve (like Foo) can be resolved out of the container.

That leaves us only needing to bind classes that have unresolvable constructor parameters—for example, our $logger class in Example 11-3, which has parameters related to our log path and log level.

For those, we'll need to learn how to explicitly bind something to the container.

Binding Classes to the Container

Binding a class to Laravel's container is essentially telling the container, "If a developer asks for an instance of Logger, here's the code to run in order to instantiate one with the correct parameters and dependencies and then return it correctly."

We're teaching the container that, when someone asks for this particular string (which is usually the FQCN of a class), it should resolve it this way.

Binding to a Closure

So, let's look at how to bind to the container. Note that the appropriate place to bind to the container is in a service provider's `register()` method (see Example 11-5).

Example 11-5. Basic container binding

```
// In service provider
public function register()
{
    $this->app->bind(Logger::class, function ($app) {
        return new Logger('\log\path\here', 'error');
    });
}
```

There are a few important things to note in this example. First, we're running `$this->app->bind()`. `$this->app` is an instance of the container that's always available on every service provider. The container's `bind()` method is what we use to bind to the container.

The first parameter of `bind()` is the "key" we're binding to. Here we've used the FQCN of the class. The second parameter differs depending on what you're doing, but essentially it should be *something* that shows the container what to do to resolve an instance of that bound key.

So, in this example, we're passing a closure. And now, any time someone runs `app(Logger::class)`, they'll get the result of this closure. The closure is passed an instance of the container itself (`$app`), so if the class you're resolving has a dependency you want resolved out of the container, you can use it in your definition:

```
$this->app->bind(UserMailer::class, function ($app) {
    return new UserMailer(
        $app->make(Mailer::class),
        $app->make(Logger::class),
        $app->make(Slack::class)
    );
});
```

Note that every time you ask for a new instance of your class, this closure will be run again and the new output returned.

Binding to Singletons, Aliases, and Instances

If you want the output of the binding closure to be cached so that this closure isn't re-run every time you ask for an instance, that's the Singleton pattern, and you can run `$this->app->singleton()` to do that:

```
public function register()
{
    $this->app->singleton(Logger::class, function () {
        return new Logger('\log\path\here', 'error');
    });
}
```

You can also get similar behavior if you already have an instance of the object you want the singleton to return:

```
public function register()
{
    $logger = new Logger('\log\path\here', 'error');
    $this->app->instance(Logger::class, $logger);
}
```

Finally, if you want to alias one class to another, bind a class to a shortcut, or bind a shortcut to a class, you can just pass two strings:

```
$this->bind(Logger::class, FirstLogger::class);
// or
$this->bind('log', FirstLogger::class);
// or
$this->bind(FirstLogger::class, 'log');
```

Note that these shortcuts are common in Laravel's core; it provides a system of shortcuts to classes that provide core functionality, using easy-to-remember keys like `log`.

Binding a Concrete Instance to an Interface

Just like we can bind a class to another class, or a class to a shortcut, we can also bind to an interface. This is extremely powerful, because we can now typehint interfaces instead of class names, like in Example 11-6.

Example 11-6. Typehinting and binding to an interface

```
...
use Interfaces\Mailer;

class UserMailer
{
    protected $mailer;

    public function __construct(Mailer $mailer)
    {
```

```
        $this->mailer = $mailer;
    }
}
// service provider
public function register()
{
    $this->app->bind(\Interfaces\Mailer::class, function () {
        return new MailgunMailer(...);
    });
}
```

You can now typehint `Mailer` or `Logger` interfaces all across your code, and then choose once in a service provider which specific mailer or logger you want to use everywhere. That's inversion of control.

Contextual Binding

Sometimes you need to change how to resolve an interface depending on the context. You might want to log events from one place to a local syslog and from others out to an external service. So, let's tell the container to differentiate—check out Example 11-7.

Example 11-7. Contextual binding

```
// In a service provider
public function register()
{
    $this->app->when(FileWrangler::class)
        ->needs(Interfaces\Logger::class)
        ->give(Loggers\Syslog::class);

    $this->app->when(Jobs\SendWelcomeEmail::class)
        ->needs(Interfaces\Logger::class)
        ->give(Loggers\PaperTrail::class);
}
```

Constructor Injection

We've covered the concept of constructor injection, and we've looked at how the container makes it easy to resolve instances of a class or interface out of the container. We saw how easy it is to use the `app()` helper to make instances, and also how the container will resolve the constructor dependencies of a class when it's creating it.

What we haven't covered yet is how the container is also responsible for resolving many of the core operating classes of your application. For example, every controller is instantiated by the container. That means if you want an instance of a logger in your controller, you can simply typehint the logger class in your controller's constructor, and when Laravel creates the controller, it will resolve it out of the container and that logger instance will be available to your controller. Take a look at Example 11-8 for an example.

Example 11-8. Injecting dependencies into a controller

```
...
class MyController extends Controller
{
    protected $logger;

    public function __construct(Logger $logger)
    {
        $this->logger = $logger;
    }

    public function index()
    {
        // Do something
        $this->logger->error('Something happened');
    }
}
```

The container is responsible for resolving controllers, middleware, queue jobs, event listeners, and any other classes that are automatically generated by Laravel in the process of your application's lifecycle—so any of those classes can typehint dependencies in their constructors and expect them to be automatically injected.

Method Injection

There are a few places in your application where Laravel doesn't just read the constructor signature: it also reads the *method* signature and will inject dependencies for you there as well.

The most common place to use method injection is in controller methods. If you have a dependency you only want to use for a single controller method, you can inject it into just that method like in Example 11-9.

Example 11-9. Injecting dependencies into a controller method

```
...
class MyController extends Controller
{
```

```
    // Method dependencies can come after or before route parameters
    public function show(Logger $logger, $id)
    {
        // Do something
        $logger->error('Something happened');
    }
}
```

This is also available on the `boot()` method of service providers, and you can also arbitrarily call a method on any class using the container, which will allow for method injection there (see Example 11-10).

Example 11-10. Manually calling a class method using the container's call() method

```
class Foo
{
    public function bar($parameter1) {}
}

$foo = new Foo;

// Calls the 'bar' method on $foo with a first parameter of "value"
app()->call($foo, 'bar', ['parameter1' => 'value']);
```

Facades and the Container

We've covered facades quite a bit so far in the book, but we haven't actually talked about how they work.

Laravel's facades are classes that provide simple access to core pieces of Laravel's functionality. There are two trademark features of facades: first, they're all available in the global namespace (`\Log` is an alias to `\Illuminate\Support\Facades\Log`), and second, they use static methods to access nonstatic resources.

Let's take a look at the `Log` facade, since we've been looking at logging already in this chapter. In your controller or views you could use this call:

```
Log::alert('Something has gone wrong!');
```

Here's what it would look like to make that same call without the facade:

```
$logger = app('log');
$logger->alert('Something has gone wrong!');
```

As you can see, facades translate static calls (any method call that you make on a class itself, using ::, instead of on an instance) to normal method calls on instances.

Importing facade namespaces

If you're in a namespaced class, you'll want to be sure to import the facade at the top:

```php
...
use Illuminate\Support\Facades\Log;

class Controller extends Controller
{
    public function index()
    {
        // ...
        Log::error('Something went wrong!');
    }
}
```

How Facades Work

So, let's take a look at the Log facade and see how it actually works.

First, open up the class Illuminate\Support\Facades\Log. You'll see something like Example 11-11.

Example 11-11. The Log facade class

```php
<?php

namespace Illuminate\Support\Facades;

class Log extends facade
{
    protected static function getFacadeAccessor()
    {
        return 'log';
    }
}
```

Every facade has a single method: getFacadeAccessor(). This defines the key that Laravel should use to look up this facade's backing instance from the container.

In this instance, we can see that every call to the Log facade is proxied to be a call to an instance of the log shortcut from the container. Of course, that's not a real class or interface name, so we know it's one of those shortcuts I mentioned earlier.

So, here's what's really happening:

```php
Log::error('Help!');

// is the same as...

app('log')->error('Help!');
```

There are a few ways to look up exactly what class each facade accessor points to, but checking the documentation is the easiest. There's a table on the facades documentation page (*https://laravel.com/docs/facades*) that shows you, for each facade, which container binding (shortcut, like `log`) it's connected to, and which class that returns. It looks like this:

Facade	Class	Service Container Binding
App	Illuminate\Foundation\Application	app
...	...	...
Log	Illuminate\Log\Writer	log

Now that you have this reference, you can do three things.

First, you can always figure out what methods are available on a facade. Just find its backing class and look at the definition of that class, and you'll know that any of its public methods are callable on the facade.

Second, you can figure out how to inject a facade's backing class using dependency injection. If you ever want the functionality of a facade but prefer to use dependency injection, just typehint the facade's backing class or get an instance of it with `app()` and call the same methods you would've called on the facade.

Third, you can see how to create your own facades. Create a class for the facade that extends `Illuminate\Support\Facades\Facade`, and give it a `getFacadeAccessor()` method, which returns a string. Make that string something that can be used to resolve your backing class out of the container—maybe just the FQCN of the class. Finally, you have to register the facade by adding it to the `aliases` array in *config/app.php*. Done! You just made your own facade.

Service Providers

We've covered the basics of service providers in the previous chapter (see "Service Providers" on page 227). What's most important with regard to the container is that you remember to register your bindings in the `register()` method of some service provider somewhere.

You can just dump loose bindings into `App\Providers\AppServiceProvider`, which is a bit of a catchall, but it's generally better practice to create a unique service provider for each group of functionality you're developing, and bind its classes in its unique `register()` method.

Testing

The ability to use inversion of control and dependency injection makes testing in Laravel extremely versatile. You can bind a different logger, for instance, depending on whether the app is live or under testing. Or you can change the transactional email service from Mailgun to a local email logger for easy inspection. Both of these swaps are actually so common that it's even easier to make them using Laravel's *.env* configuration files, but you can make similar swaps with any interfaces or classes you'd like.

The easiest way to do this is to explicitly re-bind classes and interfaces when you need them rebound, directly in the test. Example 11-12 shows how.

Example 11-12. Overriding a binding in tests

```
public function test_it_does_something()
{
    app()->bind(Interfaces\Logger, function () {
        return new DevNullLogger;
    });

    // do stuff
}
```

If you need certain classes or interfaces rebound globally for your tests (which is not a particularly common occurrence), you can do this either in the test class's setUp() method or in Laravel's TestCase base test's setUp() method, as in Example 11-13.

Example 11-13. Overriding a binding for all tests

```
class TestCase extends \Illuminate\Foundation\Testing\TestCase
{
    public function setUp()
    {
        parent::setUp();

        app()->bind('whatever', 'whatever else');
    }
}
```

When using something like Mockery, it's common to create a mock or spy or stub of a class, and then re-bind that to the container in place of its referent.

TL;DR

Laravel's service container has many names, but in the end its goal is to make it easy to define how to resolve certain string names as concrete instances. These string names are going to be the fully qualified class names of classes or interfaces, or short-cuts like log.

Each binding teaches the application, given a string key (e.g., app('log')), how to resolve a concrete instance.

The container is smart enough to do recursive dependency resolution, so if you try to resolve an instance of something that has constructor dependencies, the container will try to resolve those dependencies based on their typehints, then pass them into your class, and finally return an instance.

There are a few ways to bind to the container, but in the end they all define what to return given a particular string.

Facades are simple shortcuts that make it easy to use static calls on a root-namespaced class to call nonstatic methods on classes resolved out of the container.

## CHAPTER 12

Testing

Most developers know that testing your code is A Good Thing. We're supposed to do it. We likely have an idea of why it's good, and we might've even read some tutorials about how it's supposed to work.

But the gap between knowing *why* you should test and knowing *how* to test is wide. Thankfully, tools like PHPUnit, Mockery, and PHPSpec have provided an incredible number of options for testing in PHP—but it can still be pretty overwhelming to get everything set up.

Out of the box, Laravel comes with baked-in integrations to PHPUnit (unit testing), Behat (behavior-driven development), Mockery (mocking), and Faker (creating fake data for seeding and testing). It also comes with its own simple and powerful suite of application testing tools, which allow you to "crawl" your site's URIs, click buttons, submit forms, check HTTP status codes, and validate and assert against JSON.

Laravel's testing setup even has a sample application test that can run successfully the moment you create a new app. That means you don't have to spend any time configuring your testing environment, and that's one less barrier to writing your tests.

Testing Terms

It's hard to get any group of programmers to agree on which terms they use to define different types of tests.

In this book, I'll use three primary terms:

Unit tests
> Unit tests target small, relatively isolated units—a class or method, usually.

Integration tests

> Integration tests test the way individual units work together and pass messages.

Application tests

> Often called acceptance or functional tests, application tests test the entire behavior of the application, usually at an outer boundary by employing something like a document object model (DOM) crawler—which is exactly what Laravel's application test suite offers.

Testing Basics

Tests in Laravel live in the *tests* folder, and you can see there are two files in there by default: *TestCase.php*, which is a base class intended to be extended by any application tests, and *ExampleTest.php*, which is a ready-to-run application test that will return green on any new app.

As you can see in Example 12-1, ExampleTest "crawls" the DOM of the page returned at the root path of your application and checks for the word "Laravel." If it finds it, it'll pass; if not, it'll fail.

Example 12-1. tests/ExampleTest.php

```php
<?php

use Illuminate\Foundation\Testing\WithoutMiddleware;
use Illuminate\Foundation\Testing\DatabaseMigrations;
use Illuminate\Foundation\Testing\DatabaseTransactions;

class ExampleTest extends TestCase
{
    /**
     * A basic functional test example.
     *
     * @return void
     */
    public function testBasicExample()
    {
        $this->visit('/')
            ->see('Laravel');
    }
}
```

To run this test, go to the command line and run `./vendor/bin/phpunit` from the root folder of your application. You should see something like the output in Example 12-2.

Example 12-2. Sample ExampleTest output

```
PHPUnit 5.5.2 by Sebastian Bergmann and contributors.

.

Time: 139 ms, Memory: 12.00Mb

OK (1 test, 2 assertions)
```

You just ran your first Laravel application test! As you can see, you're set up out of the box not only with a functioning PHPUnit instance, but also a full-fledged application testing suite complete with a DOM crawler.

In case you're not familiar with PHPUnit, let's change the test to look for "Apple-sauce," like in Example 12-3, to see what an error looks like.

Example 12-3. tests/ExampleTest.php, edited to fail

```php
public function testBasicExample()
{
    $this->visit('/')
        ->see('Applesauce');
}
```

Whoops! This time the output will probably look a bit like Example 12-4.

Example 12-4. Sample failing ExampleTest output

```
PHPUnit 5.5.2 by Sebastian Bergmann and contributors.

F

Time: 115 ms, Memory: 12.00Mb

There was 1 failure:

1) ExampleTest::testBasicExample
<source of page here>
Failed asserting that the page contains the HTML [Applesauce].
Please check the content above.

/path-to-your-app/vendor/.../Foundation/Testing/Constraints/PageConstraint.php:90
/path-to-your-app/vendor/.../Foundation/Testing/Concerns/InteractsWithPages.php:271
/path-to-your-app/vendor/.../Foundation/Testing/Concerns/InteractsWithPages.php:287
/path-to-your-app/tests/ExampleTest.php:21

FAILURES!
Tests: 1, Assertions: 2, Failures: 1.
```

Let's break this down. First, we get an F instead of a . up top (just below the PHPUnit attribution information). Then, for each error, it shows us the test name (here, 1) `ExampleTest::testBasicExample`), the error message (`Failed asserting...`), *and* a full stack trace of our error, so we can see what was called. Since this was an application test, the stack trace just shows us that it was called via the `InteractsWithPages` trait, but if this were a unit or application test, we'd see the entire call stack of the test.

A Sample JSON Test

As you can see in this example, JSON testing is simple and clear—perhaps simpler than any other sort of application testing:

```
public function test_people_list_shows_person_after_creation()
{
    $this->json('post', 'people', ['name' => 'matt']);
    $this->json('get', 'people');
    $this->seeJson(['name' => 'matt']);
}
```

Just run your POST, GET, DELETE, or whatever else, and then assert that the database, or additional GET response, or anything else returns what you expect after you've performed the given action.

Let's learn more about Laravel's testing environment.

Naming Tests

By default, Laravel's testing system will run any files in the *tests* directory whose names end with the word *Test*. That's why *tests/ExampleTest.php* was run by default.

If you're not familiar with PHPUnit, you might not know that only the methods in your tests with names that start with the word `test` will be run—or methods with a `@test` docblock. See Example 12-5 for which methods will and won't run.

Example 12-5. Naming PHPUnit methods

```
class Naming
{
    public function test_it_names_things_well()
    {
        // Runs as "test it names things well"
    }

    public function testItNamesThingsWell()
    {
        // Runs as "It names things well"
```

```
    }

    /** @test */
    public function it_names_things_well()
    {
        // Runs as "it names things well"
    }

    public function it_names_things_well()
    {
        // Doesn't run
    }
}
```

The Testing Environment

Any time a Laravel application is running, it has a current "environment" name that represents the environment it's running in. This name may be set to local, staging, production, or anything else you want. You can retrieve this by running app()->environment(), or you can run something like if (app()->environment('local')) to test whether the current environment matches the passed name.

When you run tests, Laravel automatically sets the environment to testing. This means you can test for if (app()->environment('testing')) to enable or disable certain behaviors in the testing environment.

Additionally, Laravel doesn't load the normal environment variables from *.env* for testing. If you want to set any environment variables for your tests, edit *phpunit.xml* and, in the <php> section, add a new <env> for each environment variable you want to pass in—for example, <env name="DB_CONNECTION" value="sqlite"/>.

Using .env.test to Exclude Testing Environment Variables from Version Control

If you want to set environment variables for your test, you can do so in *phpunit.xml* as just described. But what if you have environment variables for your tests that you want to be different for each testing environment? Or what if you want them to be excluded from source control?

Thankfully, handling these conditions is pretty easy. First, create an *.env.test.example* file—just like Laravel's *.env.example* file—and add *.env.test* to your *.gitignore* file just below *.env*. Next, add the variables you'd like to be environment-specific to *.env.test.example*, just like they're set in *.env.example*. Then, make a copy of *.env.test.example* and name it *.env.test*.

Finally, let's load that file into our tests. In *tests/TestCase.php*, in the createApplica tion() method, paste this code just below the $app = require(...) line:

```
    if (file_exists(dirname(__DIR__) . '/.env.test')) {
        (new \Dotenv\Dotenv(dirname(__DIR__), '.env.test'))->load();
    }
```

That's it! You're now loading *.env.test* to provide environment variables to every test.

The Testing Traits

Before we get into the methods you can use for testing, you'll want to know about the three testing traits you can pull into any test class.

WithoutMiddleware

If you import `Illuminate\Foundation\Testing\WithoutMiddleware` into your test class, it will disable all middleware for any test in that class. This means you won't have to worry about the authentication middleware, or CSRF protection, or anything else that might be useful in the real application but distracting in a test.

DatabaseMigrations

Laravel provides two tools out of the box to keep your database in the right state between tests: the `DatabaseMigrations` trait and the `DatabaseTransactions` trait.

If you import the `DatabaseMigrations` trait, it will run your entire set of database migrations up before each test and down after each test. Laravel makes this happen by running `php artisan migrate` in the `setUp()` method before every test runs and `php artisan migrate:rollback` in the `tearDown()` method after each test finishes.

DatabaseTransactions

`DatabaseTransactions`, on the other hand, expects your database to be properly migrated before your tests start. Then, it wraps every test in a database transaction, which it rolls back at the end of each test. This means that, at the end of each test, your database will be returned to the exact same state it was in prior to the test.

Application Testing

Now that we've laid out the basic framework of Laravel's testing environment, let's take a look at how it actually works.

In Laravel's default `ExampleTest` (*tests/ExampleTest.php*) you can see that, with a few lines of code, we can "crawl" to particular URIs in our application and actually check the output for certain words. But how can PHPUnit navigate pages as if it were a browser?

TestCase

Any application tests should extend the `TestCase` class (*tests/TestCase.php*) that's included with Laravel by default. Your application's `TestCase` class will extend the abstract `Illuminate\Foundation\Testing\TestCase` class, which brings in quite a few goodies.

The first thing the two `TestCase` classes (yours and its abstract parent) do is handle booting the Illuminate application instance for you, so you have a fully bootstrapped application available. They also "refresh" the application between each test, which means they're not *entirely* re-creating the application between tests, but rather making sure you don't have any data lingering.

The parent `TestCase` also sets up a system of hooks that allow callbacks to be run before and after the application is created, and imports a series of traits that provide you with methods for interacting with every aspect of your application. These traits include `InteractsWithContainer`, `MakesHttpRequests`, `InteractsWithConsole`, and more, and they bring in a broad variety of custom assertions and testing methods.

As a result, your application tests have access to a fully bootstrapped application instance, application-test-minded custom assertions, and a DOM crawler, with a series of simple and powerful wrappers around each to make them easy to use.

That means you can write `$this->visit('/')->see('Laravel')` and know that your application is actually behaving as if it were responding to a normal HTTP request, and that the response is being passed to a DOM crawler that is checking for that text for you. It's pretty powerful stuff, considering how little work you had to do to get it running.

So, let's look at some basic methods this opens up to you.

Different trait structure in Laravel 5.1

In Laravel 5.1, the structure of testing traits and how the testing framework is organized is very different from what I've described here; however, the functionality is still the same.

"Visiting" Routes

The most complex of Laravel's application testing functionality is also the simplest—and most powerful—to use. Using these methods, your tests can interact with ("visit") pages in your application like never before:

`$this->visit($uri)`

Visiting a route is at the core of Laravel's application testing. When you call `$this->visit('dashboard')`, you're mimicking the action the framework takes when a web request comes in for that same route. The application will create a request object for that request, handle it like normal, and store the response object (an instance of `Illuminate\Http\Response`) in `$this->response`.

This is the same response object that would normally be returned and displayed to the browser, but it's just cached for Laravel's application testing assertions to check against (or for your code, if you want to interact with the response).

On its own, visiting doesn't do much, but now that you have a response cached in `$this->response`, you can write assertions against it.

What Makes visit() Different from the Other Visiting Methods

We're about to cover `call()`, and `get()`, and many other methods related to visiting routes. But they're much simpler than `visit()`, and it's worth seeing just what makes `visit()` different.

Here's a shortened definition of the `visit()` method:

```
public function visit($uri)
{
    $uri = $this->prepareUrlForRequest($uri);

    $this->call($method, $uri, $parameters, $cookies, $files);

    $this->clearInputs()->followRedirects()->assertPageLoaded($uri);

    $this->currentUri = $this->app->make('request')->fullUrl();

    $this->crawler = new Crawler(
        $this->response->getContent(),
        $this->currentUri
    );

    return $this;
}
```

I know this is a lot to take in, so just suffice it to say `visit()` is doing a lot. When you want to check that a page loads, when you want to crawl a page, when you want to do all this nearly magical application testing, use `visit()`.

If you just want to get a response and nothing else, or if you're using more traditional checks to POST to a page and assert certain behavior happens or something else, you'll be fine using the simpler methods like call().

`$this->call($method, $uri, $params = [], $cookies = [], $files = [], $server = [], $content = null)`

If you need to make calls against the server without worrying about crawling the returned DOM—for example, if you want to assert that a given POST has certain effects—there's a method for that. visit() is actually based on call(), but you can also use call() directly.

As you can see from the method definition, we have a lot of options available to us when we use call()—the HTTP method, the URI, parameters, cookies, and files, all pretending to be sent along with our call.

Just like when you use visit(), these requests will make a request and store the response on $this->response, but they *won't* enable any DOM-crawling-based assertions like see().

`$this->get($uri, $headers = []), ->post($uri, $data = [], $headers = []), ->put($uri, $data = [], $headers = []), ->patch(), and ->delete()`

These are a series of convenience helpers that wrap call(); they're all just shortcuts to passing a particular string to the first parameter of call(), the HTTP method. Otherwise, you can use them exactly the same as you would call().

`$this->json($method, $uri, $data = [], $headers = [])`

Just like get(), post(), and the other methods just mentioned json() is a wrapper around call(). It converts the passed data to JSON and adds JSON request headers, and then passes it all into call().

json() is exceptionally useful, unsurprisingly, for testing JSON APIs. Because you can even define your headers and data, you can use this method to fully interact with your REST APIs in your tests, like we saw in "A Sample JSON Test" on page 264.

`$this->followRedirects()`

There's actually another thing that visit() does that call() doesn't: it tells Laravel to follow any redirects using followRedirects(), and then checks that the eventual landing page loaded using assertPageLoaded().

Without followRedirects(), the response you'll get after calling a redirected page will just be the contents of the redirect, not the page that you were being redirected to.

Custom Application Testing Assertions

So, what are the new application testing assertions we've gained? There are quite a few. Let's start simple and move up:

`$this->assertPageLoaded()`

> `assertPageLoaded()` checks that you got an HTTP status code of 200 when loading the page.

`$this->see()` *and* `->dontSee()`

> Like we saw earlier in this chapter, `see()` takes a string and uses a regular expression to check that that string is present somewhere on the page that's rendered. `dontSee()` is its inverse.

`$this->seeLink()` *and* `->dontSeeLink()`

> `seeLink()` takes two parameters: first, the link text to find, and second, optionally, the URL. `dontSeeLink()` is its inverse.

`$this->seeHeader()`

> `seeHeader()` takes two parameters: first, the name of the header, and second, optionally, the value of the header.

`$this->seeCookie()`

> `seeCookie()` takes two parameters: first, the name of the cookie, and second, optionally, the value of the cookie.

`$this->seeInField()` *and* `->dontSeeInField()`

> `seeInField()` takes two parameters: first, the name or ID of the input or text area to look at, and second, the value to look for. `dontSeeInField()` is its inverse.

`$this->seeIsChecked()` *and* `->dontSeeIsChecked()`

> `seeIsChecked()` takes one parameter, the name or ID of the checkbox input to inspect. `dontSeeIsChecked()` is its inverse.

`$this->seeIsSelected()` *and* `->dontSeeIsSelected()`

> `seeIsSelected()` takes two parameters: first, the name or ID of the select box to inspect, and second, the value to check whether it is set to. `dontSeeIsSelected()` is its inverse.

`$this->seePageIs()`

> `seePageIs()` asserts that the current loaded page URI is the same as the parameter you pass to it.

`$this->seeInDatabase()` *and* `->dontSeeInDatabase()`

> To check for records in the database table, pass in the table name as the first parameter of `seeInDatabase()` and the data you're looking for as the second:

```
public function test_database_has_user_after_registration()
{
    $this
        ->visit('register')
        ->fillForm([
            'email' => 'matt@mattstauffer.co'
        ])
        ->submitForm();

    $this->seeInDatabase('emails', ['email' => 'matt@mattstauffer.co']);
}
```

> As you can see, the second "data" parameter of `seeInDatabase()` is structured like a SQL WHERE statement—you pass a key and a value (or multiple keys and values), and then Laravel looks for any records in the specified database table that match your key(s) and value(s).
>
> As always, `dontSeeInDatabase()` is the inverse.

JSON and Non-visit() Application Testing Assertions

The remaining application assertions are tied less closely to the `visit()` methodology and a little more closely to the implementation details of your application. Quite a few of these are also often used for testing JSON APIs:

`$this->seeJson()`, `->dontSeeJson()`, `->seeJsonEquals()`

> `seeJson()` with no parameters checks to make sure that the content of the response was valid JSON. Its optional parameter represents the data that you're checking for. For instance, in the following example we receive a response, and we're checking both that it is valid JSON *and* that it contains a key/value pair of `username/mattstauffer` somewhere in it:

```
public function test_api_returns_certain_json()
{
    $this->json('get', 'users');
    $this->seeJson(['username' => 'mattstauffer']);
}
```

> As always, `seeJson()` has an inverse, `dontSeeJson()`. `dontSeeJson()` still expects valid JSON, but it expects to *not* see anything passed in as data.
>
> Finally, if you want to check that the JSON maps *exactly* to your data, you can try `seeJsonEquals()`, which compares a data array to the JSON response and throws an exception if they don't match exactly.

`$this->assertResponseOK()` *and* `->assertResponseStatus($status)`

After any `call()` or `visit()`, one valuable assertion is just that the page loaded with the HTTP status you expected. `assertResponseOK()` asserts that the page returned a 200 HTTP status code, but you can also pass a specific status that you expect:

```
public function test_pages_load_the_way_we_want()
{
    $this->get('people');
    $this->assertResponseOK();

    $this->call('post', 'owners');
    $this->assertResponseStatus(405); // Method not allowed
}
```

You could even check the authorization settings for a particular route by asserting that it gives a 401 (Unauthorized) status code, then authenticate and assert it gives a 200 status code.

`$this->assertViewHas($key, $value = null)`, `->assertViewHasAll(array $bindings)`, `->assertViewMissing($key)`

Sometimes the only option you have is to assert that you see a particular phrase on a page using `see()`, but what's more likely is that you're really checking that the correct data was passed to your view. Thankfully, you can check that directly with these methods.

`assertViewHas()` checks that data with a particular key was sent to the most recently retrieved view, and if you pass the assertion a second parameter, it will assert that that data was equal to it:

```
// Route
Route::get('test', function () {
    return view('test')->with('foo', 'bar');
});

// Test
public function test_view_gets_data()
{
    $this->get('test');
    $this->assertViewHas('foo'); // true
    $this->assertViewHas('foo', 'bar'); // true
    $this->assertViewHas('foo', 'baz'); // false
}
```

You can also check for multiple view variables at once using `assertViewHasAll()`, which expects an array of key/value pairs:

```
// Route
Route::get('test', function () {
    return view('test')
```

```
        ->with('foo', 'bar')
        ->with('baz', 'qux');
});

// Test
public function test_view_gets_data()
{
    $this->get('test');
    $this->assertViewHasAll([
        'foo' => 'bar',
        'baz' => 'qux'
    ]); // true
}
```

You can ensure that the view *hasn't* been passed a particular key by passing that key to `assertViewMissing()`.

In Laravel 5.3, as shown in the following example, you can pass a closure to the second parameter of `assertViewHas()`. This gives you the opportunity to perform much more nuanced checks of the data your view is provided:

```
public function test_events_are_owned_by_user_1()
{
    $this->get('events');
    $this->assertViewHas('events', function ($events) {
        return $events->reject(function ($event) {
            return $event->user_id === 1;
        })->isEmpty();
    });
}
```

`$this->assertRedirectedTo()`, `->assertRedirectedToRoute()`, `->assertRedirectedToAction()`

If you want to ensure that the user not only ends up at a particular page but was sent there as a redirect, these methods provide that functionality. You can check by URL (`to()`), route name (`toRoute()`), or controller and method (`toAction()`):

```
// Route
Route::get('redirector', function () {
    return redirect('/');
});

Route::get('/', 'HomeController@index')->name('home');

// Test
public function test_redirector_works()
{
    $this->get('redirector');
    $this->assertRedirectedTo('/');
    $this->assertRedirectedToRoute('home');
```

```
    $this->assertRedirectedToAction('HomeController@index');
}
```

$this->assertSessionHas(*$key, $value* = *''*),
->assertSessionHasAll(*$bindings*), ->assertSessionHasErrors(*$bindings* =
[], $format = *null*), ->assertHasOldInput()

These methods make it easy to check for specific values in the session.
assertSessionHas() and assertSessionHasAll() are shaped just like
assertViewHas() and assertViewHasAll().

When passed just one parameter, assertSessionHas() asserts that there is a session value with that key; if you pass it two parameters, it asserts that the value of
that session key is equal to the session parameter. assertSessionHasAll() takes
an array of key/value pairs and asserts that each key exists in the session and is
set to its corresponding value:

```
public function test_session_has_stuff()
{
    Session::put('foo', 'bar');
    Session::put('baz', 'qux');
    $this->assertSessionHas('foo');
    $this->assertSessionHas('foo', 'bar');
    $this->assertSessionHasAll([
        'foo' => 'bar',
        'baz' => 'qux'
    ]);
}
```

assertSessionHasErrors() with no parameters asserts that there's at least one
error set in Laravel's special errors session container. Its first parameter can be
an array of key/value pairs that define the errors that should be set and its second
parameter can be the string format that the checked errors should be formatted
against, as demonstrated here:

```
public function test_posting_empty_errors_out()
{
    // assuming the "/form" route requires an email field, and we're
    // posting an empty form to it to trigger the error
    $this->post('form', []);
    $this->assertSessionHasErrors();
    $this->assertSessionHasErrors(['email' => 'The email field is required.']);
    $this->assertSessionHasErrors(
        ['email' => '<p>The email field is required.</p>'],
        '<p>:message</p>'
    );
}
```

Finally, assertHasOldInput() asserts that some old input has been saved from a
form that was submitted, likely using redirect()->withOldInput().

Clicking and Forms

Let's move into some magical yet terrifying powers: navigating through forms, clicking and filling and unchecking, and even attaching files. Laravel provides the following methods for working with forms:

`$this->click($name)`

Given a link with the provided *$name* as either the body of the link or its name or ID, `click()` grabs the URI from that link and visits it.

`$this->type($text, $element)`

Given an input on the page with the provided *$element* as the name or ID, `type()` "types" the provided text into it.

Manipulating Forms

With this talk of clicking links and typing into form fields, it may seem like Laravel is running some sort of JavaScript-based application test where it's actually driving a browser interacting with the page. But it's not, really.

It's storing up this "input" you're creating, and if at any point you "submit" the form, it'll gather together your input and post it to the target of the form. In theory it's very different from the user's experience, but in practice it's a beautifully eloquent syntax for writing tests that mimic form submissions.

`$this->check($element)`

Given a checkbox on the page with the provided *$element* as the name or ID, `check()` "checks" it.

`$this->uncheck($element)`

Given a checkbox on the page with the provided *$element* as the name or ID, `uncheck()` "unchecks" it.

`$this->select($option, $element)`

Given a select box on the page with the provided *$element* as the name or ID, `select()` sets its value to *$option*.

`$this->attach($filePath, $element)`

Given a file upload input on the page with the provided *$element* as the name or ID, `attach()` attaches a file from the given local file path to it, marked to upload when the form is submitted.

`$this->press($buttonText)`

Given a button on the page with the provided text, `press()` submits the form that button is a part of.

`$this->submitForm($buttonText, $inputs = [], $uploads = [])`

Given a button on the page with the provided text, `submitForm()` submits the form that button is a part of. You can also optionally set or override all of the inputs and file uploads using the second and third parameters.

`$this->fillForm($buttonText, $inputs = [])`

Given a button on the page with the provided text, `fillForm()` finds the form that button is a part of and sets all the values to be the provided values.

`$this->clearInputs()`

`clearInputs()` wipes any inputs or uploads that have been previously set.

Jobs and Events

We'll cover these job- and event-related tests in more depth in Chapter 16, but let's take a quick look at how they work:

`$this->expectsEvents($eventClassName)`

If you want to assert that a particular class of event was fired during your test, you can pass the class name to `expectsEvents()`:

```
public function test_usersubscribed_event_fires_when_subscribing()
{
    $this->expectsEvents(App\Events\UserSubscribed::class);

    $this->visit('subscribe')->type('me@me.com', 'email')->press('Subscribe');
}
```

`$this->withoutEvents()`

`withoutEvents()` is not actually an assertion; rather, it disables Laravel's event handling system so that, during this test, you don't have to worry about the effects of any of your events taking place—for example, sending any emails or writing any logs.

`$this->expectsJobs()`

If you want to assert that a particular class of job was fired during your test, you can pass that class name to `expectsJobs()`:

```
public function test_number_of_subscriptions_crunches_reports()
{
    $this->expectsJobs(App\Jobs\CrunchReports::class);

    $this->visit('subscribe')->type('me@me.com', 'email')->press('Subscribe');
}
```

Authentication and Sessions

Laravel makes it simple to set up a test environment for your tests, even making it easy to control the session and authenticate as a given user:

`$this->session(['key' => 'value'])`

session() starts the session and saves any key/value pairs of data in the provided array to the session. You can run this multiple times during a test to add different pieces of session data, if you'd like.

`$this->flushSession()`

flushSession() wipes all of the data in the current session.

`$this->be($authenticatable)`

be() takes any object that fulfills the Illuminate\Contracts\Auth\Authentic able interface (including, of course, the base App\User class) and authenticates every page request or interaction in the test as that user. This means you can write tests like this:

```
public function test_members_cant_see_admin_dashboard()
{
    $member = factory(\App\User::class, 'member')->create();
    $this->be($member);

    $this->get('admin-dashboard');
    $this->assertResponseStatus(403);
}

public function test_admins_can_see_admin_dashboard()
{
    $admin = factory(\App\User::class, 'admin')->create();
    $this->be($admin);

    $this->get('admin-dashboard');
    $this->assertResponseOK();
}
```

Artisan and Seed

Almost done. There are two more test methods you might want to take a look at:

`$this->artisan($command, $parameters = [])`

If you want to use an Artisan command in a test, artisan() makes it easy. Just pass the command name as the first parameter and, optionally, pass any parameters as an array as the second.

Doing so will save the response code to $this->code in case you'd like to assert against it, but it will also return it. So, this functions the same as Artisan::call() with the addition of saving the response to $this->code:

```
public function test_returns_certain_code()
{
    $this->artisan('do:thing', ['--flagOfSomeSort' => true]);
    $this->assertEquals(0, $this->code); // 0 means "no errors were returned"
}
```

$this->seed($seederClassName = 'DatabaseSeeder')

If you want to seed your database, seed() will do that for you; and if you pass an argument, you can choose to only run a single seeder.

seed() provides the same functionality as running $this->artisan('db:seed').

Model factories

Model factories are amazing tools that make it easy to seed randomized, well-structured database data for testing (or other purposes).

We've already covered them in depth, so check out "Model Factories" on page 143 to learn more.

Mocking

Mocks (and their brethren, spies and stubs and dummies and fakes and who knows what else) are common tools in testing. I won't go into great detail here, but it's unlikely you can thoroughly test an application of any size without mocking at least one thing or another.

Essentially, mocks and other similar tools make it possible to create an object that in some way mimics a real class, but for testing purposes isn't the real class. Sometimes this is done because the real class is too difficult to instantiate just to inject it into a test, or maybe the real class communicates with an external service.

As you can probably tell from these examples, Laravel encourages working with the real application as much as possible—which means avoiding too great of a dependence on mocks. But they have their place, which is why Laravel includes Mockery, a mocking library, out of the box.

Mockery

Mockery allows you to quickly and easily create mocks from any PHP class in your application. Imagine you have a class that depends on a Slack client, but you don't want the calls to actually go out to Slack. Mockery makes it simple to create a fake Slack client to use in your tests, like you can see in Example 12-6.

Example 12-6. Using Mockery in Laravel

```
// app/SlackClient.php
class SlackClient
{
    ...
    public function send($message, $channel)
    {
        // Actually sends a message to Slack
    }
}

// app/Notifier.php
class Notifier
{
    private $slack;

    public function __construct(SlackClient $slack)
    {
        $this->slack = $slack;
    }

    public function notifyAdmins($message)
    {
        $this->slack->send($message, 'admins');
    }
}

// tests/NotifierTest.php
public function test_notifier_notifies_admins()
{
    $slackMock = Mockery::mock(SlackClient::class)->shouldIgnoreMissing();

    $notifier = new Notifier($slackMock);
    $notifier->notifyAdmins('Test message');
}
```

There are a lot of moving pieces here, but let's break it down. We have a class named `Notifier` that we're testing. It has a dependency named `SlackClient` that does something that we don't want it to do when we're running our tests: it sends actual Slack notifications. So we're going to mock it.

We use Mockery to get a mock of our `SlackClient` class. If we don't care about what happens to that class—if it should simply exist to keep our tests from throwing errors —we can just use `shouldIgnoreMissing()`:

```
$slackMock = Mockery::mock(SlackClient::class)-shouldIgnoreMissing();
```

No matter what Notifier calls on $slackMock, it'll just accept it and return null.

But take a look at test_notifier_notifies_admins(). At this point, it doesn't actually *test* anything.

We could just keep shouldIgnoreMissing() and then write some assertions below it. That's usually what we do with shouldIgnoreMissing(), which makes this object a "fake" or a "stub."

But what if we want to actually assert that a call was made to the send() method of SlackClient? That's when we drop shouldIgnoreMissing() and reach for the should* methods (Example 12-7).

Example 12-7. Using the shouldReceive method on a Mockery mock

```
public function test_notifier_notifies_admins()
{
    $slackMock = Mockery::mock(SlackClient::class);
    $slackMock->shouldReceive('send')->once();

    $notifier = new Notifier($slackMock);
    $notifier->notifyAdmins('Test message');
}
```

shouldReceive('send')->once() is the same as saying "assert that $slackMock will have its send() method called once and only once." So, we're now asserting that Notifier, when we call notifyAdmins(), must make a single call to the send method on SlackClient.

We could also use something like shouldReceive('send')->times(3) or shouldReceive('send')->never().

What if we wanted to use the IoC container to resolve our instance of the Notifier? This might be useful if Notifier had several other dependencies that we didn't need to mock.

We can do that! We just use the instance() method on the container, as in Example 12-8, to tell Laravel to provide an instance of our mock to any classes that request it (which, in this example, will be Notifier).

Example 12-8. Binding a Mockery instance to the container

```
public function test_notifier_notifies_admins()
{
    $slackMock = Mockery::mock(SlackClient::class);
    $slackMock->shouldReceive('send')->once();

    app()->instance(SlackClient::class, $slackMock);
```

```
    $notifier = app(Notifier::class);
    $notifier->notifyAdmins('Test message');
}
```

There's a lot more you can do with Mockery: you can use spies, and partial spies, and much more. Going deeper into how to use Mockery is out of the scope of this book, but I encourage you to learn more about the library and how it works.

Mocking Facades

Let's say you have a controller method that calls a facade. Now, you want to test that controller method, and assert that that facade call should be made. How do you do it? Thankfully, it's simple: treat the facade like an instance of Mockery in your test. Example 12-9 shows how this works.

Example 12-9. Mocking a facade

```
// PeopleController
public function index()
{
    return Cache::remember('people', function () {
        return Person::all();
    });
}

// PeopleTest
public function test_all_people_route_should_be_cached()
{
    $person = factory(Person::class)->make();

    Cache::shouldReceive('remember')
        ->once()
        ->andReturn(collect([$person]));

    $this->visit('people')->seeJson(['name' => $person->name]);
}
```

As you can see, you can use methods like shouldReceive() on the facades, just like you do on a Mockery object.

As of Laravel 5.3, you can also use your facades as spies, which means you can set your assertions at the end and use shouldHaveReceived() instead of shouldReceive(). Example 12-10 illustrates this.

Example 12-10. Facade spies

```
public function test_queue_job_should_be_pushed_after_regisration()
{
    Cache::spy();

    $this->post('register', ['email' => 'joaquin@me.com']);

    Cache::shouldHaveReceived('push')
        ->with(SendWelcomeEmail::class, ['email' => 'joaquin@me.com']);
}
```

TL;DR

Laravel can work with any modern PHP testing framework, but it brings in a lot of framework-specific power if you use PHPUnit and if your tests extend Laravel's Test Case. Laravel's application testing framework makes it simple to send fake requests through your application and inspect the results, even "typing" in inputs and "clicking" buttons before submitting a form.

The TestCase class brings in a group of methods that make it easy to customize how your tests interact with your database, disable the effects of events, and make assertions against framework-level structures like jobs and facades.

Laravel brings in Mockery in case you need mocks, stubs, spies, dummies, or anything else, but the testing philosophy of Laravel is to use real collaborators as much as possible. Don't fake it unless you have to.

## CHAPTER 13

Writing APIs

One of the most common tasks Laravel developers are given is to create an API, usually JSON and REST or REST-like, that allows third parties to interact with the Laravel application's data.

Laravel makes it incredibly easy to work with JSON, and its resource controllers are already structured around REST verbs and patterns. In this chapter we'll learn about some basic API-writing concepts, the tools Laravel provides for writing APIs, and some external tools and organizational systems you'll want to consider when writing your first Laravel API.

The Basics of REST-Like JSON APIs

Representational State Transfer (REST) is an architectural style for building APIs. Technically, REST is a broad definition that could apply to almost the entirety of the Internet, so don't let yourself get overwhelmed by the definition or caught in an argument with a pedant. When we talk about RESTful or REST-like APIs in the Laravel world, we're generally talking about APIs with a few common characteristics:

- Structured around "resources" that can be uniquely represented by URIs, like `/cats` for all cats, `/cats/15` for a single cat with the ID of 15, etc.

- Interactions with resources primarily take place using HTTP verbs (`GET /cats/15` versus `DELETE /cats/15`)

- Stateless, meaning there's no persistent session authentication between requests; each request must uniquely authenticate itself

- Cacheable and consistent, meaning each request (except for a few authenticated-user-specific requests) should return the same result regardless of who the requester is
- Return JSON

The most common API pattern is to have a unique URL structure for each of your Eloquent models that's exposed as an API resource, and allow for users to interact with that resource with specific verbs and get JSON back. Example 13-1 shows a few possible examples.

Example 13-1. Common REST API endpoint structures

```
GET /api/cats
[
    {
        id: 1,
        name: 'Fluffy'
    },
    {
        id: 2,
        name: 'Killer'
    }
]

GET /api/cats/2
{
    id: 2,
    name: 'Killer'
}

DELETE /api/cats/2
deletes cat

POST /api/cats with body:
{
    name: 'Mr Bigglesworth'
}
(creates new cat)

PATCH /api/cats/3 with body:
{
    name: 'Mr. Bigglesworth'
}
(updates cat)
```

You can see the basic set of interactions we are likely to have with our APIs. Let's dig into how to make them happen with Laravel.

Controller Organization and JSON Returns

Laravel's resource controllers are structured very similarly to a RESTful API controller, so let's get started there. First we'll create a new controller for our resource, which we'll route at */api/dogs*:

```
php artisan make:controller Api/\DogsController --resource
```

Remember, the `--resource` flag generates a resource controller instead of a plain controller.

 Escaping slashes in Artisan commands

Note that in order to put the `DogsController` in the `Api` namespace, we had to escape the \ namespace backslash with a forward slash.

Example 13-2 shows what that controller will look like.

Example 13-2. A generated resource controller

```php
<?php

namespace App\Http\Controllers\Api;

use Illuminate\Http\Request;

use App\Http\Requests;
use App\Http\Controllers\Controller;

class DogsController extends Controller
{
    /**
     * Display a listing of the resource.
     *
     * @return \Illuminate\Http\Response
     */
    public function index() {}

    /**
     * Show the form for creating a new resource.
     *
     * @return \Illuminate\Http\Response
     */
    public function create() {}

    /**
     * Store a newly created resource in storage.
     *
     * @param  \Illuminate\Http\Request  $request
```

```
 * @return \Illuminate\Http\Response
 */
public function store(Request $request) {}

/**
 * Display the specified resource.
 *
 * @param  int  $id
 * @return \Illuminate\Http\Response
 */
public function show($id) {}

/**
 * Show the form for editing the specified resource.
 *
 * @param  int  $id
 * @return \Illuminate\Http\Response
 */
public function edit($id) {}

/**
 * Update the specified resource in storage.
 *
 * @param  \Illuminate\Http\Request  $request
 * @param  int  $id
 * @return \Illuminate\Http\Response
 */
public function update(Request $request, $id) {}

/**
 * Remove the specified resource from storage.
 *
 * @param  int  $id
 * @return \Illuminate\Http\Response
 */
public function destroy($id) {}
}
```

The docblocks pretty much tell the story. index() lists all of the dogs, show() lists a single dog, create() shows the create view, store() stores a dog, edit() shows the edit view, update() updates a dog, and destroy() removes a dog.

Since this is an API, we can delete create() and edit() off the bat; we're not showing views here.

Let's quickly make a model and a migration so we can work with it:

```
php artisan make:model Dog --migration
php artisan migrate
```

Great! Now we can fill out our controller methods.

We can take advantage of a great feature of Eloquent here: if you echo an Eloquent results collection, it'll automatically convert itself to JSON (using the __toString() magic method, if you're curious). That means if you return a collection of results from a route, you'll in effect be returning JSON.

So, as Example 13-3 demonstrates, this will be some of the simplest code you'll ever write.

Example 13-3. A sample resource controller for the Dog entity

```
...
class DogsController extends Controller
{
    public function index()
    {
        return Dog::all();
    }

    public function store(Request $request)
    {
        Dog::create($request->all());
    }

    public function show($id)
    {
        return Dog::findOrFail($id);
    }

    public function update(Request $request, $id)
    {
        $dog = Dog::findOrFail($id);
        $dog->update($request->all());
    }

    public function destroy($id)
    {
        $dog = Dog::findOrFail($id);
        $dog->delete();
    }
}
```

Example 13-4 shows how we can link this up in our routes file.

Example 13-4. Binding the routes for a resource controller

```
// Routes.php
Route::group(['prefix' => 'api', 'namespace' => 'Api', function () {
    Route::resource('dogs', 'DogsController');
}]);
```

There you have it! Your first RESTful API in Laravel.

Of course, we'll need much more nuance: pagination, sorting, authentication, more defined response headers. But this is the foundation of everything else.

Reading and Sending Headers

REST APIs often read, and send, non-content information using headers. For example, any request to GitHub's API will return headers detailing the current user's rate limiting status:

```
X-RateLimit-Limit: 5000
X-RateLimit-Remaining: 4987
X-RateLimit-Reset: 1350085394
```

X-* headers

You might be wondering why the GitHub rate limiting headers are prefixed with X-, especially if you see them in the context of other headers returned with the same request:

```
HTTP/1.1 200 OK
Server: nginx
Date: Fri, 12 Oct 2012 23:33:14 GMT
Content-Type: application/json; charset=utf-8
Connection: keep-alive
Status: 200 OK
ETag: "a00049ba79152d03380c34652f2cb612"
X-GitHub-Media-Type: github.v3
X-RateLimit-Limit: 5000
X-RateLimit-Remaining: 4987
X-RateLimit-Reset: 1350085394
Content-Length: 5
Cache-Control: max-age=0, private, must-revalidate
X-Content-Type-Options: nosniff
```

Any header whose name starts with X- is a header that's not in the HTTP spec. It might be entirely made up (e.g., X-How-Much-Matt-Loves-This-Page), or part of a common convention that hasn't made it into the spec yet (e.g., X-Requested-With).

Similarly, many APIs allow developers to customize their requests using request headers. For example, GitHub's API makes it easy to define which version of the API you'd like to use with the Accept header:

```
Accept: application/vnd.github.v3+json
```

If you were to change v3 to v2, GitHub would pass your request to version 2 of its API instead.

Let's learn quickly how to do both in Laravel.

Sending Response Headers in Laravel

We already covered this topic quite a bit in Chapter 10, but here's a quick refresher. Once you have a response object, you can add a header using header(*$headerName*, *$headerValue*), as seen in Example 13-5.

Example 13-5. Adding a response header in Laravel

```
Route::get('dogs', function () {
    return response(Dog::all())
        ->header('X-Greatness-Index', 9);
});
```

Nice and easy.

Reading Request Headers in Laravel

If we have an incoming request, it's also simple to read any given header. Example 13-6 illustrates this.

Example 13-6. Reading a request header in Laravel

```
Route::get('dogs', function (Request $request) {
    echo $request->header('Accept');
});
```

Now that you can read incoming request headers and set headers on your API responses, let's take a look at how you might want to customize your API.

Eloquent Pagination

Pagination is one of the first places where most APIs need to consider special instructions. Eloquent comes out of the box with a pagination system that hooks directly into the query parameters of any page request. We already covered the paginator component a bit in Chapter 5, but here's a quick refresher.

Any Eloquent call provides a paginate() method, which you can pass the number of items you'd like to return per page. Eloquent then checks the URL for a page query parameter and, if it's set, treats that as an indicator of how many pages the user is into a paginated list.

To make your API route ready for automated Laravel pagination, use paginate() instead of all() or get() in your route; something like Example 13-7.

Example 13-7. A paginated API route

```
Route::get('dogs', function () {
    return Dog::paginate(20);
});
```

We've defined that Eloquent should get 20 results from the database. Depending on what the `page` query parameter is set to, Laravel will know exactly *which* 20 results to pull for us:

```
GET /dogs        - Return results 1-20
GET /dogs?page=1 - Return results 1-20
GET /dogs?page=2 - Return results 21-40
```

Note that the `paginate()` method is also available on query builder calls, as seen in Example 13-8.

Example 13-8. Using the paginate() method on a query builder call

```
Route::get('dogs', function () {
    return DB::table('dogs')->paginate(20);
});
```

Here's something interesting, though: this isn't just going to return 20 results when you convert it to JSON. Instead, it's going to build a response object that automatically passes some useful pagination-related details to the end user, *along with* the paginated data. Example 13-9 shows a possible response from our call, truncated to only three records to save space.

Example 13-9. Sample output from a paginated database call

```
{
    "total": 50,
    "per_page": 3,
    "current_page": 1,
    "last_page": 17,
    "next_page_url": "http://myapp.com/api/dogs?page=2",
    "prev_page_url": null,
    "from": 1,
    "to": 3,
    "data": [
        {
            'name': 'Fido'
        },
        {
            'name': 'Pickles'
        },
        {
            'name': 'Spot'
        }
```

```
        ]
}
```

Sorting and Filtering

While there is a convention and some built-in tooling for pagination in Laravel, there isn't any for sorting, so you have to figure that out on your own. I'll give a quick code sample here, and I'll style our query parameters similarly to the JSON API spec (described in the following sidebar).

The JSON API Spec

The JSON API (*http://jsonapi.org/*) is a standard for how to handle many of the most common tasks in building JSON-based APIs: filtering, sorting, pagination, authentication, embedding, links, metadata, and more.

Laravel's default pagination doesn't work *exactly* according to the JSON API spec, but it gets you started in the right direction. And the majority of the rest of the JSON API spec is something you'll just have to choose (or not) to implement manually.

For example, here's a piece of the JSON API spec that helpfully handles how to structure data versus error returns:

> A document MUST contain at least one of the following top-level members:
>
> - `data`: the document's "primary data"
> - `errors`: an array of error objects
> - `meta`: a meta object that contains non-standard meta-information.
>
> The members `data` and `errors` MUST NOT coexist in the same document.

Be warned, however: it's wonderful to have the JSON API as a spec, but it also takes quite a bit of groundwork to get running with it. We won't use it entirely in these examples, but I'll use its general ideas as inspiration.

Sorting Your API Results

First, let's set up the ability to sort our results. We start in Example 13-10 with the ability to sort by only a single column, and in only a single direction.

Example 13-10. Simplest API sorting

```
// Handles /dogs?sort=name
Route::get('dogs', function (Request $request) {
    // Get the sort query parameter (or fall back to default sort "name")
    $sortCol = $request->input('sort', 'name');
```

```
    return Dog::orderBy($sortCol)->paginate(20);
});
```

We add the ability to invert it (e.g., `?sort=-weight`) in Example 13-11.

Example 13-11. Single-column API sorting, with direction control

```
// Handles /dogs?sort=name and /dogs?sort=-name
Route::get('dogs', function (Request $request) {
    // Get the sort query parameter (or fall back to default sort "name")
    $sortCol = $request->input('sort', 'name');

    // Set the sort direction based on whether the key starts with -
    // using Laravel's starts_with() helper function
    $sortDir = starts_with($sortCol, '-') ? 'desc' : 'asc';
    $sortCol = ltrim($sort, '-');

    return Dog::orderBy($sortCol, $sortDir)
        ->paginate(20);
});
```

Finally, we do the same for multiple columns (e.g., `?sort=name,-weight`) in Example 13-12.

Example 13-12. JSON API–style sorting

```
// Handles ?sort=name,-weight
Route::get('dogs', function (Request $request) {
    // Grab the query parameter and turn it into an array exploded by ,
    $sorts = explode(',', $request->input('sort', ''));

    // Create a query
    $query = Dog::query();

    // Add the sorts one by one
    foreach ($sorts as $sortCol) {
        $sortDir = starts_with($sortCol, '-') ? 'desc' : 'asc';
        $sortCol = ltrim($sort, '-');

        $query->orderBy($sortCol, $sortDir);
    }

    // Return
    return $query->paginate(20);
});
```

As you can see, it's not the simplest process ever, and you'll likely want to build some helper tooling around the repetitive processes, but we're building up the customizability of our API piece by piece using logical and simple features.

Filtering Your API Results

Another common task in building APIs is filtering out all but a certain subset of data. For example, the client might ask for a list of the dogs that are female.

The JSON API doesn't give us any great ideas for syntax here, other than that we should use the `filter` query parameter. Let's think along the lines of the sort syntax, where we're putting everything into a single key—maybe `?filter=sex:female`. You can see how to do this in Example 13-13.

Example 13-13. Single filter on API results

```
Route::get('dogs', function (Request $request) {
    $query = Dog::query();

    if ($request->has('filter')) {
        list($criteria, $value) = explode(':', $request->input('filter'));
        $query->where($criteria, $value);
    }

    return $query->paginate(20);
});
```

And, just for kicks, in Example 13-14 we allow for multiple filters, like `?filter=sex:female,color:brown`.

Example 13-14. Multiple filters on API results

```
Route::get('dogs', function (Request $request) {
    $query = Dog::query();

    if ($request->has('filter')) {
        $filters = explode(',', $request->input('filter'));
        foreach ($filters as $filter) {
            list($criteria, $value) = explode(':', $filter);
            $query->where($criteria, $value);
        }
    }

    return $query->paginate(20);
});
```

Transforming Results

We've covered how to sort and filter our result sets. But right now, we're relying on Eloquent's JSON serialization, which means we get every field on every model.

Eloquent provides a few convenience tools for defining which fields to show when you're serializing an array. You can read more in Chapter 8, but the gist is that if you set a `$hidden` array property on your Eloquent class, any field listed in that array will not be shown in the serialized model output. You can alternatively set a `$visible` array that defines the fields that are allowed to be shown. You could also either overwrite or mimic the `toArray()` function on your model, crafting a custom output format.

Another common pattern is to create a transformer for each data type. There's a fantastic package for this, Fractal (*http://bit.ly/2fEt8Nr*), that sets up a series of convenience structures and classes for transforming your data, but let's cover a simple implementation to show what a transformer is and why you might want to do this.

Writing Your Own Transformer

The general concept of a transformer is that we are going to run every instance of our model through another class that *transforms* its data to a different state. It might add fields, rename fields, delete fields, manipulate fields, add nested children, or whatever else. Let's start with a simple example (Example 13-15).

Example 13-15. A simple transformer

```
Route::get('users/{id}', function ($userId) {
    return (new UserTransformer(User::findOrFail($userId)));
});

class UserTransformer
{
    protected $user;

    public function __construct($user)
    {
        $this->user = $user;
    }

    public function toArray()
    {
        return [
            'id' => $this->user->id,
            'name' => sprintf(
                "%s %s",
                $this->user->first_name,
                $this->user->last_name
            ),
            'friendsCount' => $this->user->friends->count()
        ];
    }
}
```

```
public function toJson()
{
    return json_encode($this->toArray());
}

public function __toString()
{
    return $this->toJson();
}
}
```

Classic transformers

A more classic transformer would probably offer a `transform()` method that takes a `$user` parameter. This would likely spit out an array or JSON directly.

However, I've been using this pattern, which we sometimes call "API objects," for a few years and really love how much more power and flexibility it provides.

As you can see in Example 13-15, transformers accept the model they're transforming as a parameter and then manipulate that model—and its relationships—to create the final output that you want to send to the API.

This gives you more control, isolates API-specific logic away from the model itself, and allows you to provide a more consistent API even when the models and their relationships change down the road.

Nesting and Relationships

Whether, and how, to nest relationships in APIs is an issue of much debate. Thankfully, people more experienced than me have written on this at length; I'd recommend reading Phil Sturgeon's *Build APIs You Won't Hate* (*https://apisyouwonthate.com/*) (Leanpub) to learn more about this and about REST APIs in general.

There are a few primary ways to approach nesting relationships. These examples will assume your primary resource is a `user` and your related resource is a `friend`:

- Embed related resources directly in the primary resource (e.g., the `users/5` resource has its friends nested in it).
- Embed just the foreign keys in the primary resource (e.g., the `users/5` resource has an array of friend IDs nested in it).
- Allow the user to query the related resource filtered by the originating resource (e.g., `/friends?user=5`, or "give me all friends who are related to user #5").
- Create a subresource (e.g., `/users/5/friends`).

- Allow optional embedding (e.g., /users/5 does not embed, but /users/5? embed=friends does embed; so does /users/5?embed=friends,dogs).

Let's assume for a minute that we want to (optionally) embed the relationships. How would we do that? Our transformer example in Example 13-15 gives us a great head start. Let's adjust it in Example 13-16 to add optional embedding.

Example 13-16. Allowing for optional embedding of a resource in a transformer

```php
Route::get('users/{id}', function ($userId, Request $request) {
    // Get the embeds query parameter and split by commas
    $embeds = explode(',', $request->input('embed', ''));
    // Pass both user and embeds to the user transformer
    return (new UserTransformer(User::findOrFail($userId), $embeds));
});

class UserTransformer
{
    protected $user;
    protected $embeds;

    public function __construct($user, $embeds = [])
    {
        $this->user = $user;
        $this->embeds = $embeds;
    }

    public function toArray()
    {
        $append = [];

        if (in_array('friends', $this->embeds)) {
            // If you have more than one embed, you'll want to generalize this
            $append['friends'] = $this->user->friends->map(function ($friend) {
                return (new FriendTransformer($friend))->toArray();
            });
        }

        return array_merge([
            'id' => $this->user->id,
            'name' => sprintf(
                "%s %s",
                $this->user->first_name,
                $this->user->last_name
            )
        ], $append);
    }
...
```

We'll learn more about the map() functionality when we look at collections in Chapter 17, but everything else in here should be pretty familiar.

In the route, we're splitting the embed query parameter by commas and passing it into our transformer. Currently our transformer can just handle the friends embed, but it could be abstracted to handle others. If the user has requested the friends embed, the transformer maps over each friend (using the *has many* friends relationship on the user model), passes that friend to the FriendTransformer, and embeds the array of all transformed friends in the user response.

API Authentication with Laravel Passport

Most APIs require some form of authentication to access some or all of the data. Laravel 5.2 introduced a simple "token" authentication scheme, which we'll cover shortly, but in Laravel 5.3 we got a new tool called Passport (by way of a separate package, brought in via Composer) that makes it easy to set up a full-featured OAuth 2.0 server in your application, complete with an API and UI components for managing clients and tokens. Passport and the features it relies on are only compatible with Laravel 5.3 and above.

A Brief Introduction to OAuth 2.0

OAuth is by far the most common auth system used in RESTful APIs. Unfortunately, it's far too complex a topic for us to cover here in depth. For further reading, Matt Frost has written a great book on OAuth and PHP titled *Integrating Web Services with OAuth and PHP* (php[architect]).

If you're working with Laravel 5.1 or 5.2, there's a Laravel package called OAuth 2.0 Server for Laravel (*http://bit.ly/2e2lFYi*) that makes it relatively easy to add a basic OAuth 2.0 authentication server to your Laravel application. It's a Laravel convenience bridge to a PHP package called PHP OAuth 2.0 Server (*http://bit.ly/2f1dUyP*).

However, if you're on Laravel 5.3, Passport gives you everything provided by that package and much more, with a simpler and more powerful API and interface.

Installing Passport

Passport is a separate package, so your first step is to install it. I'll sum up the steps here, but you can get more in-depth installation instructions in the docs (*http://bit.ly/2fEBjtk*).

First, bring it in with Composer:

```
composer require laravel/passport
```

Next, add `Laravel\Passport\PassportServiceProvider::class` to the providers array of *config/app.php*. This will make Passport boot up every time your app loads.

Passport imports a series of migrations, so run those with `php artisan migrate` to create the tables necessary for OAuth clients, scopes, and tokens.

Next, run the installer with `php artisan passport:install`. This is going to create encryption keys for the OAuth server (*storage/oauth-private.key* and *storage/oauth-public.key*) and insert OAuth clients into the database for our personal and password grant type tokens (which we'll cover later).

You'll need to import the `Laravel\Passport\HasApiTokens` trait into your `User` model; this will add OAuth client- and token-related relationships to each `User`, as well as a few token-related helper methods. Next, add a call to `Laravel\Passport \Passport::routes()` in the `boot()` method of the `AuthServiceProvider`. This will add the following routes:

- `oauth/authorize`
- `oauth/clients`
- `oauth/clients/{client_id}`
- `oauth/personal-access-tokens`
- `oauth/personal-access-tokens/{token_id}`
- `oauth/scopes`
- `oauth/token`
- `oauth/token/refresh`
- `oauth/tokens`
- `oauth/tokens/{token_id}`

Finally, look for the `api` guard in *config/auth.php*. By default this guard will use the token driver (which we'll cover shortly), but we'll change that to be the `passport` driver instead.

You now have a fully functional OAuth 2.0 server! You can create new clients with `php artisan passport:client`, and you have an API for managing your clients and tokens available under the `/oauth` route prefix.

To protect a route behind your Passport auth system, add the `auth:api` middleware to the route or route group, as shown in Example 13-17.

Example 13-17. Protecting an API route with the Passport auth middleware

```
// routes/api.php
Route::get('/user', function (Request $request) {
    return $request->user();
})->middleware('auth:api');
```

In order to authenticate to these protected routes, your client apps will need to pass a token (we'll cover how to get one next) as a `Bearer` token in the `Authorization` header. Example 13-18 shows what this would look like if you were making a request using the Guzzle HTTP library.

Example 13-18. Making a sample API request with a Bearer token

```
$http = new GuzzleHttp\Client;
$response = $http->request('GET', 'http://speakr.dev/api/user', [
    'headers' => [
        'Accept' => 'application/json',
        'Authorization' => 'Bearer ' . $accessToken,
    ],
]);
```

Now, let's learn a little more about how it all works.

Passport's API

Passport exposes an API in your application under the `/oauth` route prefix. The API provides two primary functions: first, to authorize users with OAuth 2.0 authorization flows (`/oauth/authorize` and `/oauth/token`), and second, to allow users to manage their clients and tokens (the rest of the routes).

This is an important distinction, especially if you're unfamiliar with OAuth. Every OAuth server needs to expose the ability for consumers to authenticate with your server; that's the entire point of the service. But Passport *also* exposes an API for managing the state of your OAuth server's clients and tokens. This means you can easily build a frontend to let your users manage their information in your OAuth application, and Passport actually comes with Vue-based manager components that you can either use or use for inspiration.

We'll cover the API routes that allow you to manage clients and tokens, and the Vue components that Passport ships with to make it easy, but first let's dig into the various ways your users can authenticate with your Passport-protected API.

Passport's Available Grant Types

Passport makes it possible for you to authenticate users in four different ways. Two are traditional OAuth 2.0 grants (the password grant and authorization code grant) and two are convenience methods that are unique to Passport (the personal token and synchronizer token).

Password grant

The password grant, while less common than the authorization code grant, is much simpler. If you want users to be able to authenticate directly with your API using their username and password—for example, if you have a mobile app for your company consuming your own API—you can use the password grant.

 Creating a password grant client

In order to use the password grant flow, you need a password grant client in your database. One will have been added when you ran php artisan passport:install, but if you ever need to generate a new password grant client for any reason, you can:

```
php artisan passport:client --password

What should we name the password grant client?
  [My Application Password Grant Client]:
> SpaceBook_internal

Password grant client created successfully.
```

With the password grant type, there is just one step to getting a token: sending the user's credentials to the /oauth/token route, like in Example 13-19.

Example 13-19. Making a request with the password grant type

```
// Assuming SpaceBook is not an external app, but actually
// a trusted internal app... this is SpaceBook's routes/web.php
Route::get('speakr/password-grant-auth', function () {
    $http = new GuzzleHttp\Client;

    $response = $http->post('http://speakr.dev/oauth/token', [
        'form_params' => [
            'grant_type' => 'password',
            'client_id' => config('speakr.id'),
            'client_secret' => config('speakr.secret'),
            'username' => 'matt@mattstauffer.co',
            'password' => 'my-speakr-password',
        ],
    ]);

    $thisUsersTokens = json_decode((string) $response->getBody(), true);
    // do stuff with the tokens
});
```

This route will return an `access_token` and a `refresh_token`. You can now save those tokens to use to authenticate with the API (access token) and to request more tokens later (refresh token).

Note that the ID and secret we'd use for the password grant type would be those in the `clients` database table of our Passport app in the row with the name `Space Book_internal`.

Authorization code grant

The most common OAuth 2.0 auth workflow is also the most complex one Passport supports. Let's imagine we're developing an application that's like Twitter but for sound clips; we'll call it Speakr. And we'll imagine another website, a social network for science fiction fans, called SpaceBook. SpaceBook's developer wants to let people embed their Speakr data into their SpaceBook newsfeeds. We're going to install Passport in our app so that other apps—SpaceBook, for example—can allow their mutual users to authenticate with their Speakr information.

In the authorization code grant type, each consuming website—SpaceBook, in this example—needs to create a "client" in our Passport-enabled app. In most scenarios, the other sites' admins will have user accounts at Speakr, and we'll build tools for them to create clients there. But for starters, we can just manually create a client for the SpaceBook admins:

```
php artisan passport:client
Which user ID should the client be assigned to?:
> 1 ❶

What should we name the client?:
> SpaceBook

Where should we redirect the request after authorization?
  [http://passport.dev/auth/callback]:
> http://spacebook.dev/auth/callback

New client created successfully.
Client ID: 3
Client secret: RiQstsWDqd9SqQY3lQhiZF50ulKdw4iPhPAdke03
```

❶ Every client needs to be assigned to a user in your app. Imagine Jill, user #1, is writing SpaceBook; she'll be the "owner" of this client we're creating.

Now we have the ID and secret for the SpaceBook client. At this point, SpaceBook can use this ID and secret to build tooling allowing an individual SpaceBook user (who is also a Speakr user) to get an auth token from Speakr for use when SpaceBook wants to make API calls to Speakr on that user's behalf. Example 13-20 illustrates this. (This and the following examples assume SpaceBook is a Laravel app, too; they also assume we've created a file at *config/speakr.php* that returns the ID and secret we just created.)

Example 13-20. A consumer app redirecting a user to our OAuth server

```php
// In SpaceBook's routes/web.php:
Route::get('speakr/redirect', function () {
    $query = http_build_query([
        'client_id' => config('speakr.id'),
        'redirect_uri' => url('speakr/callback'),
        'response_type' => 'code',
    ]);

    // Builds a string like:
    // client_id={$client_id}&redirect_uri={$redirect_uri}&response_type=code

    return redirect('http://speakr.dev/oauth/authorize?' . $query);
});
```

When users hit that route in SpaceBook, they'll now be redirected to the /oauth/ authorize Passport route on our Speakr app. At this point they'll see a confirmation page; you can use the default Passport confirmation page by running this command:

```
php artisan vendor:publish --tag=passport-views
```

This will publish the view to *resources/views/vendor/passport/authorize.blade.php*, and your users will see the page shown in Figure 13-1.

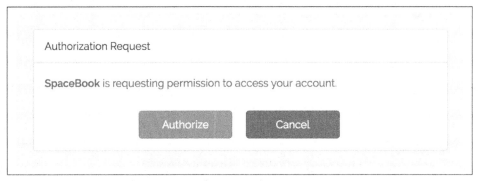

Figure 13-1. OAuth authorization code approval page

Once a user chooses to accept or reject the authorization, Passport will redirect that user back to the provided redirect_uri. In Example 13-20 we set a redirect_uri of url('speakr/callback'), so the user will be redirected back to *http://spacebook.dev/ speakr/callback*.

An approval request will contain a code that our consumer app's callback route can now use to get a token back from our Passport-enabled app, Speakr. A rejection request will contain an error. SpaceBook's callback route might look something like Example 13-21.

Example 13-21. The authorization callback route in our sample consuming app

```
// In SpaceBook's routes/web.php:
Route::get('speakr/callback', function (Request $request) {
    if ($request->has('error')) {
        // handle error condition
    }

    $http = new GuzzleHttp\Client;

    $response = $http->post('http://speakr.dev/oauth/token', [
        'form_params' => [
            'grant_type' => 'authorization_code',
            'client_id' => config('speakr.id'),
            'client_secret' => config('speakr.secret'),
            'redirect_uri' => url('speakr/callback'),
            'code' => $request->code,
        ],
    ]);

    $thisUsersTokens = json_decode((string) $response->getBody(), true);
    // do stuff with the tokens
});
```

What we're doing here is building a Guzzle HTTP request to the /oauth/token Passport route on Speakr. We send a POST request containing the authorization code we received when the user approved access, and Speakr will return a JSON response containing a few keys:

- access_token is the token SpaceBook will want to save for this user. This token is what the user will use to authenticate in future requests to Speakr.

- refresh_token is a token SpaceBook will need *if* you decide to set your tokens to expire. By default, Passport's access tokens never need to be refreshed, so you don't need to concern yourself with this and can just ignore it.

- expires_in is the number of seconds until an access_token expires (needs to be refreshed).

Using Refresh Tokens

If you'd like to force users to reauthenticate more often, you need to set a shorter refresh time on the tokens, and then you can use the `refresh_token` to request a new `access_token`.

To set a shorter refresh time:

```php
// AuthServiceProvider's boot() method
public function boot()
{
    $this->registerPolicies();

    Passport::routes();

    // How long a token lasts before needing refreshing
    Passport::tokensExpireIn(
        Carbon::now()->addDays(15)
    );

    // How long a refresh token will last before re-auth
    Passport::refreshTokensExpireIn(
        Carbon::now()->addDays(30)
    );
}
```

To request a new token using a refresh token, you need to have first saved the `refresh_token` from the initial auth response in Example 13-21. Once it's time to refresh, you'll make a call similar to that example, but modified slightly:

```php
// In SpaceBook's routes/web.php:
Route::get(
    'speakr/request-refresh',
    function (Request $request) {
        $http = new GuzzleHttp\Client;

        $params = [
            'grant_type' => 'refresh_token',
            'client_id' => config('speakr.id'),
            'client_secret' => config('speakr.secret'),
            'redirect_uri' => url('speakr/callback'),
            'refresh_token' => $theTokenYouSavedEarlier,
        ];

        $response = $http->post(
            'http://speakr.dev/oauth/token',
            ['form_params' => $params,]
        );

        $thisUsersTokens = json_decode(
            (string) $response->getBody(),
```

```
                    true
              );

              // do stuff with the tokens
          }
      );
```
In the response, you'll receive a fresh set of tokens to save to your user.

You now have all the tools you need to perform basic authorization code flows. We'll cover how to build an admin panel for your clients and tokens later, but first, let's take a quick look at the other grant types.

Personal access tokens

The authorization code grant is great for your users' apps and the password code grant is great for your own apps, but what if your users want to create tokens for themselves to test out your API or to use when they're developing their apps? That's what personal tokens are for.

Creating a personal access client

In order to create personal tokens, you need a personal access client in your database. Running `php artisan passport:install` will have added one already, but if you ever need to generate a new personal access client for any reason, you can run `php artisan passport:client --personal`:

```
php artisan passport:client --personal

What should we name the password grant client?
  [My Application Personal Access Client]:
> My Application Personal Access Client

Personal access client created successfully.
```

Personal access tokens are not quite a "grant" type; there's no OAuth-prescribed flow here. Rather, they're a convenience method that Passport adds to make it easy to have a single client registered in your system that exists solely for the easy creation of convenience tokens for your users who are developers.

For example, maybe you have a user who's developing a competitor to SpaceBook named RaceBook (it's for marathon runners), and he wants to toy around with the Speakr API a bit to figure out how it works *before* starting to code. Does this developer have the facility to create tokens using the authorization code flow? Not yet—he hasn't even written any code yet! That's what personal access tokens are for.

You can create personal access tokens through the JSON API, which I'll cover shortly, but you can also create one for your user directly in code:

```
// Creating a token without scopes
$token = $user->createToken('Token Name')->accessToken;

// Creating a token with scopes...
$token = $user->createToken('My Token', ['place-orders'])->accessToken;
```

Your users can use these tokens just as if they were tokens created with the authorization code grant flow.

Tokens from Laravel session authentication (synchronizer tokens)

There's one final way for your users to get tokens to access your API, and it's another convenience method that Passport adds but which normal OAuth servers don't provide. This method is for when your users are already authenticated because they've logged in to your Laravel app like normal, and you want the JavaScript on your Laravel app to be able to access the API. It'd be a pain to have to reauthenticate the users with the authorization code or password grant flow, so Laravel provides a helper for that.

If you add the `Laravel\Passport\Http\Middleware\CreateFreshApiToken` middleware to your `web` middleware group (in *app/Http/Kernel.php*), every response Laravel sends to your authenticated users will have a cookie named `laravel_token` attached to it. This cookie is a JSON Web Token (JWT) that contains encoded information about the CSRF token. Now, if you send the normal CSRF token with your JavaScript and send it along in the `X-CSRF-TOKEN` header on any API requests you make, the API will compare your CSRF token with this cookie and this will authenticate your users to the API just like any other token.

JSON Web Tokens (JWT)

JWT is a newer format that is just beginning to gain prominence. A JSON Web Token is a JSON object containing all of the information necessary to determine a user's authentication state and access permissions. This JSON object is digitally signed using a keyed-hash message authentication code (HMAC) or RSA, which is what makes it trustworthy.

The token is usually encoded and then delivered via URL, `POST` request, or in a header. Once a user authenticates with the system somehow, every HTTP request after that will contain the token, describing the user's identity and authorization.

JSON Web Tokens consist of three Base64-encoded strings separated by dots (`.`); something like *xxx.yyy.zzz*. The first section is a Base64-encoded JSON object containing information about which hashing algorithm is being used; the second section is a series of "claims" about the user's authorization and identity; and the third is the

---

signature, or the first and second sections encrypted and signed using the algorithm specified in the first section.

To learn more about JWT, check out JWT.io (*https://jwt.io/*) or the `jwt-auth` Laravel package (*https://github.com/tymondesigns/jwt-auth*).

The default Vue setup that Laravel comes bundled with sets up this header for you, but if you're using a different framework, you'll need to set it up manually. Example 13-22 shows how to do it with jQuery.

Example 13-22. Setting jQuery to pass Laravel's CSRF tokens with all Ajax requests

```
$.ajaxSetup({
    headers: {
        'X-CSRF-TOKEN': "{{ csrf_token() }}"
    }
});
```

If you add the `CreateFreshApiTokens` middleware to your `web` middleware group and pass that header with every JavaScript request, your JavaScript requests will be able to hit your Passport-protected API routes without worrying about any of the complexity of the authorization code or password grants.

Managing Clients and Tokens with the Passport API and the Vue Components

Now that we've covered how to manually create clients and tokens and how to authorize as a consumer, let's take a look at the aspects of the Passport API that make it possible to build user interface elements allowing your users to manage their clients and tokens.

The routes

The easiest way to dig into the API routes is by looking at how the sample provided Vue components work and which routes they rely on, so I'll just give a brief overview:

```
/oauth/clients (GET, POST)
/oauth/clients/{id} (DELETE, PUT)
/oauth/personal-access-tokens (GET, POST)
/oauth/personal-access-tokens/{id} (DELETE)
/oauth/scopes (GET)
/oauth/tokens (GET)
/oauth/tokens/{id} (DELETE)
```

As you can see, we have a few entities here (clients, personal access tokens, scopes, and tokens). We can list all of them; we can create some (you can't create scopes, since they're defined in code, and you can't create tokens, because they're created in the authorization flow); and we can delete and update some.

The Vue components

Passport comes with a set of Vue components out of the box that make it easy to allow your users to administer their clients (those they've created), authorized clients (those they've allowed access to their account), and personal access tokens (for their own testing purposes).

To publish these components into your application, run this command:

```
php artisan vendor:publish --tag=passport-components
```

You'll now have three new Vue components in *resources/assets/js/components/passport*. To add them to your Vue bootstrap so they're accessible in your templates, register them in your *resources/assets/js/app.js* file as shown in Example 13-23.

Example 13-23. Importing Passport's Vue components into app.js

```
require('./bootstrap');

Vue.component(
    'passport-clients',
    require('./components/passport/Clients.vue')
);

Vue.component(
    'passport-authorized-clients',
    require('./components/passport/AuthorizedClients.vue')
);

Vue.component(
    'passport-personal-access-tokens',
    require('./components/passport/PersonalAccessTokens.vue')
);

const app = new Vue({
    el: 'body'
});
```

You now get three components that you can use anywhere in your application:

```
<passport-clients></passport-clients>
<passport-authorized-clients></passport-authorized-clients>
<passport-personal-access-tokens></passport-personal-access-tokens>
```

`<passport-clients>` shows your users all of the clients they've created. This means SpaceBook's creator will see the SpaceBook client listed here when she logs in to Speakr.

`<passport-authorized-clients>` shows your users all of the clients they've authorized to have access to their accounts. This means any users of both SpaceBook and Speakr who have given SpaceBook access to their Speakr account will see SpaceBook listed here.

`<passport-personal-access-tokens>` shows your users any personal access tokens they've created here. This means the creator of RaceBook, the SpaceBook competitor, will see his personal access token here that he's been using to test out the Speakr API.

If you are on a fresh install of Laravel and want to test these out, there are a few steps to take to get it working:

- Follow the instructions given earlier in this chapter to get Passport installed.
- In your terminal, run the following commands:
  - `php artisan vendor:publish --tag=passport-components`
  - `npm install`
  - `gulp`
  - `php artisan make:auth`
- Open *resources/views/home.blade.php* and add the Vue component references (e.g., `<passport-clients>`) just below the `<div class="panel">`.

If you'd like, you can just use those components as they are. But you can also use them as reference points to understand how to use the API and create your own frontend components in whatever format you'd like.

Passport Scopes

If you're familiar with OAuth, you probably noticed we haven't talked about scopes. Everything we've covered so far can be customized by scope, but first let's quickly cover what scopes are.

In OAuth, scopes are defined sets of privileges that are something other than "can do everything." If you've ever gotten a GitHub API token before, for example, you might've noticed that some apps want access just to your name and email address, some want access to all of your repos, and some want access to your gists. Each of these is a "scope," which allows both the user and the consumer app to define what access the consumer app needs to perform its job.

As shown in Example 13-24, you can define the scopes for your application in the `boot()` method of your `AuthServiceProvider`.

Example 13-24. Defining Passport scopes

```
// AuthServiceProvider
use Laravel\Passport\Passport;
...
    public function boot()
    {
        ...

        Passport::tokensCan([
            'list-clips' => 'List sound clips',
            'add-delete-clips' => 'Add new and delete old sound clips',
            'admin-account' => 'Administer account details',
        ]);
    }
```

Once you have your scopes defined, the consumer app can define which scopes it's asking for access to. Just add a space-separated list of tokens in the "token" field to the initial redirect, in the scope field, as shown in Example 13-25.

Example 13-25. Requesting authorization to access specific scopes

```
// In SpaceBook's routes/web.php:
Route::get('speakr/redirect', function () {
    $query = http_build_query([
        'client_id' => config('speakr.id'),
        'redirect_uri' => url('speakr/callback'),
        'response_type' => 'code',
        'scope' => 'list-clips add-delete-clips'
    ]);

    return redirect('http://speakr.dev/oauth/authorize?' . $query);
});
```

When the user tries to authorize with this app, it'll present the list of requested scopes. This way, the user will see the difference between "SpaceBook is requesting to see your email address" and "SpaceBook is requesting access to post as you and delete your posts and message your friends."

You can check for scope using middleware or on the User instance.

Example 13-26 shows how to check on the User.

Example 13-26. Checking whether the token a user authenticated with can perform a given action

```
Route::get('/events', function () {
    if (auth()->user()->tokenCan('add-delete-clips')) {
        //
```

```
    }
});
```

There are two middleware you can use for this too, scope and scopes. To use these in your app, add them to $routeMiddleware in your *app/Http/Kernel.php* file:

```
'scopes' => \Laravel\Passport\Http\Middleware\CheckScopes::class,
'scope' => \Laravel\Passport\Http\Middleware\CheckForAnyScope::class,
```

You can now use the middleware as illustrated in Example 13-27. scopes requires *all* of the defined scopes to be on the user's token in order for the user to access the route, while scope requires *at least one* of the defined scopes to be on the user's token.

Example 13-27. Using middleware to restrict access based on token scopes

```
// routes/api.php
Route::get('clips', function () {
    // Access token has both the "list-clips" and "add-delete-clips" scopes
})->middleware('scopes:list-clips,add-delete-clips');

// or

Route::get('clips', function () {
    // Access token has at least one of the listed scopes
})->middleware('scope:list-clips,add-delete-clips')
```

If you haven't defined any scopes, the app will just work as if they don't exist. The moment you use scopes, however, your consumer apps will have to explicitly define which scopes they're requesting access with. The one exception to this rule is that if you're using the password grant type your consumer app can request the * scope, which gives the token access to everything.

Laravel 5.2+ API Token Authentication

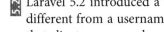 Laravel 5.2 introduced a simple API token authentication mechanism. It's not much different from a username and password: there's a single token assigned to each user that clients can pass along with a request to authenticate that request for that user.

This API token mechanism is not nearly as secure as OAuth 2.0, so make sure you know it's the right fit for your application before deciding to use it. But if it is, it couldn't be much simpler to implement.

First, add a 60-character unique api_token column to your users table:

```
$table->string('api_token', 60)->unique();
```

Next, update whatever method creates your new users and ensure it sets a value for this field for each new user. Laravel has a helper for generating random strings, so if you want to use that, just set the field to `str_random(60)` for each. You'll also need to do this for preexisting users if you're adding this to a live application.

To wrap any routes with this authentication method, use the `auth:api` route middleware, as in Example 13-28.

Example 13-28. Applying the API auth middleware to a route group

```
Route::group(['prefix' => 'api', 'middleware' => 'auth:api'], function () {
    //
});
```

Note that, since you're using an authentication guard other than the standard guard, you'll need to specify that guard any time you use any `auth()` methods:

```
$user = auth()->guard('api')->user();
```

Testing

Fortunately, testing APIs is actually simpler than testing almost anything else in Laravel.

We cover this in more depth in Chapter 12, but there are a series of methods for making assertions against JSON. Combine that capability with the simplicity of full-stack application tests and you can put together your API tests quickly and easily. Take a look at the common API testing pattern in Example 13-29.

Example 13-29. A common API testing pattern

```
...
class DogsApiTest extends TestCase
{
    use WithoutMiddleware, DatabaseMigrations;

    public function test_it_gets_all_dogs()
    {
        $this->be(factory(User::class)->create());
        $dog1 = factory(Dog::class)->create();
        $dog2 = factory(Dog::class)->create();

        $this->visit('api/dogs');
        $this->seeJson([
            'name' => $dog1->name
        ]);
        $this->seeJson([
            'name' => $dog2->name
        ]);
    }
}
```

Note that we're using `WithoutMiddleware` to avoid worrying about the authentication. You'll want to test that separately, if at all (for more on authentication, see Chapter 9).

We generate a user and authenticate as that user with `$this->be()`. We then insert two dogs into the database, and then visit the API route for listing all dogs and make sure both are present in the output.

You can cover all of your API routes simply and easily here, including modifying actions like `POST` and `PATCH`.

TL;DR

Laravel is geared toward building APIs and makes it simple to work with JSON and RESTful APIs. There are some conventions, like for pagination, but much of the definition of exactly how your API will be sorted, or authenticated, or whatever else is up to you.

Laravel provides tools for authentication and testing, easy manipulation and reading of headers, and working with JSON, even automatically encoding all Eloquent results to JSON if they're returned directly from a route.

Laravel Passport is a separate package that makes it simple to create and manage an OAuth server in your Laravel apps.

## CHAPTER 14

Storage and Retrieval

We covered how to store data in relational databases in Chapter 8, but there's a lot more that can be stored, both locally and remotely. In this chapter we'll cover filesystem and in-memory storage, file uploads and manipulation, nonrelational data stores, sessions, the cache, cookies, and full-text search.

Local and Cloud File Managers

Laravel provides a series of file manipulation tools through the `Storage` facade, and a few helper functions.

Laravel's filesystem access tools can connect to the local filesystem as well as S3, Rackspace, and FTP. The S3 and Rackspace file drivers are provided by Flysystem (*https://github.com/thephpleague/flysystem*), and it's simple to add additional Flysystem providers to your Laravel app—for example, Dropbox or WebDAV.

Configuring File Access

The definitions for Laravel's file manager live in *config/filesystems.php*. Each connection is called a "disk," and Example 14-1 lists the disks that are available out of the box.

Example 14-1. Default available storage disks

```
...
'disks' => [
    'local' => [
        'driver' => 'local',
        'root' => storage_path('app'),
    ],
```

```
    'public' => [
        'driver' => 'local',
        'root' => storage_path('app/public'),
        'visibility' => 'public',
    ],

    's3' => [
        'driver' => 's3',
        'key' => 'your-key',
        'secret' => 'your-secret',
        'region' => 'your-region',
        'bucket' => 'your-bucket',
    ],
],
```

The storage_path() helper

The `storage_path()` helper used in Example 14-1 links to Laravel's configured storage directory, *storage/*. Anything you pass to it is added to the end of the directory name, so `storage_path('public')` will return the string `storage/public`.

The `local` disk connects to your local storage system and presumes it will be interacting with the *app* directory of the storage path, which is *storage/app*.

The `public` disk is also a local disk (although you can change it if you'd like), which is intended for use with any files you intend to be served by your application. It defaults to the *storage/app/public* directory, and if you want to use this directory to serve files to the public, you'll need to add a symbolic link (symlink) to somewhere within the *public/* directory. Thankfully, there's an Artisan command for that:

```
# Maps public/storage to serve the files from storage/app/public
php artisan storage:link
```

The `s3` disk shows how Laravel connects to cloud-based file storage systems. If you've ever connected to S3 or any other cloud storage provider, this will be familiar; pass it your key and secret and some information defining the "folder" you're working with, which in S3 is the region and the bucket.

Using the Storage Facade

In *config/filesystem.php* you can set the default disk, which is what will be used any time you call the `Storage` facade without specifying a disk. To specify a disk, call `disk('diskname')` on the facade:

```
Storage::disk('s3')->get('file.jpg');
```

The filesystems each provide the following methods:

get('*file.jpg*')
> Retrieves the file at *file.jpg*

put('*file.jpg*', *$contentsOrStream*)
> Puts the given file contents to *file.jpg*

putFile('*myDir*', *$file*)
> Puts the contents of a provided file (in the form of an instance of either Illumi nate\Http\File or Illuminate\Http\UploadedFile) to the *myDir* directory, but with Laravel managing the entire streaming process and naming the file

exists('*file.jpg*')
> Returns a boolean of whether *file.jpg* exists

copy('*file.jpg*', '*newfile.jpg*')
> Copies *file.jpg* to *newfile.jpg*

move('*file.jpg*', '*newfile.jpg*')
> Moves *file.jpg* to *newfile.jpg*

prepend('*my.log*', '*log text*')
> Adds content at the beginning of *my.log*

append('*my.log*', '*log text*')
> Adds content to the end of *my.log*

delete('*file.jpg*')
> Deletes *file.jpg*

deleteDirectory('*myDir*')
> Deletes *myDir*

size('*file.jpg*')
> Returns the size in bytes of *file.jpg*

lastModified('*file.jpg*')
> Returns the Unix timestamp of when *file.jpg* was last modified

files('*myDir*')
> Returns an array of filenames in the directory *myDir*

allFiles('*myDir*')
> Returns an array of filenames in the directory *myDir* and all subdirectories

```
directories('myDir')
```
Returns an array of directory names in the directory *myDir*

```
allDirectories('myDir')
```
Returns an array of directory names in the directory *myDir* and all subdirectories

Injecting an instance

If you'd prefer injecting an instance instead of using the `File` facade, typehint or inject `Illuminate\Filesystem\Filesystem` and you'll get all the same methods available to you.

Adding Additional Flysystem Providers

If you want to add an additional Flysystem provider, you'll need to "extend" Laravel's native storage system. In a service provider somewhere—it could be the `boot()` method of `AppServiceProvider`, but it'd be more appropriate to create a unique service provider for each new binding—use the `Storage` facade to add new storage systems, as seen in Example 14-2.

Example 14-2. Adding additional Flysytem providers

```
// Some service provider
public function boot()
{
    Storage::extend('dropbox', function ($app, $config) {
        $client = new DropboxClient(
            $config['accessToken'], $config['clientIdentifier']
        );

        return new Filesystem(new DropboxAdapter($client));
    });
}
```

Basic File Uploads and Manipulation

One of the more common usages for the `Storage` facade is accepting file uploads from your application's users. Let's look at a common workflow for that, in Example 14-3.

Example 14-3. Common user upload workflow

```
...
class DogsController
{
    public function updatePicture(Request $request, Dog $dog)
```

```
    {
        Storage::put(
            'dogs/' . $dog->id,
            file_get_contents($request->file('picture')->getRealPath())
        );
    }
```

We put() to a file named *dogs/{id}*, and we grab our contents from the uploaded file. Every uploaded file is a descendant of the SplFileInfo class, which provides a getRealPath() method that returns the path to the file's location. So, we get the temporary upload path for the user's uploaded file, read it with file_get_contents(), and pass it into Storage::put().

Since we have this file available to us here, we can do anything we want to the file before we store it—use an image manipulation package to resize it if it's an image, validate it and reject it if it doesn't meet our criteria, or whatever else we like.

If we wanted to upload this same file to S3 and we had our credentials stored in *config/filesystems.php*, we could just adjust Example 14-3 to call Storage::disk('s3')->put(); we'll now be uploading to S3. Take a look at Example 14-4 to see a more complex upload example.

Example 14-4. A more complex example of file uploads, using Intervention

```
...
class DogsController
{
    public function updatePicture(Request $request, Dog $dog)
    {
        $original = $request->file('picture');

        // Resize image to max width 150
        $image = Image::make($original)->resize(150, null, function ($constraint) {
            $constraint->aspectRatio();
        })->encode('jpg', 75);

        Storage::put(
            'dogs/thumbs/' . $dog->id,
            $image->getEncoded()
        );
    }
}
```

I used an image library called Intervention (*http://image.intervention.io/*) in Example 14-4 just as an example; you can use any library you want. The important point is that you have the freedom to manipulate the files however you want before you store them.

Sessions

Session storage is the primary tool we use in web applications to store state between page requests. Laravel's session manager supports session drivers using files, cookies, a database, Memcached or Redis, or in-memory arrays (which expire after the page request and are only good for tests).

You can configure all of your session settings and drivers in *config/session.php*. You can choose whether or not to encrypt your session data, select which driver to use (file is the default), and specify more connection-specific details like the length of session storage and which files or database tables to use. Take a look at the session docs (*https://laravel.com/docs/master/session*) to learn about specific dependencies and settings you need to prepare for whichever driver you choose to use.

The general API of the session tools allows you to save and retrieve data based on individual keys: session()->put('*user_id*') and session()->get('*user_id*'), for example. Make sure to avoid saving anything to a flash session key, since Laravel uses that internally for flash (only available for the next page request) session storage.

Accessing the Session

The most common way to access the session is using the Session facade:

```
session()->get('user_id');
```

But you can also use the session() method on any given Illuminate Request object, as in Example 14-5.

Example 14-5. Using the session() method on a Request object

```
Route::get('dashboard', function (Request $request) {
    $request->session()->get('user_id');
});
```

Or you can inject an instance of Illuminate\Session\Store, as in Example 14-6.

Example 14-6. Injecting the backing class for sessions

```
Route::get('dashboard', function (Illuminate\Session\Store $session) {
    return $session->get('user_id');
});
```

Finally, you can use the global `session()` helper. Use it with no parameters to get a session instance, with a single string parameter to "get" from the session, or with an array to "put" to the session, as demonstrated in Example 14-7.

Example 14-7. Using the global session() helper

```
// get
$value = session()->get('key');
$value = session('key');
// put
session()->put('key', 'value');
session(['key', 'value']);
```

If you're new to Laravel and not sure which to use, I'd recommend using the global helper.

The Methods Available on Session Instances

The two most common methods are `get()` and `put()`, but let's take a look at each of the available methods and their parameters:

`session()->get($key, $fallbackValue)`
> `get()` pulls the value of the provided key out of the session. If there is no value attached to that key, it will return the fallback value instead (and if you don't provide a fallback, it will return `null`). The fallback value can be a string or a closure, as you can see in the following examples.

```
$points = session()->get('points');

$points = session()->get('points', 0);

$points = session()->get('points', function () {
    return (new PointGetterService)->getPoints();
});
```

`session()->put($key, $value)`
> `put()` stores the provided value in the session at the provided key:

```
session()->put('points', 45);

$points = session()->get('points');
```

`session()->push($key, $value)`
> If any of your session values are arrays, you can use `push()` to add a value onto the array:

```
session()->put('friends', ['Saúl', 'Quang', 'Mechteld']);

session()->push('friends', 'Javier');
```

```
session()->has($key)
```
has() checks whether there's a value set at the provided key:

```
if (session()->has('points')) {
    // do something
}
```

You can also pass an array of keys, and it only returns true if all of the keys exist.

session()->has() and null values

If a session value is set, but the value is null, session()->has() will return false.

```
session()->all()
```
all() returns an array of everything that's in the session, including those values set by the framework. You'll likely see values under keys like _token (CSRF tokens), _previous (previous page, for back() redirects), and flash (for flash storage).

```
session()->forget($key) and session()->flush()
```
forget() removes a previously set session value. flush() removes every session value, even those set by the framework:

```
session()->put('a', 'awesome');
session()->put('b', 'bodacious');

session()->forget('a');
// a is no longer set, b is still set
session()->flush();
// session is now empty
```

```
session()->pull($key, $fallbackValue)
```
pull() is the same as get(), except that it deletes the value from the session after pulling it.

```
session()->regenerate()
```
It's not common, but if you need to regenerate your session ID, regenerate() is there for you.

Flash Session Storage

There are three more methods we haven't covered yet, and they all have to do with something called "flash" session storage.

One very common pattern for session storage is to set a value that you only want available for the next page load. For example, you might want to store a message like

"Updated post successfully." You could manually get that message and then wipe it on the next page load, but if you use this pattern a lot it can get wasteful. Enter flash session storage: keys that are expected to only last for a single page request.

Laravel handles the work for you, and all you need to do is use `flash()` instead of `put()`. The useful methods here are:

`session()->flash($key, $value)`
> `flash()` sets the session key to the provided value for just the next page request.

`session()->reflash()` *and* `session()->keep($key)`
> If you need the previous page's `flash()` session data to stick around for one more request, you can use `reflash()` to restore the entire flash contents for the next request or `keep($key)` to just restore a single flash value for the next request. `keep()` can also accept an array of keys to reflash.

Cache

Caches are structured very similarly to sessions. You provide a key and Laravel stores it for you. The biggest difference is that the data in a cache is cached per application and the data in a session is cached per user. That means caches are more commonly used for storing large database results, API calls, or other slow queries that can stand to get a little bit "stale."

The cache configuration settings are available at *config/cache.php*. Just like with a session, you can set the specific configuration details for any of your drivers, and also choose which will be your default. Laravel uses the `file` cache driver by default, but you can also use Memcached or Redis, APC, or a database, or write your own cache driver. Take a look at the cache docs (*https://laravel.com/docs/master/cache*) to learn about specific dependencies and settings you need to prepare for whichever driver you choose to use.

Accessing the Cache

Just like with sessions, there are a few different ways to access a cache. You can use the facade:

```
$users = Cache::get('users');
```

You can get an instance from the container, as in Example 14-8.

Example 14-8. Injecting an instance of the cache

```
Route::get('users', function (Illuminate\Contracts\Cache\Repository $cache) {
    return $cache->get('users');
});
```

Or you can use the global cache() helper (introduced in Laravel 5.3), as in Example 14-9.

Example 14-9. Using the global cache() helper

```
// get from cache
$users = cache('key', 'default value');
$users = cache()->get('key', 'default value');
// put for $minutes duration
$users = cache(['key' => 'value'], $minutes);
$users = cache()->put('key', 'value', $minutes);
```

If you're new to Laravel and not sure which to use, I'd recommend using the global helper.

The Methods Available on Cache Instances

Let's take a look at the methods you can call on a Cache instance:

cache()->get($key, $fallbackValue) *and*
cache()->pull($key, $fallbackValue)
> get() makes it easy to retrieve the value for any given key. pull() is the same as get() except it removes the cached value after retrieving it.

cache()->put($key, $value, $minutesOrExpiration)
> put() sets the value of the specified key for a given number of minutes. If you'd prefer setting an expiration date/time instead of a number of minutes, you can pass a Carbon object as the third parameter:
>
> ```
> cache()->put('key', 'value', Carbon::now()->addDay());
> ```

cache()->add($key, $value)
> add() is similar to put(), except if the value already exists, it won't set it. Also, the method returns a boolean of whether or not the value was actually added:
>
> ```
> $someDate = Carbon::now();
> cache()->add('someDate', $someDate); // returns true
> $someOtherDate = Carbon::now()->addHour();
> cache()->add('someDate', $someOtherDate); // returns false
> ```

cache()->forever($key, $value)
> forever() saves a value to the cache for a specific key; it's the same as put(), except the values will never expire (until they're removed with forget()).

cache()->has($key)
> has() returns a boolean of whether or not there's a value at the provided key.

```
cache()->remember($key, $minutes, $closure) and
cache()->rememberForever($key, $closure)
```
remember() provides a single method to handle a very common flow: look up whether a value exists in the cache for a certain key, and if it doesn't, get that value somehow, save it to the cache, and return it.

remember() lets you provide a key to look up, the number of minutes it should be saved for, and a closure to define how to look it up, in case the key has no value set. rememberForever() is the same, except it doesn't need you to set the number of minutes it should expire after. Take a look at the following example to see a common user scenario for remember():

```
// Either returns the value cached at "users" or gets "User::all()",
// caches it at "users", and returns it
$users = cache()->remember('users', 120, function () {
    return User::all();
});
```

```
cache()->increment($key, $amount) and cache()->decrement($key, $amount)
```
increment() and decrement() allow you to increment and decrement integer values in the cache. If there is no value at the given key, it'll be treated as if it were 0, and if you pass a second parameter to increment or decrement, it'll increment or decrement by that amount instead of by 1.

```
cache()->forget($key) and cache()->flush()
```
forget() works just like Session's forget() method: pass it a key and it'll wipe that key's value. flush() wipes the entire cache.

Cookies

You might expect cookies to work the same as the session and the cache. A facade and a global helper are available for these too, and our mental models of all three are similar: you can get or set their values in the same way.

But because cookies are inherently attached to the requests and responses, you'll need to interact with cookies differently. Let's look really briefly at what makes cookies different.

Cookies in Laravel

Cookies can exist in three places in Laravel. They can come in via the request, which means the user had the cookie when she visited the page. You can read that with the Cookie facade, or you can read it off of the request object.

They can also be sent out with a response, which means the response will instruct the user's browser to save the cookie for future visits. You can do this by adding the cookie to your response object before returning it.

And lastly, a cookie can be *queued*. If you use the `Cookie` facade to set a cookie, you have put it into a "CookieJar" queue, and it will be removed and added to the response object by the `AddQueuedCookiesToResponse` middleware.

Accessing the Cookie Tools

You can get and set cookies in three places: the `Cookie` facade, the `cookie()` global helper, and the request and response objects.

The Cookie facade

The `Cookie` facade is the most full-featured option, allowing you to not only read and make cookies, but also to queue them to be added to the response. It provides the following methods:

`Cookie::get($key)`
> To pull the value of a cookie that came in with the request, you can just run `Cookie::get('cookie-name')`. This is the simplest option.

`Cookie::has($key)`
> You can check whether a cookie came in with the request using `Cookie::has('cookie-name')`, which returns a boolean.

`Cookie::make(...params)`
> If you want to *make* a cookie without queueing it anywhere, you can use `Cookie::make()`. The most likely use for this would be to make a cookie and then manually attach it to the response object, which we'll cover in a bit.
>
> Here are the parameters for `make()`, in order:
>
> - `$name` is the name of the cookie
> - `$value` is the content of the cookie
> - `$minutes` specifies how many minutes the cookie should live
> - `$path` is the path under which your cookie should be valid
> - `$domain` lists the domains for which your cookie should work
> - `$secure` indicates whether the cookie should only be transmitted over a secure (HTTPS) connection
> - `$httpOnly` indicates whether the cookie will be made accessible only through the HTTP protocol

`Cookie::make()`

Returns an instance of `Symfony\Component\HttpFoundation\Cookie`.

Default settings for cookies

The `CookieJar` that the `Cookie` facade instance uses reads its defaults from the *session* config. So, if you change any of the configuration values for the session cookie in *config/session.php*, those same defaults will be applied to all of your cookies that you create using the `Cookie` facade.

`Cookie::queue(Cookie || ...params)`

If you use `Cookie::make()`, you'll still need to attach the cookie to your response, which we'll cover shortly. `Cookie::queue()` has the same syntax as `Cookie::make()`, but it enqueues the created cookie to be automatically attached to the response by middleware.

If you'd like, you can also just pass a cookie you've created yourself into `Cookie::queue()`.

Here's the simplest possible way to add a cookie to the response in Laravel:

```
Cookie::queue('dismissed-popup', true, 15);
```

When your queued cookies won't get set

Cookies can only be returned as a part of a response. So, if you enqueue cookies with the `Cookie` facade and then your response isn't returned correctly—for example, if you use PHP's `exit()` or something halts the execution of your script —your cookies won't be set.

The cookie() global helper

The `cookie()` global helper will return a `CookieJar` instance if you call it with no parameters. However, two of the most convenient methods on the `Cookie` facade—`has()` and `get()`—exist *only* on the facade, not on the `CookieJar`. So, in this context, I think the global helper is actually less useful than the other options.

The one task for which the `cookie()` global helper is useful is creating a cookie. If you pass parameters to `cookie()`, they'll be passed directly to the equivalent of `Cookie::make()`, so this is the fastest way to create a cookie:

```
$cookie = cookie('dismissed-popup', true, 15);
```

Injecting an instance

You can also inject an instance of `Illuminate\Cookie\CookieJar` anywhere in the app, but you'll have the same limitations discussed here.

Cookies on request and response objects

Since cookies come in as a part of the request and are set as a part of the response, those Illuminate objects are the places they actually live. The `Cookie` facade's `get()`, `has()`, and `queue()` methods are just proxies to interact with the request and response objects.

So, the simplest way to interact with cookies is to pull cookies from the request and set them on the response.

Reading cookies from request objects. Once you have a copy of your request object—if you don't know how to get one, just try `app('request')`—you can use the request object's `cookie()` method to read its cookies, as shown in Example 14-10.

Example 14-10. Reading a cookie from a request object

```
Route::get('dashboard', function (Illuminate\Http\Request $request) {
    $userDismissedPopup = $request->cookie('dismissed-popup', false);
});
```

As you can see in this example, the `cookie()` method has two parameters: the cookie's name and, optionally, the fallback value.

Setting cookies on response objects. Whenever you have your response object ready, you can use the `cookie()` method (or the `withCookie()` method in Laravel prior to 5.3) on it to add a cookie to the response, like in Example 14-11.

Example 14-11. Setting a cookie on a response object

```
Route::get('dashboard', function () {
    $cookie = cookie('saw-dashboard', true);

    return Response::view('dashboard')
        ->cookie($cookie);
});
```

If you're new to Laravel and not sure which option to use, I'd recommend setting cookies on the request and response objects. It's a bit more work, but will lead to fewer surprises if future developers don't understand the `CookieJar` queue.

Full-Text Search with Laravel Scout

Laravel Scout is a separate package that you can bring into your Laravel apps to add full-text search to your Eloquent models. Scout makes it easy to index and search the contents of your Eloquent models; it ships with Algolia and Elasticsearch drivers, but there are also community packages for other providers. I'll assume you're using Algolia.

Installing Scout

First, pull in the package in any Laravel 5.3+ app:

```
composer require laravel/scout
```

Next, add `Laravel\Scout\ScoutServiceProvider::class,` to the `providers` section of *config/app.php*.

You'll want to set up your Scout configuration. Run `php artisan vendor:publish` and paste your Algolia credentials in *config/scout.php*.

Finally, install the Algolia SDK:

```
composer require algolia/algoliasearch-client-php
```

Marking Your Model for Indexing

In your model (we'll use `Review`, for a book review, for this example), import the `Laravel\Scout\Searchable` trait.

You can define which properties are searchable using the `toSearchableArray()` method (it defaults to mirroring `toArray()`), and define the name of the model's index using the `searchableAs()` method (it defaults to the table name).

Scout subscribes to the create/delete/update events on your marked models. When you create, update, or delete any rows, Scout will sync those changes up to Algolia. It'll either make those changes synchronously with your updates or, if you configure Scout to use a queue, queue the updates.

Searching Your Index

Scout's syntax is simple. For example, to find any `Review` with the word `Llew` in it:

```
Review::search('Llew')->get();
```

You can also modify your queries as you would with regular Eloquent calls:

```
// Get all records from the Review that match the term "Llew",
// limited to 20 per page and reading the page query parameter,
// just like Eloquent pagination
Review::search('Llew')->paginate(20);
```

```
// Get all records from the Review that match the term "Llew"
// and have the account_id field set to 2
Review::search('Llew')->where('account_id', 2)->get();
```

What comes back from these searches? A collection of Eloquent models, rehydrated from your database. The IDs are stored in Algolia, which returns a list of matched IDs; Scout then pulls the database records for those and returns them as Eloquent objects.

You don't have full access to the complexity of SQL WHERE commands, but it provides a basic framework for comparison checks like you can see in the code samples here.

Queues and Scout

At this point your app will be making HTTP requests to Algolia on every request that modifies any database records. This can slow down your application quickly, which is why Scout makes it easy to push all of its actions onto a queue.

In *config/scout.php*, set queue to true so that these updates are set to be indexed asynchronously. Your full-text index is now operating under "eventual consistency"; your database records will receive the updates immediately, and the updates to your search indexes will be queued and updated as fast as your queue worker allows.

Perform Operations Without Indexing

If you need to perform a set of operations and avoid triggering the indexing in response, wrap the operations in the withoutSyncingToSearch() method on your model:

```
Review::withoutSyncingToSearch(function () {
    // make a bunch of reviews, e.g.
    factory(Review::class, 10)->create();
});
```

Manually Trigger Indexing via Code

If you want to manually trigger indexing your model, you can do it using code in your app or via the command line.

To manually trigger indexing from your code, add searchable() to the end of any Eloquent query and it will index all of the records that were found in that query:

```
Review::all()->searchable();
```

You can also choose to scope the query to only those you want to index. However, Scout is smart enough to insert new records and update old records, so you may choose to just reindex the entire contents of the model's database table.

You can also run `searchable()` on relationship methods:

```
$user->reviews()->searchable();
```

If you want to unindex any records with the same sort of query chaining, just use `unsearchable()` instead:

```
Review::where('sucky', true)->unsearchable();
```

Manually Trigger Indexing via the CLI

You can also trigger indexing with an Artisan command:

```
php artisan scout:import App\\Review
```

This will chunk all of the `Review` models and index them all.

Testing

Testing most of these features is as simple as just using them in your tests; no need to mock or stub. The default configuration will already work—for example, take a look at *phpunit.xml* to see that your session driver and cache driver have been set to values appropriate for tests.

However, there are a few convenience methods and a few gotchas that you should know about before you attempt to test them all.

File Storage

Testing file uploads can be a bit of a pain, but follow these steps and it will be clear.

Uploading fake files

First, let's look at how to manually create a Symfony `UploadedFile` object for use in our application testing (Example 14-12). Note that this assumes we have a *storage/ tests* directory where we're placing a file named *for-tests.jpg* that we'll use for our tests.

Example 14-12. Creating a fake UploadedFile for testing

```
public function test_file_should_be_stored()
{
    $path = storage_path('tests/for-tests.jpg');
    $file = new UploadedFile(
        $path, // file path
        'for-tests.jpg', // original file name
        'image/jpg', // MIME type
        filesize($path), // file size; best to get once & hardcode into your test,
        null, // error code
        true // whether we're in test mode
    );
```

```
    $this->call('post', 'upload-route', [], [], ['upload' => $file]);

    $this->assertResponseOk();
}
```

We've created a new instance of `UploadedFile` that refers to our testing file, and we can now use it to test our routes.

Returning fake files

If your route is expecting a real file to exist, sometimes the best way to make it testable is to make that real file actually exist. Let's say every user must have a profile picture.

First, let's set up the model factory for the user to use Faker to make a copy of the picture, as in Example 14-13.

Example 14-13. Returning fake files with Faker

```
$factory->define(User::class, function (Faker\Generator $faker) {
    return [
        'picture' => $faker->file(
            storage_path('tests'), // source directory
            storage_path('app'), // target directory
            false // return just filename, not full path
        ),
        'name' => $faker->name,
    ];
});
```

Faker's `file()` method picks a random file from the source directory and copies it to the target directory, and then returns the filename. So we've just picked a random file from the *storage/tests* directory, copied it to the *storage/app* directory, and set its filename as the `picture` property on our `User`. At this point we can use a `User` in tests on routes that expect the `User` to have a picture, as seen in Example 14-14.

Example 14-14. Asserting that an image's URL is echoed

```
public function test_user_profile_picture_echoes_correctly()
{
    $user = factory(User::class)->create();

    $this->visit("users/{$user->id}");
    $this->see($user->picture);
}
```

Of course, in many contexts you can just generate a random string there without even copying a file. But if your routes check for the file's existence or run any operations on the file, this is your best option.

Session

If you need to assert something has been set in the session, you can use some convenience methods Laravel makes available in every test. All of these methods are available in your tests on the $this object:

assertSessionHas($key, $value = null)
> Asserts that the session has a value for a particular key, and, if the second parameter is passed, that that key is a particular value:

```
public function test_some_thing()
{
    // do stuff
    $this->assertSessionHas('key', 'value');
}
```

assertSessionHasAll(array $bindings)
> If passed an array of key/value pairs, asserts that all of the keys are equal to all of the values. If one or more of the array entries is just a value (with PHP's default numeric key), it will just be checked for existence in the session:

```
$check = [
    'has',
    'hasWithThisValue' => 'thisValue',
]

$this->assertSessionHasAll($check);
```

assertSessionMissing($key)
> Asserts that the session does *not* have a value for a particular key.

assertSessionHasErrors($bindings = [], $format = null)
> Asserts that the session has an errors value. This is the key Laravel uses to send errors back from validation failures.

> If the array contains just keys, it will check that errors are set with those keys:

```
$this->post('test-route', ['failing' => 'data']);
$this->assertSessionHasErrors(['name', 'email']);
```

> You can also pass values for those keys, and optionally a *$format*, to check that the messages for those errors came back the way you expected:

```
$this->post('test-route', ['failing' => 'data']);
$this->assertSessionHasErrors([
```

```
        'email' => '<strong>The email field is required.</strong>'
    ], '<strong>:message</strong>');
```

assertHasOldInput()

Since you can flash the previous page's input to the session, you may want to assert that it's been flashed correctly:

```
$this->post('test-route', ['failing' => 'data']);
$this->assertHasOldInput();
```

Cache

There's nothing special about testing your features that use cache—just do it:

```
Cache::put('key', 'value', 15);

$this->assertEquals('value', Cache::get('key'));
```

Laravel uses the "array" cache driver by default in your testing environment, which just stores your cache values in memory.

Cookies

If you need to set a cookie before testing a route in your application tests, you can manually pass cookies to one of the parameters of the call() method. To learn more about call(), check out Chapter 12.

Excluding your cookie from encryption during testing

Your cookies won't work in your tests unless you exclude them from Laravel's cookie encryption middleware. You can do this by teaching the EncryptCookies middleware to temporarily disable itself for that cookie:

```
use Illuminate\Cookie\Middleware\EncryptCookies;
...

$this->app->resolving(
    EncryptCookies::class,
    function ($object) {
        $object->disableFor('cookie-name');
    }
);

// ...run test
```

That means you can set and check against a cookie with something like Example 14-15.

Example 14-15. Running unit tests against cookies

```php
public function test_cookie()
{
    $this->app->resolving(EncryptCookies::class, function ($object) {
        $object->disableFor('my-cookie');
    });

    $this->call('get', 'route-echoing-my-cookie-value', [], ['my-cookie' => 'baz']);
    $this->see('baz');
}
```

If, for some reason, you'd rather not disable encryption, you can instead set the encrypted value of the cookie like in Example 14-16.

Example 14-16. Manually encrypting a cookie before setting it

```php
use Illuminate\Contracts\Encryption\Encrypter;
...

public function test_cookie()
{
    $encryptedBaz = app(Encrypter::class)->encrypt('baz');

    $this->call(
        'get',
        'route-echoing-my-cookie-value',
        [],
        ['my-cookie' => $encryptedBaz]
    );

    $this->see('baz');
}
```

If you want to test that a response has a cookie set, you can use either seeCookie() to test for the cookie:

```php
$this->visit('cookie-setting-route');
$this->seeCookie('cookie-name');
```

or seePlainCookie() to test for the cookie and to assert that it's not encrypted.

TL;DR

Laravel provides simple interfaces to many common storage operations: filesystem access, sessions, cookies, the cache, and search. Each of these APIs is the same regardless of which provider you use, which Laravel enables by allowing multiple "drivers" to serve the same public interface. This makes it simple to switch providers depending on the environment, or as the needs of the application change.

## CHAPTER 15

Mail and Notifications

Sending an application's users notifications via email, Slack, SMS, or another notification system is a common but surprisingly complex requirement. Laravel's mail and notification features provide consistent APIs that abstract away the need to pay too close attention to any particular provider. Just like in Chapter 14, you'll write your code once and choose at the configuration level which provider you'll use to send your email or notifications.

Mail

Laravel's mail functionality is a convenience layer on top of SwiftMailer (*http://swift mailer.org/*), and out of the box Laravel comes with drivers for Mailgun, Mandrill, Sparkpost, SES, SMTP, PHP Mail, and Sendmail.

For all of the cloud services, you'll set your authentication information in *config/services.php*. However, if you take a look you'll see there are already keys there —and in *config/mail.php*—that allow you to customize your application's mail functionality in *.env* using variables like MAIL_DRIVER and MAILGUN_SECRET.

Cloud-based API driver dependencies

If you're using any of the cloud-based API drivers, you'll need to bring Guzzle in with Composer. You can run the following command to add it:

```
composer require guzzlehttp/guzzle:"~5.3|~6.0"
```

If you use the SES driver, you'll need to run the following command:

```
composer require aws/aws-sdk-php:~3.0
```

"Classic" Mail

There are two different syntaxes in Laravel for sending mail: classic and mailable. The mailable syntax is the preferred syntax from 5.3 onward, so we're going to focus on that in this book. But for those who are working in 5.1 or 5.2, here's a quick look at how the classic syntax (Example 15-1) works.

Example 15-1. Basic "classic" mail syntax

```
Mail::send(
    'emails.assignment',
    ['trainer' => $trainer, 'trainee' => $trainee],
    function ($m) use ($trainer, $trainee) {
        $m->from($trainer->email, $trainer->name);
        $m->to($trainee->email, $trainee->name)->subject('A New Assignment!');
    }
);
```

The first parameter of `Mail::send()` is the name of the view. Remember, `emails.assignment` means *resources/views/emails/assignment.blade.php* or *resources/views/emails/assignment.php*.

The second parameter is an array of data that you want to pass to the view.

The third parameter is a closure, in which you define how and where to send the email: from, to, CC, BCC, subject, and any other metadata. Make sure to `use` any variables you want access to within the closure. And note that the closure is passed one parameter, which we've named `$m`; this is the message object.

Take a look at the old docs (*https://laravel.com/docs/5.2/mail*) to learn about the classic mail syntax.

Basic "Mailable" Mail Usage

Laravel 5.3 introduced a new mail syntax called the "mailable." It works the same as the classic mail syntax, but instead of defining your mail messages in a closure, you instead create a specific PHP class to represent each mail.

To make a mailable, use the `make:mail` Artisan command:

```
php artisan make:mail Assignment
```

Example 15-2 shows what that class looks like.

Example 15-2. An autogenerated mailable PHP class

```php
<?php

namespace App\Mail;
```

```php
use Illuminate\Bus\Queueable;
use Illuminate\Mail\Mailable;
use Illuminate\Queue\SerializesModels;
use Illuminate\Contracts\Queue\ShouldQueue;

class Assignment extends Mailable
{
    use Queueable, SerializesModels;

    /**
     * Create a new message instance.
     *
     * @return void
     */
    public function __construct()
    {
        //
    }

    /**
     * Build the message.
     *
     * @return $this
     */
    public function build()
    {
        return $this->view('view.name');
    }
}
```

This class probably looks familiar—it's shaped almost the same as a Job. It even imports the Queueable trait for queuing your mail and the SerializesModels trait so any Eloquent models you pass to the constructor will be serialized correctly.

So, how does this work? The build() method on a mailable is where you're going to define which view to use, what the subject is, and anything else you want to tweak about the mail *except who it's going to*. The constructor is the place where you'll pass in any data, and any public properties on your mailable class will be available to the template.

Take a look at Example 15-3 to see how we might update the autogenerated mailable for our assignment example.

Example 15-3. A sample mailable

```php
<?php

namespace App\Mail;
```

```
use Illuminate\Bus\Queueable;
use Illuminate\Mail\Mailable;
use Illuminate\Queue\SerializesModels;
use Illuminate\Contracts\Queue\ShouldQueue;

class Assignment extends Mailable
{
    use Queueable, SerializesModels;

    public $trainer;
    public $trainee;

    public function __construct($trainer, $trainee)
    {
        $this->trainer = $trainer;
        $this->trainee = $trainee;
    }

    public function build()
    {
        return $this->subject('New assignment from ' . $this->trainer->name)
            ->view('emails.assignment');
    }
}
```

Example 15-4 shows how to send a mailable.

Example 15-4. A few ways to send mailables

```
// Simple send
Mail::to($user)->send(new Assignment($trainer, $trainee));

// With CC/BCC/etc.
Mail::to($user1))
    ->cc($user2)
    ->bcc($user3)
    ->send(new Assignment($trainer, $trainee));

// With collections
Mail::to('me@app.com')
    ->bcc(User::all())
    ->send(new Assignment($trainer, $trainee))
```

Mail Templates

Mail templates are just like any other template. They can extend other templates, use sections, parse variables, contain conditional or looping directives, and do anything else you can do in a normal Blade view.

Take a look at Example 15-5 to see a possible `emails.assignments` template for Example 15-3.

Example 15-5. Sample assignment email template

```
<!-- resources/views/emails/assignment.blade.php -->
<p>Hey {{ $trainee->name }}!</p>

<p>You have received a new training assignment from <b>{{ $trainer->name }}</b>.
Check out your <a href="{{ route('training-dashboard') }}">training
dashboard</a> now!</p>
```

In Example 15-3, both `$trainer` and `$trainee` are public properties on your mailable, which makes them available to the template.

If you want to explicitly define which variables are passed to the template, you can chain the `with()` method onto your `build()` call as in Example 15-6.

Example 15-6. Customizing the template variables

```
public function build()
{
    return $this->subject('You have a new assignment!')
        ->view('emails.assignment')
        ->with(['assignment' => $this->event->name]);
}
```

HTML versus plain-text emails

So far we've used the `view()` method in our `build()` call stacks. This expects the template we're referencing to pass back HTML. If you'd like to pass a plain-text version, the `text()` method defines your plain-text view:

```
public function build()
{
    return $this->view('emails.reminder')
        ->text('emails.reminder_plain');
}
```

Methods Available in build()

Here are a few of the methods available to you to customize your message in the `build()` method of your mailable:

`from($address, $name = null)`
    Sets the "from" name and address—represents the author

`subject($subject)`
    Sets the email subject

`attach($pathToFile, array $options = [])`

Attaches a file; valid options are `mime` for MIME type and `as` for display name

`attachData($data, $name, array $options = [])`

Attaches a file from a raw string; same options as `attach()`

`priority($priority)`

Set the email's priority, where 1 is the highest and 5 is the lowest

Finally, if you want to perform any manual modifications on the underlying Swift message, you can do that using `withSwiftMessage()`, as shown in Example 15-7.

Example 15-7. Modifying the underlying SwiftMessage object

```
public function build()
{
    return $this->subject('Howdy!')
        ->withSwiftMessage(function ($swift) {
            $swift->setReplyTo('noreply@email.com');
        })
        ->view('emails.howdy');
}
```

Attachments and Inline Images

Example 15-8 shows two options for how to attach files or raw data to your email.

Example 15-8. Attaching files or data to mailables

```
// Attach a file using the local filename
public function build()
{
    return $this->subject('Your whitepaper download')
        ->attach(storage_path('pdfs/whitepaper.pdf'), [
            'mime' => 'application/pdf', // Optional
            'as' => 'whitepaper-barasa.pdf' // Optional
        ])
        ->view('emails.whitepaper');
}

// Attach a file passing the raw data
public function build()
{
    return $this->subject('Your whitepaper download')
        ->attachData(
            file_get_contents(storage_path('pdfs/whitepaper.pdf')),
            'whitepaper-barasa.pdf',
            [
                'mime' => 'application/pdf' // Optional
            ]
```

```
    )
    ->view('emails.whitepaper');
}
```

And you can see how to embed images directly into your email in Example 15-9.

Example 15-9. Inlining images

```
<!-- emails/image.blade.php --!>
Here is an image:

<img src="{{ $message->embed(storage_path('embed.jpg')) }}">

Or, the same image embedding the data:

<img src="{{ $message->embedData(
    file_get_contents(storage_path('embed.jpg')), 'embed.jpg'
) }}">
```

Queues

Sending email is a time-consuming task that can cause applications to slow down, so it's common to move sending email to a background queue. It's so common, in fact, that Laravel has a set of built-in tools to make it easier to queue your messages without writing queue jobs for each email.

 Configuring queues

Everything we'll cover here requires your queues to be configured correctly. Take a look at Chapter 16 to learn more about how queues work and how to get them running in your application.

queue()

To queue a mail object instead of sending it immediately, simply pass your mailable object to `Mail::queue()` instead of `Mail::send()`:

```
Mail::queue(new Assignment($trainer, $trainee));
```

later()

`Mail::later()` works the same as `Mail::queue()`, but it allows you to add a delay—either in minutes, or at a specific time by passing an instance of `DateTime` or `Carbon` —to when the email will be pulled from the queue and sent:

```
$when = Carbon::now()->addMinutes(30);
Mail::later($when, new Assignment($trainer, $trainee));
```

Specifying the queue or connection

For both `queue()` and `later()`, if you'd like to specify which queue or queue connection your mail is added to, use the `onConnection()` and `onQueue()` methods on your mailable object:

```
$message = (new Assignment($trainer, $trainee))
    ->onConnection('sqs')
    ->onQueue('emails');

Mail::to($user)->queue($message);
```

Local Development

This is all well and good for sending mail in your production environments. But how do you test this all out? There are three primary tools you'll want to consider: Laravel's `log` driver, a Software as a Service (SaaS) app named Mailtrap, and the "universal *to*" configuration option.

The log driver

Laravel provides a `log` driver that logs every email you try to send to your local *laravel.log* file (which is, by default, in *storage/logs*).

If you want to use this, edit *.env* and set `MAIL_DRIVER` to `log`. Now open up or tail *storage/logs/laravel.log* and send an email from your app. You'll see something like this:

```
Message-ID: <04ee2e97289c68f0c9191f4b04fc0de1@localhost>
Date: Tue, 17 May 2016 02:52:46 +0000
Subject: Welcome to our app!
From: Matt Stauffer <matt@mattstauffer.co>
To: freja@jensen.no
MIME-Version: 1.0
Content-Type: text/html; charset=utf-8
Content-Transfer-Encoding: quoted-printable

Welcome to our app!
```

Mailtrap.io

Mailtrap (*https://mailtrap.io*) is a service for capturing and inspecting emails in development environments. You send your mail to the Mailtrap servers via SMTP, but instead of sending those emails off to the intended recipients, Mailtrap captures them all and provides you with a web-based email client for inspecting them, regardless of which email address is in the to field.

To set up Mailtrap, sign up for a free Mailtrap account and visit the base dashboard for your demo. Copy your username and password from the SMTP column.

Now edit your app's *.env* file and set the following values in the `mail` section:

```
MAIL_DRIVER=smtp
MAIL_HOST=mailtrap.io
MAIL_PORT=2525
MAIL_USERNAME=your_username_from_mailtrap_here
MAIL_PASSWORD=your_password_from_mailtrap_here
MAIL_ENCRYPTION=null
```

Now, any email you send from your app will show up in your Mailtrap inbox.

Universal to

If you'd like to inspect the emails in your preferred client, you can override the `to` field on each message with the "universal `to`" configuration setting. To set this up, add a "to" key to your *config/mail.php* file that looks something like this:

```
'to' => [
    'address' => 'matt@mattstauffer.co',
    'name' => 'Matt Testing My Application'
],
```

Note that you'll need to actually set up a real email driver with something like Mailgun or Sendmail in order to use this.

Notifications

Most of the mail that's sent from web apps really has the purpose of notifying users that a particular action has happened or needs to happen. As users' communication preferences grow more and more diverse, we gather ever more—and more disparate—packages to communicate via Slack, SMS, and other means.

Laravel 5.3 introduced a new concept in Laravel called, fittingly, *notifications*. Just like mailables, a notification is a PHP class that represents a single communication that you might want to send to your users. For now, let's imagine we're notifying users of our physical training app that they have a new workout available on our app.

Each class represents all of the information necessary to send notifications to your users *using one or many notification channels*. A single notification could send an email, send an SMS via Nexmo, send a WebSockets ping, add a record to a database, send a message to a Slack channel, and much more.

So, let's create our notification:

```
php artisan make:notification WorkoutAvailable
```

Example 15-10 shows what that gives us.

Example 15-10. An autogenerated notification class

```php
<?php

namespace App\Notifications;

use Illuminate\Bus\Queueable;
use Illuminate\Notifications\Notification;
use Illuminate\Contracts\Queue\ShouldQueue;
use Illuminate\Notifications\Messages\MailMessage;

class WorkoutAvailable extends Notification
{
    use Queueable;

    /**
     * Create a new notification instance.
     *
     * @return void
     */
    public function __construct()
    {
        //
    }

    /**
     * Get the notification's delivery channels.
     *
     * @param  mixed  $notifiable
     * @return array
     */
    public function via($notifiable)
    {
        return ['mail'];
    }

    /**
     * Get the mail representation of the notification.
     *
     * @param  mixed  $notifiable
     * @return \Illuminate\Notifications\Messages\MailMessage
     */
    public function toMail($notifiable)
    {
        return (new MailMessage)
                    ->line('The introduction to the notification.')
                    ->action('Notification Action', 'https://laravel.com')
                    ->line('Thank you for using our application!');
    }

    /**
     * Get the array representation of the notification.
```

```
 *
 * @param  mixed  $notifiable
 * @return array
 */
public function toArray($notifiable)
{
    return [
        //
    ];
}
}
```

We can learn a few things here. First, we're going to pass in relevant data to the constructor. Second, there's a `via()` method that allows us to define, for a given user, which notification channels to use (`$notifiable` represents whatever entities you want to notify in your system; for most apps, it'll be a user, but that's not always the case). And third, there are individual methods for each notification channel that allow you to specifically define how to send one of these notifications through that channel.

When would a $notifiable not be a user?

While the most common notification targets will be users, it's possible you may want to notify something else. This may simply be because your application has multiple user types—so, you might want to be able to notify both "trainers" and "trainees." But you also might find yourself wanting to notify a "group," a "company," or a "server."

So, let's modify this class for our `WorkoutAvailable` example. Take a look at Example 15-11.

Example 15-11. Our WorkoutAvailable notification class

```
...
class WorkoutAvailable extends Notification
{
    use Queueable;

    public $workout;

    public function __construct($workout)
    {
        $this->workout = $workout;
    }

    public function via($notifiable)
    {
```

```
    // This method doesn't exist on the User... we're going to make it up
    return $notifiable->preferredNotificationChannels();
}

public function toMail($notifiable)
{
    return (new MailMessage)
        ->line('You have a new workout available!')
        ->action('Check it out now', route('workout', [$this->workout]))
        ->line('Thank you for training with us!');
}

public function toArray($notifiable)
{
    return [];
}
}
```

Defining the via() Method for Your Notifiables

As you can see in Example 15-11, we're somehow responsible for deciding, for each notification and each notifiable, which notification channels we're going to use.

You could just send everything as mail or just send everything as SMS (Example 15-12).

Example 15-12. Simplest possible via() method

```
public function via($notifiable)
{
    return 'nexmo';
}
```

You could also let each user choose their one preferred method and save that on the User itself (Example 15-13).

Example 15-13. Customizing the via() method per user

```
public function via($notifiable)
{
    return $notifiable->preferred_notification_channel;
}
```

Or, as we imagined in Example 15-11, you could create a method on each notifiable that allows for some complex notification logic. For example, you could notify the user over certain channels during work hours and other channels in the evening. What is important is that via() is a PHP class method, so you can do whatever complex logic you want there.

Sending Notifications

There are two ways to send a notification: using the Notification facade, or adding the Notifiable trait to an Eloquent class (likely your User class).

Sending notifications using the Notifiable trait

Any model that imports the Laravel\Notifications\Notifiable trait (which the App\User class does by default) has a notify() method that can be passed a notification, which will look like Example 15-14.

Example 15-14. Sending a notification using the Notifiable trait

```
use App\Notifications\WorkoutAvailable;
...
$user->notify(new WorkoutAvailable($workout));
```

Sending notifications with the Notification facade

The Notification facade is the clumsier of the two methods, since you have to pass both the notifiable and the notification. However, it's helpful because you can choose to pass more than one notifiable in at the same time, like you can see in Example 15-15.

Example 15-15. Sending notifications using the Notification facade

```
use App\Notifications\WorkoutAvailable;
...
Notification::send($users, new WorkoutAvailable($workout));
```

Queueing Notifications

Most of the notification drivers need to send HTTP requests to send their notifications, which could slow down your user experience, so you probably want to queue your notifications. All notifications import the Queueable trait by default, so all you need to do is add implements ShouldQueue to your notification and Laravel will instantly move it to a queue.

As with any other queued features, you'll need to make sure you have your queue settings configured correctly and a queue worker running.

If you'd like to delay the delivery of your notifcation, you can run the delay() method on the notification:

```
$delayUntil = Carbon::now()->addMinutes(15);

$user->notify((new WorkoutAvailable($workout))->delay($delayUntil));
```

Out-of-the-Box Notification Types

Out of the box, Laravel comes with notification drivers for email, database, broadcast, Nexmo SMS, and Slack. I'll cover each briefly, but I'd recommend referring to the docs (*https://laravel.com/docs/notifications*) for more thorough introductions to each.

It's also easy to create your own notification drivers, and dozens of people already have; you can find them at Laravel Notification Channels website (*http://laravel-notification-channels.com/*).

Email notifications

Let's take a look at how the email from our earlier example, Example 15-11, is built:

```
public function toMail($notifiable)
{
    return (new MailMessage)
        ->line('You have a new workout available!')
        ->action('Check it out now', route('workout', [$this->workout]))
        ->line('Thank you for training with us!');
}
```

The result is shown in Figure 15-1. The email notification system puts your application's name in the header of the email; you can customize that app name in the name key of *config/app.php*.

This email is automatically sent to the email property on the notifiable, but you can customize this behavior by adding a method to your notifiable class named routeNotificationForMail() that returns the email address you'd like email notifications sent to.

The email's subject is set by parsing the notification class name and converting it to words. So, our WorkoutAvailable notification would have the default subject of Work out Available. We can also customize this by chaining the subject() method on our MailMessage in the toMail() method.

If you want to modify the templates, publish them and edit to your heart's content:

```
php artisan vendor:publish --tag=laravel-notifications
```

You can also change the style of the default template to be an "error" message, which uses a bit of different language and changes the primary button color to red. Just add a call to the error() method to your MailMessage call chain in the toMail() method.

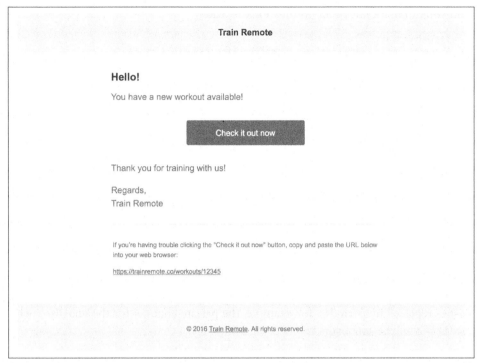

Figure 15-1. An email sent with the default notification template

Database notifications

You can send notifications to a database table using the `database` notification channel. First, create your table with `php artisan notifications:table`. Next, create a `toDatabase()` method on your notification and return an array of data there. This data will be encoded as JSON and stored in the database table's `data` column.

The `Notifiable` trait adds a `notifications` relationship to any model it's imported in, allowing you to easily access records in the notifications table. So if you're using database notifications, you could so something like this:

```
User::first()->notifications->each(function ($notification) {
    // do something
});
```

The `database` notification channel also has the concept of whether or not a notification is "read." You can scope to only the "unread" notifications:

```
User::first()->unreadNotifications->each(function ($notification) {
    // do something
});
```

And you can mark one or all notifications as read:

```
// Individual
User::first()->notifications->each(function ($notification) {
    if ($condition) {
        $notification->markAsRead();
    }
});

// All
User::first()->unreadNotifications->markAsRead();
```

Broadcast notifications

The `broadcast` channel sends notifications out using Laravel's event broadcasting features (Echo).

Create a `toBroadcast()` method on your notification and return array of data, and if your app is correctly configured for event broadcasting, that data will be broadcast on a private channel named `{notifiable}.{id}`. The `{id}` will be the ID of the notifiable, and `{notifiable}` will be the notifiable's fully qualified class name, with the slashes replaced by periods—for example, the private channel for the `App\User` with the ID of 1 will be `App.User.1`.

SMS notifications

SMS notifications are sent via Nexmo, so if you want to send SMS notifications, sign up for a Nexmo account and follow the instructions in the docs (*https://laravel.com/ docs/notifications*). Like with the other channels, you'll be setting up a `toNexmo()` method and customizing the SMS message there.

Slack notifications

The `slack` notification channel allows you to customize the appearance of your notifications and even attach files to your notifications. Like with the other channels, you'll set up a `toSlack()` method and customize the message there.

Testing

Let's take a look at how to test mail and notifications.

Mail

There are two options for testing mail in Laravel. If you're using the traditional mail syntax, I'd recommend using a tool called MailThief (*https://github.com/tightenco/ mailthief*), which Adam Wathan wrote for Tighten. Once you bring MailThief into your application with Composer, you can use `MailThief::hijack()` in your tests to make MailThief capture any calls to the `Mail` facade or any mailer classes.

MailThief then makes it possible to make assertions against the senders, recipients, CC and BCC values, and even content and attachments of your mail. Take a look at the GitHub repo to learn more, or bring it into your app:

```
composer require tightenco/mailthief --dev
```

If you are using mailables, there's a simple syntax for writing assertions against your sent mail (Example 15-16).

Example 15-16. Asserting against mailables

```
public function test_signup_triggers_welcome_email()
{
    ...

    Mail::assertSent(WelcomeEmail::class, function ($e) {
        return $e->subject == 'Welcome!';
    });

    // You can also use assertSentTo() to explicitly test the recipients
}
```

Notifications

Laravel provides a built-in set of assertions for testing your notifications. Example 15-17 demonstrates.

Example 15-17. Asserting notifications were sent

```
public function test_new_signups_triggers_admin_notification()
{
    ...

    Notification::assertSentTo($user, NewUsersSignedup::class,
        function ($n, $channels) {
            return $n->user->email == 'user-who-signed-up@gmail.com'
            && $channels == ['mail'];
    });

    // You can also use assertNotSentTo()
}
```

TL;DR

Laravel's mail and notification features provide simple, consistent interfaces to a variety of messaging systems. Laravel's mail system uses "mailables," PHP classes that represent emails, to provide a consistent syntax to different mail drivers. The notification system makes it easy to build a single notification that can be delivered in many different media—from emails to SMS messages to physical postcards.

## CHAPTER 16

Queues, Jobs, Events, Broadcasting, and the Scheduler

So far we've covered some of the most common structures that power web applications: databases, mail, filesystems, and more. Each of these are common across a majority of applications and frameworks.

Laravel also provides facilities for some less common architecture patterns and application structures. In this chapter we'll cover Laravel's tools for implementing queues, queued jobs, events, and WebSocket event publishing. We'll also cover Laravel's scheduler, which makes cron a thing of the past.

Queues

To understand what a queue is, just think about the idea of "queueing up" in a line at the bank. Even if there are multiple lines—queues—only one person is being served at a time from each queue, and each person will eventually reach the front and be served. In some banks, it's a strict first-in-first-out sort of policy, but in other banks, there's not an exact guarantee that someone won't cut ahead of you in line at some point. Essentially, someone can get added to the queue, be removed from the queue prematurely, or be successfully "processed" and then removed. Someone might even hit the front of the queue, not be able to be served correctly, return to the queue for a time, and then be processed again.

Queues in programming are very similar. Your application adds a "job" to a queue, which is a chunk of code that tells the application how to perform a particular behavior. Then some other separate application structure, usually a "queue worker," takes the responsibility for pulling jobs off of the queue one at a time and performing the appropriate behavior. Queue workers can delete the jobs, return them to the queue with a delay, or mark them as successfully processed.

Laravel makes it easy to serve your queues using Redis, *beanstalkd*, Amazon's SQS (Simple Queue Service), or a database table. You can also choose the `sync` driver to have the jobs run right in your application without actually being queued, or the `null` driver for jobs to just be discarded; these two are usually used in local development or testing environments.

Why Queues?

Queues make it easy to remove a costly or slow process from any synchronous call. The most common example is sending mail—doing so can be slow, and you don't want your users to have to wait for mail to send in response to their actions. Instead, trigger a "send mail" queued job and let the users get on with their day. Sometimes you may not just want to save your users time, but you might have a process like a cron job or a webhook that has a lot of work to process; rather than letting it all run at once (and potentially time out), you may choose to queue its individual pieces and let the queue worker process them one at a time.

Additionally, if you have some heavy processing that's more than your server can handle, you can spin up more than one queue worker to work through your queue faster than your normal application server could on its own.

Basic Queue Configuration

Like many other Laravel features that abstract multiple providers, queues have their own dedicated config file (*config/queue.php*) that allows you to set up multiple drivers and define which will be the default. This is also where you'll store your SQS, Redis, or *beanstalkd* authentication information.

Simple beanstalkd queues on Laravel Forge

We haven't covered Laravel Forge (*http://forge.laravel.com/*) in much depth, but it's a hosting service provided by Taylor Otwell, the creator of Laravel. Every server you create has *beanstalkd* configured automatically, so if you visit any site's Forge console, you can just go to the Queue Workers tab and hit Start Worker and you're ready to use *beanstalkd* as your queue driver; you can leave all the default settings, and no other work is necessary.

Queued Jobs

Remember our bank analogy? Each person in the bank "queue" (line) is, in programming terms, a job. This job could be shaped any way; it could just be a string, or an array, or an object. In Laravel, it's a collection of information containing the job name, the data payload, the number of attempts that have been made so far to process this job, and some other simple metadata.

But you don't need to worry about that in your interactions with Laravel. Laravel provides a structure called a Job, which is intended to encapsulate a single task—a behavior that your application can be commanded to do—and allow it to be added to and pulled from a queue. There are also simple helpers to make it easy to queue Artisan commands and mail.

Let's start with an example where, every time a user changes his plan with your SaaS app, you want to rerun some calculations about your overall profit.

Creating a job

As always, there's an Artisan command for that:

```
php artisan make:job CrunchReports
```

Take a look at Example 16-1 to see what you'll get.

Example 16-1. The default template for jobs in Laravel

```php
<?php

use Illuminate\Bus\Queueable;
use Illuminate\Queue\SerializesModels;
use Illuminate\Queue\InteractsWithQueue;
use Illuminate\Contracts\Queue\ShouldQueue;

class CrunchReports implements ShouldQueue
{
    use InteractsWithQueue, Queueable, SerializesModels;

    /**
     * Create a new job instance.
     *
     * @return void
     */
    public function __construct()
    {
        //
    }

    /**
     * Execute the job.
     *
     * @return void
     */
    public function handle()
    {
```

```
        //
    }
}
```

As you can see, this template imports the `Queueable`, `InteractsWithQueue`, and `SerializesModels` traits, and implements the `ShouldQueue` interface. Prior to Laravel 5.3, some of this functionality came in through the parent `App\Jobs` class.

We also get two methods from this template: the constructor, which you'll want to use to attach data to the job, and the `handle()` method, which is where the job's logic should reside (and is also the method signature you'll use to inject dependencies).

The traits and interface provide the class with the ability to be added to, and interact with, the queue. `Queueable` allows you to specify how Laravel should push this job to the queue; `InteractsWithQueue` allows each job, while being handled, to control its relationship with the queue, including deleting or requeueing itself; and `Serializes Models` gives the job the ability to serialize and deserialize Eloquent models.

Serializing models

The `SerializesModels` trait gives the jobs the ability to serialize injected models so that your job's `handle()` method will have access to them. However, because it's too difficult to reliably serialize an entire Eloquent object, the trait ensures that just the primary keys of any attached Eloquent objects are serialized when the job is pushed onto the queue. When the job is deserialized and handled, the trait pulls those Eloquent models fresh from the database by their primary key. This means that when your job runs it will be pulling a fresh instance of this model, not whatever state it was in when you queued the job.

Let's fill out the methods for our sample class, as in Example 16-2.

Example 16-2. An example job

```
...
use App\ReportGenerator;
use Illuminate\Log\Writer as Logger;

class CrunchReports implements ShouldQueue
{
    use InteractsWithQueue, SerializesModels;

    protected $user;

    public function __construct($user)
    {
```

```
        $this->user = $user;
    }

    public function handle(ReportGenerator $generator, Logger $logger)
    {
        $generator->generateReportsForUser($this->user);

        $logger->info('Generated reports.');
    }
}
```

We're expecting the User instance to be injected when we create the job, and then when it's handled we're typehinting a ReportGenerator class (which we presumably wrote) and a Logger (which Laravel provides). Laravel will read both typehints and inject those dependencies automatically.

Pushing a job onto a queue

There are two primary ways you can push a job onto a queue: the global dispatch() helper and the methods provided by the DispatchesJobs trait, which is imported by default in every controller.

With each, create an instance of your job, attach any necessary data by passing it to the constructor, and pass it to the dispatch() method (see Example 16-3).

Example 16-3. Dispatching jobs

```
// In a controller
public function index()
{
    $user = auth()->user();
    $this->dispatch(new \App\Jobs\CrunchReports($user));
}

// Elsewhere
dispatch(new \App\Jobs\CrunchReports($user));
```

There are three settings you can control in order to customize exactly how you dispatch a job: the connection, the queue, and the delay.

Customizing the connection. If you ever have multiple queue connections in place at once, you can customize the connection by running onConnection() on your instantiated job:

```
dispatch((new DoThingJob)->onConnection('redis'));
```

Customizing the queue. Within queue servers, you can specify which named queue you're pushing a job onto. For example, you may differentiate your queues based on their importance, naming one `low` and one `high`.

You can customize which queue you're pushing a job onto with the `onQueue()` method:

```
dispatch((new DoThingJob)->onQueue('high'));
```

Customizing the delay. You can customize the amount of time your queue workers should wait before processing a job with the `delay()` method, which accepts an integer representing the number of seconds to delay a job:

```
// Delays one minute before releasing the job to queue workers
dispatch((new DoThingJob)->delay(60));
```

Note that Amazon SQS doesn't allow delays longer than 15 minutes.

Running a Queue Worker

So what is a queue worker, and how does it work? In Laravel, it's an Artisan command that stays running forever (until it's stopped manually) and takes the responsibility for pulling down jobs from your queue and running them:

```
php artisan queue:work
```

This command starts a daemon "listening" to your queue; every time there are jobs on the queue, it will pull down the first job, handle it, delete it, and move on to the next. If at any point there are no jobs, it "sleeps" for a configurable amount of time before checking again to see if there are any more jobs.

You can define how many seconds a job should be able to run before the queue listener stops it (`--timeout`), how many seconds the listener should "sleep" when there are no jobs left (`--sleep`), how many tries each job should be allowed before being deleted (`--tries`), which connection the worker should listen to (the first parameter after `queue:work`), and which queues it should listen to (`--queue=`):

```
php artisan queue:work redis --timeout=60 --sleep=15 --tries=3
--queue=high,medium
```

You can also process just a single job with `php artisan queue:work`.

Handling Errors

So, what happens when something goes wrong with your job when it's in the middle of processing?

Exceptions in handling

If an exception is thrown, the queue listener will release that job back onto the queue. That job will be rereleased to be processed again and again until it is able to finish successfully or until it has been attempted the maximum number of times allowed by your queue listener.

Limiting the number of tries

The maximum number of tries is defined by the `--tries` switch passed to the `queue:listen` or `queue:work` Artisan commands.

The danger of infinite retries

If you don't set `--tries`, or if you set it to 0, the queue listener will allow for infinite retries. That means if there are any circumstances in which a job could just *never* be satisfied—for example, if it relies on a tweet that has since been deleted—your app will slowly crawl to a halt as it forever retries uncompletable jobs.

The documentation and Laravel Forge both show 3 as the default starting point for the maximum number of retries. So, in case of confusion, start there and adjust:

```
php artisan queue:listen --tries=3
```

If at any point you'd like to check how many times a job has been attempted already, use the `attempts()` method on the job itself, as in Example 16-4.

Example 16-4. Checking how many times a job has already been tried

```
public function handle()
{
    ...
    if ($this->attempts() > 3) {
        //
    }
}
```

Handling failed jobs

Once a job has exceeded its allowable number of retries, it's considered a "failed" job. Before you do anything else—even if all you want to do is limit the number of times a job can be tried—you'll need to create the "failed jobs" database table.

There's an Artisan command to create the migration (and you'll then want to migrate):

```
php artisan queue:failed-table
php artisan migrate
```

Any job that has surpassed its maximum number of allowed attempts will be dumped there. But there are quite a few things you can do with your failed jobs.

First, you can define a `failed()` method on the job itself, which will run when that job fails (see Example 16-5).

Example 16-5. Defining a method to run when a job fails

```
...
class CrunchReports implements ShouldQueue
{
    ...

    public function failed()
    {
        // Do whatever you want
    }
}
```

Next, you can register a global handler for failed jobs. Somewhere in the application's bootstrap—if you don't know where to put it, just put it in the `boot()` method of `AppServiceProvider`—place the code in Example 16-6 code to define a listener.

Example 16-6. Registering a global handler to handle failed jobs

```
// Some service provider
use Illuminate\Support\Facades\Queue;
...
    public function boot()
    {
        Queue::failing(function ($connection, $job, $data) {
            // Do whatever you want
        });
    }
```

There is also a suite of Artisan tools for interacting with the failed jobs table.

`queue:failed` shows you a list of your failed jobs:

```
php artisan queue:failed
```

The list will look something like this:

```
+----+------------+---------+---------------------+---------------------+
| ID | Connection | Queue   | Class               | Failed At           |
+----+------------+---------+---------------------+---------------------+
| 9  | database   | default | App/Jobs/AlwaysFails | 2016-01-26 03:42:55 |
+----+------------+---------+---------------------+---------------------+
```

From there, you can grab the ID of any individual failed job and retry it with `queue:retry`:

```
php artisan queue:retry 9
```

If you'd rather retry all of the jobs, pass `all` instead of an ID:

```
php artisan queue:retry all
```

You can delete an individual failed job with `queue:forget`:

```
php artisan queue:forget 5
```

And you can delete all of your failed jobs with `queue:flush`:

```
php artisan queue:flush
```

Controlling the Queue

Sometimes, from within the handling of a job, you'll want to add conditions that will potentially either release the job to be restarted later or delete the job forever.

To release a job back into the queue, use the `release()` command, as in Example 16-7.

Example 16-7. Releasing a job back onto the queue

```
public function handle()
{
    ...
    if (condition) {
        $this->release($numberOfSecondsToDelayBeforeRetrying);
    }
}
```

If you want to delete a job during its handling, you can just `return` at any point, as seen in Example 16-8; that's the signal to the queue that the job was handled appropriately and should not be returned to the queue.

Example 16-8. Deleting a job

```
public function handle()
{
    ...
```

```
    if ($jobShouldBeDeleted) {
        return;
    }
}
```

Queues Supporting Other Functions

The primary use for queues is to push jobs onto, but you can also queue mail using the `Mail::queue` functionality. You can learn more about this in "queue()" on page 343. You can also queue Artisan commands, which we covered in Chapter 7.

Events

With jobs, the calling code informs the application that it should *do something*: `CrunchReports`, or `NotifyAdminOfNewSignup`.

With an event, the calling code instead informs the application that *something happened*: `UserSubscribed`, or `UserSignedUp`, or `ContactWasAdded`. Events are notifications that something has taken place.

Some of these events may be "fired" by the framework itself. For example, Eloquent models fire events when they are saved, or created, or deleted. But some events are also manually triggered by the application's code.

An event being fired doesn't do anything on its own. However, you can bind event listeners, whose sole purpose is to listen for the broadcasting of specific events and to act in response. Any event can have anywhere from zero to many event listeners.

Laravel's events are structured like the observer, or "pub/sub," pattern. Many events are fired out into the application; some may never be listened for, and others may have a dozen listeners. The events don't know or care.

Firing an Event

There are three ways to fire an event. You can use the `Event` facade, inject the `Dispatcher`, or use the `event()` global helper:

```
Event::fire(new UserSubscribed($user, $plan));
// or
$dispatcher = app(Illuminate\Contracts\Events\Dispatcher);
$dispatcher->fire(new UserSubscribed($user, $plan));
// or
event(new UserSubscribed($user, $plan));
```

If in doubt, I'd recommend using the global helper function.

To create an event to fire, use the `make:event` Artisan command:

```
php artisan make:event UserSubscribed
```

That'll make a file that looks something like Example 16-9.

Example 16-9. The default template for a Laravel event

```php
<?php

namespace App\Events;

use Illuminate\Broadcasting\Channel;
use Illuminate\Queue\SerializesModels;
use Illuminate\Broadcasting\PrivateChannel;
use Illuminate\Broadcasting\PresenceChannel;
use Illuminate\Broadcasting\InteractsWithSockets;
use Illuminate\Contracts\Broadcasting\ShouldBroadcast;

class UserSubscribed
{
    use InteractsWithSockets, SerializesModels;

    /**
     * Create a new event instance.
     *
     * @return void
     */
    public function __construct()
    {
        //
    }

    /**
     * Get the channels the event should be broadcast on.
     *
     * @return Channel|array
     */
    public function broadcastOn()
    {
        return new PrivateChannel('channel-name');
    }
}
```

Let's take a look at what we get here. `SerializesModels` works just like with jobs; it allows you to accept Eloquent models as parameters. `InteractsWithSockets`, `Should Broadcast`, and the `broadcastOn()` method provide the backing functionality for broadcasting events using WebSockets, which we'll cover in a bit.

It might seem strange that there's no `handle()` or `fire()` method here. But remember, this object exists not to determine a particular action, but just to encapsulate some data. The first piece of data is its name; `UserSubscribed` tells us that a particular event happened (a user subscribed). The rest of the data is any data we pass into the constructor and associate with this entity.

Example 16-10 shows what we might want to do with our `UserSubscribed` event.

Example 16-10. Injecting data into an event

```
...
class UserSubscribed
{
    use InteractsWithSockets, SerializesModels;

    public $user;
    public $plan;

    public function __construct($user, $plan)
    {
        $this->user = $user;
        $this->plan = $plan;
    }
}
```

Now we have an object that appropriately represents the event that happened: `$event->user` subscribed to the `$event->plan` plan.

Listening for an Event

We have an event, and the ability to fire it. Now let's look at how to listen for it.

First, we'll create an event listener. Let's say we want to email the app's owner every time a new user subscribes:

```
php artisan make:listener EmailOwnerAboutSubscription --event=UserSubscribed
```

That gives us the file in Example 16-11.

Example 16-11. The default template for a Laravel event listener

```php
<?php

namespace App\Listeners;

use App\Events\UserSubscribed;
use Illuminate\Queue\InteractsWithQueue;
use Illuminate\Contracts\Queue\ShouldQueue;

class EmailOwnerAboutSubscription
{
    /**
     * Create the event listener.
     *
     * @return void
     */
    public function __construct()
```

```
    {
        //
    }

    /**
     * Handle the event.
     *
     * @param  UserSubscribed  $event
     * @return void
     */
    public function handle(UserSubscribed $event)
    {
        //
    }
}
```

This is where the action happens—where the handle() method lives. This method expects to be passed an event of type UserSubscribed and act in response to it.

So, let's make it send an email (Example 16-12).

Example 16-12. A sample event listener

```
...
use Illuminate\Contracts\Mail\Mailer;

class EmailOwnerAboutSubscription
{
    protected $mailer;

    public function __construct(Mailer $mailer)
    {
        $this->mailer = $mailer;
    }

    public function handle(UserSubscribed $event)
    {
        $this->mailer->send(
            new OwnerSubscriptionEmail($event->user, $event->plan)
        );
    }
}
```

Great! Now, one last task: we need to set this listener up to listen to the UserSubscri bed event. We'll set that up in the $listen property of the EventServiceProvider class (see Example 16-13).

Example 16-13. Binding listeners to events in EventServiceProvider

```php
class EventServiceProvider extends ServiceProvider
{
    protected $listen = [
        \App\Events\UserSubscribed::class => [
            \App\Listeners\EmailOwnerAboutSubscription::class,
        ],
    ];
```

As you can see, the key of each array entry is the class name of the event, and the value is an array of listener class names. We can add as many class names as we want under the UserSubscribed key and they will all listen and respond to each User Subscribed event.

Event subscribers

There's one more structure you can use to define the relationship between your events and their listeners. Laravel has a concept called an *event subscriber*, which is a class that contains a collection of methods that act as separate listeners to unique events, and also contains the mapping of which method should handle which event. In this case, it's easier to show than to tell; take a look at Example 16-14.

Example 16-14. A sample event subscriber

```php
<?php

namespace App\Listeners;

class UserEventSubscriber
{
    public function onUserSubscription($event)
    {
        // Handles the UserSubscribed event
    }

    public function onUserCancellation($event)
    {
        // Handles the UserCancelled event
    }

    public function subscribe($events)
    {
        $events->listen(
            \App\Events\UserSubscribed::class,
            'App\Listeners\UserEventSubscriber@onUserSubscription'
        );

        $events->listen(
            \App\Events\UserCancelled::class,
```

```
                    'App\Listeners\UserEventSubscriber@onUserCancellation'
        );
    }
}
```

Subscribers need to define a `subscribe()` method, which is passed an instance of the event dispatcher. We'll use that to pair events with their listeners, but in this case, those are methods on this class, instead of entire classes. As a refresher, any time you see an `@` inline like this means the class name is to the left of the `@` and the method name is to the right.

So, in Example 16-14, we're defining that the `onUserSubscription()` method of this subscriber will listen to any `UserSubscribed` events.

There's one last thing we need to do: in `App\Providers\EventServiceProvider`, we need to add our subscriber's class name to the `$subscribe` property, as seen in Example 16-15.

Example 16-15. Registering an event subscriber

```
...
class EventServiceProvider extends ServiceProvider
{
    ...
    protected $subscribe = [
        \App\Listeners\UserEventSubscriber::class
    ];
}
```

Broadcasting Events over WebSockets, and Laravel Echo

WebSocket (often called WebSockets) is a protocol, popularized by Pusher, that makes it simple to provide near-real-time communication between web devices. Rather than relying on information passing via HTTP requests, WebSockets libraries open a direct connection between the client and the server. WebSockets are behind tools like the chat boxes in Gmail and Facebook.

WebSockets work best with small pieces of data passed in a pub/sub structure—just like Laravel's events. Laravel has a built-in set of tools that make it easy to define that one or more of your events should be broadcast to a WebSocket server; this makes it easy, for example, to have a `MessageWasReceived` event that is published to the notifications box of a certain user or set of users, the instant a message arrives at your application.

Laravel Echo

Laravel also has a more powerful tool designed for more complex event broadcasting. If you need presence notification, or want to keep your rich frontend data model in sync with your Laravel app, check out Laravel Echo, which we'll cover toward the end of this chapter. Much of what comprises Echo is built into the Laravel core, which we cover in "Advanced Broadcasting Tools" on page 375, but some of it requires pulling in the external JavaScript Echo library, which we cover in "Laravel Echo (the JavaScript Side)" on page 378.

Configuration and Setup

Take a look at *config/broadcasting.php* to find the configuration settings for your event broadcasting. Laravel supports three drivers for broadcasting: Pusher, a paid SaaS offering; Redis, for locally run WebSocket servers; and log, for local development and debugging.

Queue listeners

In order for event broadcasting to move quickly, Laravel pushes the instruction to broadcast them onto a queue. That means you'll need to have a queue worker running (or use the sync queue driver for local development). See "Running a Queue Worker" on page 360 to learn how to run a queue worker.

Laravel suggests a default delay of three seconds before the queue worker looks for new jobs. However, with event broadcasting, you may notice some events take a second or two to broadcast. To speed this up, update your queue settings to only wait one second before looking for new jobs.

Broadcasting an Event

To broadcast an event, you need to mark that event as a broadcast event by having it implement the Illuminate\Contracts\Broadcasting\ShouldBroadcast interface. This interface requires you to add the broadcastOn() method, which will return an array of either strings or Channel objects, each representing a WebSocket channel.

The Structure of WebSocket events

Every event you send with WebSockets can have three primary characteristics: the name, the channel, and the data.

The *name* of an event might be something like user-was-subscribed, but Laravel's default is to use the fully qualified class name of the event; i.e., so something like App \Events\UserSubscribed. You can customize this by passing the name to the optional broadcastAs() method in your event class.

The *channel* is the way of describing *which* clients should receive this message. It's a very common pattern to have a channel for each user (e.g., users.1, users.2, etc.), and possibly a channel for all users (e.g., users), and maybe one for just users who are members of a certain account (accounts.1). If the channel you're targeting is a private channel, preface the channel name with private-, and if it's a presence channel, preface the channel name with presence-. So, a private Pusher channel named groups.5 should be, instead, private-groups.5. If you use Laravel's PrivateChannel and PresenceChannel objects in your broadcastOn() method, they'll take care of adding those prefaces to your channel names for you.

The *data* is a payload, usually JSON, of information relevant to the event—the message, maybe, or information about the user or plan that can be acted upon by the consuming JavaScript.

Example 16-16 shows our UserSubscribed event, modified to broadcast on two channels: one for the user (to confirm the user's subscription) and one for admins (to notify them of a new subscription).

Example 16-16. An event broadcasting on multiple channels

```
...
use Illuminate\Contracts\Broadcasting\ShouldBroadcast;

class UserSubscribed extends Event implements ShouldBroadcast
{
    use InteractsWithSockets, SerializesModels;

    public $user;
    public $plan;

    public function __construct($user, $plan)
    {
        $this->user = $user;
        $this->plan = $plan;
    }
```

```
public function broadcastOn()
{
    // String syntax
    return [
        'users.' . $this->user->id,
        'admins'
    ];

    // Channel object syntax
    return [
        new Channel('users.' . $this->user->id),
        new Channel('admins'),
        // If it were a private channel: new PrivateChannel('admins'),
        // If it were a presence channel: new PresenceChannel('admins'),
    ];
}
}
```

By default, any public properties of your event will be serialized as JSON and sent along as the data of your broadcast event. That means the data of one of our broadcast `UserSubscribed` events might look like Example 16-17.

Example 16-17. Sample broadcast event data

```
{
    'user': {
        'id': 5,
        'name': 'Fred McFeely',
        ...
    },
    'plan': 'silver'
}
```

You can override this by returning an array of data from the `broadcastWith()` method on your event, as in Example 16-18.

Example 16-18. Customizing the broadcast event data

```
public function broadcastWith()
{
    return [
        'userId' => $this->user->id,
        'plan' => $this->plan
    ];
}
```

Finally, you can customize which queue your event is pushed onto with its `onQueue()` method, as in Example 16-19. You may choose to do this so you can keep other queue items from slowing down your event broadcast; real-time WebSockets aren't much fun if a long-running job that's higher in the queue keeps the events from going out in time.

Example 16-19. Specifying the queue a job should run on

```
public function onQueue()
{
    return 'websockets-for-faster-processing'
}
```

Receiving the Message

If you choose to host your own Redis WebSockets server, the Laravel docs (*http://bit.ly/2f5lmce*) have a great walkthrough on how to set that up using socket.io and ioredis.

However, it's much more common to use Pusher (*https://pusher.com/*). Plans over a certain size cost money, but there's a generous free plan. Pusher makes it incredibly simple to set up a simple WebSocket server, and its JavaScript SDK handles all of the authentication and channel management with almost no work on your part. SDKs are available for iOS, Android, and many more platforms, languages, and frameworks.

To Echo or not to Echo?

The next section covers how to write a JavaScript frontend to interact with Laravel over WebSockets both with and without Echo. It's helpful to understand how to do this without Echo even if you choose to use it in the end, but because much of the code here is not necessary if you use Echo, I'd recommend reading the following section, then the Echo section, "Laravel Echo (the JavaScript Side)" on page 378, before you start implementing any of it; you can decide which way you prefer and then write your code from there.

To get started, pull in Pusher's library, get an API key from your Pusher account, and subscribe to any events on any channels with code like that in Example 16-20.

Example 16-20. Basic usage of Pusher JS

```
...
<script src="https://js.pusher.com/3.1/pusher.min.js"></script>
<script>
// Globally, perhaps; just a sample of how to get data in
var App = {
    'userId': 5,
    'pusherKey': 'your-pusher-api-key-here'
```

```
};

// Locally
var pusher = new Pusher(App.pusherKey);

var pusherChannel = pusher.subscribe('users.' + App.userId);

pusherChannel.bind('App\\Events\\UserSubscribed', (data) => {
    console.log(data.user, data.plan);
});
</script>
```

Escaping backslashes in JavaScript

Since \ is a control character in JavaScript, you need to write \\ to represent a backslash in your strings, which is why there are two backslashes between each namespace segment in Example 16-20.

To publish to Pusher from Laravel, get your Pusher key, secret, and app ID from your Pusher account dashboard, and then set them in your *.env* file under the keys PUSHER_KEY, PUSHER_SECRET, and PUSHER_APP_ID.

If you serve your app, visit a page with the JavaScript from Example 16-20 embedded in it in one window, push a broadcast event in another window or from your terminal, have a queue listener running or are using the sync driver, and all of your authentication information is set up correctly, you should see event logs popping up in your JavaScript window's console in near real time.

With this power, it's now easy for you to keep your users up-to-date with what's happening with their data any time they're in your app. You can notify users of the actions of other users, of long-running processes that have just finished, or of your application's responses to external actions like incoming emails or webhooks. The possibilities are endless.

Requirements

If you want to broadcast with Pusher or Redis, you'll need to bring in these dependencies:

- Pusher: pusher/pusher-php-server:~2.0
- Redis: predis/predis:~1.0

Advanced Broadcasting Tools

Laravel has a few more tools to make it possible to perform more complex interactions in event broadcasting. These tools, a combination of framework features and a JavaScript library, are called *Laravel Echo*.

These framework features work best when you use Laravel Echo in your JavaScript frontend (which we'll cover in "Laravel Echo (the JavaScript Side)" on page 378), but you can still enjoy some of the benefits of Echo without using the JavaScript components. Echo will work with both Pusher and Redis, but I'm going to use Pusher for any examples.

Excluding the current user from broadcast events

Every connection to Pusher is assigned a unique "socket ID" identifying that socket connection. And it's easy to define that any given socket (user) should be excluded from receiving a specified broadcast event.

This feature makes it possible to define that certain events should not be broadcast to the user who fired them. Let's say every user in a team gets notified when other users create a task; would you want to be notified of a task you just created? No, and that's why we have the `toOthers()` method.

To implement this, there are two steps to follow. First, you need to set up your JavaScript to send a certain `POST` to `/broadcasting/socket` when your WebSocket connection is initialized. This attaches your `socket_id` to your Laravel session. Echo does this for you, but you can also do it manually—take a look at the Echo source (*https://github.com/laravel/echo/*) to see how it works.

Next, you'll want to update every request that your JavaScript makes to have an `X-Socket-ID` header that contains that `socket_id`. Example 16-21 shows how to do that in Vue or jQuery.

Example 16-21. Sending the socket ID along with each Ajax request in Vue or jQuery

```
// Run this right after you initialize echo
// Vue
Vue.http.interceptors.push((request, next) => {
    request.headers['X-Socket-Id'] = Echo.socketId();

    next();
});

// jQuery
$.ajaxSetup({
    headers: {
        'X-Socket-Id': Echo.socketId()
```

```
    }
});
```

Once you've handled this, you can exclude any event from being broadcast to the user who triggered it by using the broadcast() global helper instead of the event() global helper and then chaining toOthers() after it:

```
broadcast(new UserSubscribed($user, $plan))->toOthers();
```

The broadcast service provider

All of the other features that Echo provides require your JavaScript to authenticate with the server. Take a look at App\Providers\BroadcastServiceProvider, where you'll define how to authorize users' access to your private and presence channels.

The two primary actions you can take are to define the middleware that will be used on your broadcasting auth routes, and to define the authorization settings for your channels.

If you're going to use these features, you'll need to uncomment the App\Providers \BroadcastServiceProvider::class line in *config/app.php*.

And if you'll be using these features *without* Laravel Echo, you'll either need to manually handle sending CSRF tokens along with your authentication requests, or exclude /broadcasting/auth and /broadcasting/socket from CSRF protection by adding them to the $except property of the VerifyCsrfToken middleware.

Binding authorization definitions for WebSocket channels. Private and presence Web-Socket channels need to be able to ping your application to learn whether the current user is authorized for that channel. You'll use the Broadcast::channel() method to define the rules for this authorization.

Public, private, and presence channels

There are three types of channels in WebSockets: public, private, and presence.

Public channels can be subscribed to by any user, authenticated or not.

Private channels require the end user's JavaScript to authenticate against the application to prove that the user is both authenticated and authorized to join this channel.

Presence channels are a type of private channel, but instead of allowing for message passing, they simply keep track of which users join and leave the channel, and make this information available to the application's frontend.

`Broadcast::channel()` takes two parameters: first, a string representing the channel(s) you want it to match, and second, a closure that defines how to authorize users for any channel matching that string. The closure will be passed an Eloquent model of the current user as its first parameter, and any matched * segments as additional parameters. For example, a channel authorization definition with a string of `teams.*`, when matched against the channel `teams.5`, will pass its closure `$user` as the first parameter and 5 as the second parameter.

If you're defining the rules for a private channel, your `Broadcast::channel()` closure will need to return a boolean: is this user authorized for this channel or not? If you're defining the rules for a presence channel, your closure should return an array of data you want available to the presence channel for any users that you want to show up in the channel. Example 16-22 illustrates defining rules for both kinds of channel.

Example 16-22. Defining authorization rules for private and presence WebSocket channels

```
...
class BroadcastServiceProvider extends ServiceProvider
{
    public function boot()
    {
        ...

        // Define how to authenticate a private channel
        Broadcast::channel('teams.*', function ($user, $teamId) {
            return $user->team_id == $teamId;
        });

        // Define how to authenticate a presence channel; return any data
        // you want the app to have about the user in the channel
        Broadcast::channel('rooms.*', function ($user, $roomId) {
            if ($user->rooms->contains($roomId)) {
                return [
                    'name' => $user->name
                ];
            }
        });
```

You might be wondering how this information gets from your Laravel application to your JavaScript frontend. Pusher's JavaScript library sends a `POST` to your application; by default it will hit `/pusher/auth`, but you can customize that (and Echo customizes it for you) to hit Laravel's authentication route, `/broadcasting/auth`:

```
var pusher = new Pusher(App.pusherKey, {
    authEndpoint: '/broadcasting/auth'
});
```

Example 16-23 shows how we can tweak Example 16-20 for private and presence channels, *without* Echo's frontend components.

Example 16-23. Basic usage of Pusher JS for private and presence channels

```
...
<script src="https://js.pusher.com/3.1/pusher.min.js"></script>
<script>
    // Globally, perhaps; just a sample of how to get data in
    var App = {
        'userId': {{ auth()->user()->id }},
        'pusherKey': 'your pusher key here'
    };

    // Locally
    var pusher = new Pusher(App.pusherKey, {
        authEndpoint: '/broadcasting/auth'
    });

    // Private channel
    var privateChannel = pusher.subscribe('private-teams.1');

    privateChannel.bind('App\\Events\\UserSubscribed', (data) => {
        console.log(data.user, data.plan);
    });

    // Presence channel
    var presenceChannel = pusher.subscribe('presence-rooms.5');

    console.log(presenceChannel.members);
</script>
```

We now have the ability to send WebSocket messages to users depending on whether they pass a given channel's authorization rules. We can also keep track of which users are active in a particular group or section of the site, and display relevant information to each user about other users in the same group.

Laravel Echo (the JavaScript Side)

Laravel Echo is comprised of two pieces: the advanced framework features we just covered, and a JavaScript package that takes advantage of those features and drastically reduces the amount of boilerplate code you need to write powerful WebSocket-based frontends. The Echo JavaScript package makes it easy to handle authentication, authorization, and subscribing to private and presence channels. Echo can be used with the SDKs for either Pusher JS (for Pusher) or socket.io (for Redis).

Bringing Echo into your project

To use Echo in your project's JavaScript, add it to *package.json* using `npm install --save` (be sure to bring in the appropriate Pusher or socket.io SDK as well):

```
npm install pusher-js --save
npm install laravel-echo --save
```

Let's assume you have a basic Gulp file running your *app.js* file through Webpack, like in Example 16-24.

Example 16-24. Compiling app.js through Webpack

```
const elixir = require('laravel-elixir');

elixir(mix => {
    mix.webpack('app.js');
});
```

Now, create a basic *resources/assets/js/app.js* file (Example 16-25) to bring in your dependencies and initialize Echo.

Example 16-25. Initializing Echo in app.js

```
import Echo from "laravel-echo"

window.Echo = new Echo({
    broadcaster: 'pusher',
    key: 'your-pusher-key'
});

// Add your Echo bindings here
```

For CSRF protection, you'll also need to add a `csrf-token` `<meta>` tag to your HTML template:

```
<meta name="csrf-token" content="{{ csrf_token() }}">
```

And, of course, remember to link to your compiled *app.js* in your HTML template:

```
<script src="/js/app.js"></script>
```

Now we're ready to get started.

Using Echo for basic event broadcasting

This is nothing different from what we've already used Pusher JS for, but Example 16-26 is a simple code sample to show how to use Echo to listen to public channels for basic event information.

Example 16-26. Listening to a public channel with Echo

```
var currentTeamId = 5; // Likely set elsewhere

Echo.channel('teams.' + currentTeamId)
    .listen('UserSubscribed', (data) => {
        console.log(data);
    });
```

Echo provides a few methods for subscribing to various types of channels; `channel()` will subscribe you to a public channel. Note that when you listen to an event with Echo, you can ignore the full event namespace and just listen for the unique name of this event. And now we now have access to the public data that's passed along with our event.

We can also chain `listen()` handlers, as in Example 16-27.

Example 16-27. Chaining event listeners in Echo

```
Echo.channel('teams.' + currentTeamId)
    .listen('UserSubscribed', (data) => {
        console.log(data);
    })
    .listen('UserCanceled', (data) => {
        console.log(data);
    });
```

Remember to compile and include!

Did you try these code samples and not see anything change in your browser? Make sure to run `gulp` (if you're running it once) or `gulp watch` (to run a listener) to compile your code. And, if you haven't yet, be sure to actually include *app.js* in your template somewhere.

Private channels and basic authentication

Echo also has a method for subscribing to private channels: `private()`. It works the same as `channel()`, but it requires you to have set up channel authorization definitions in `BroadcastServiceProvider`, like we covered earlier. Additionally, unlike with the SDKs, you don't need to put `private-` in front of your channel name.

Example 16-28 shows what it looks like to listen to a private channel named `private-teams.5`.

Example 16-28. Listening to a private channel with Echo

```
var currentTeamId = 5; // Likely set elsewhere

Echo.private('teams.' + currentTeamId)
    .listen('UserSubscribed', (data) => {
        console.log(data);
    });
```

Presence channels

Echo makes it much simpler to join and listen to events in presence channels. This time you'll want to use the join() method to bind to this channel, as in Example 16-29.

Example 16-29. Joining a presence of channel

```
var currentTeamId = 5; // Likely set elsewhere

Echo.join('teams.' + currentTeamId)
    .here((members) => {
        console.log(members);
    });
```

join() subscribes to the presence channel, and here() allows you to define the behavior when the user joins and also when any other users join or leave the presence channel.

You can think of a presence channel like a "who's online" sidebar in a chat room. When you first join a presence channel, your here() callback will be called and provided a list of all the members at that time. And any time any members join or leave, that callback will be called again with the updated list. There's no messaging happening here, but you can play sounds, update the on-page list of members, or do whatever else you want in response to these actions.

There are also specific methods for individual events, which you can use individually or chained (see Example 16-30).

Example 16-30. Listening for specific presence events

```
var currentTeamId = 5; // Likely set elsewhere

Echo.join('teams.' + currentTeamId)
    .then((members) => {
        // runs when you join
        console.table(members);
    })
    .joining((joiningMember, members) => {
        // runs when another member joins
```

```
        console.table(joiningMember);
    })
    .leaving((leavingMember, members) => {
        // runs when another member leaves
        console.table(leavingMember);
    });
```

Excluding the current user

We covered this previously in the chapter, but if you want to exclude the current user, use the broadcast() global helper instead of the event() global helper and then chain the toOthers() method after your broadcast call.

As you can see, the Echo JavaScript library doesn't do anything you couldn't do on your own—but it makes a lot of common tasks much simpler, and provides a cleaner, more expressive syntax for common WebSocket tasks.

Subscribing to notifications with Echo

Laravel's notifications come with a broadcast driver out of the box that pushes notifications out as broadcast events. You can subscribe to these notifications with Echo using Echo.notification, as in Example 16-31.

Example 16-31. Subscribing to a notification with Echo

```
Echo.private('App.User.' + userId)
    .notification((notification) => {
        console.log(notification.type);
    });
```

Scheduler

If you've ever written a cron job before, you likely already wish for a better tool. Not only is the syntax onerous and frustratingly difficult to remember, but it's one significant aspect of your application that can't be stored in version control.

Laravel's scheduler makes handling scheduled tasks simple. You'll write your scheduled tasks in code, and then point one cron job at your app: once per minute, run php artisan schedule:run. Every time this Artisan command is run, Laravel checks your schedule definitions to find out if any scheduled tasks should run.

Here's the cron job to define that command:

```
* * * * * php /home/myapp.com/artisan schedule:run >> /dev/null 2>&1
```

There are many task types you can schedule and many time frames you can use to schedule them.

---

app/Console/Kernel.php has a method named `$schedule`, which is where you'll define any tasks you'd like to schedule.

Available Task Types

First, let's take a look at the simplest option: a closure, run every minute (Example 16-32). That means that, every time the cron job hits the `schedule:run` command, it will call this closure.

Example 16-32. Scheduling a closure to run once every minute

```
// app/Consoles/Kernel.php
public function schedule($schedule)
{
    $schedule->call(function () {
        dispatch(new CalculateTotals);
    })->everyMinute();
}
```

There are two other types of tasks you can schedule: Artisan and shell commands.

You can schedule Artisan commands by passing their syntax exactly as you would call them from the command line:

```
$schedule->command('scores:tally --reset-cache')->everyMinute();
```

And you can run any shell commands that you could run with PHP's `exec()` method:

```
$schedule->exec('/home/myapp.com/bin/build.sh')->everyMinute();
```

Available Time Frames

The beauty of the scheduler isn't just that you can define your tasks in code; it's that you can schedule them in code, too. Laravel keeps track of time passing and evaluates whether it's time for any given task to run. That's easy with `everyMinute()` because the answer is always simple: run the task. But Laravel keeps the rest simple for you, too, even for the most complex of requests.

Let's take a look at your options by starting with a monstrous definition that's simple in Laravel:

```
$schedule->call(function () {
    // Runs once a week on Sunday at 23:50
})->weekly()->sundays()->at('23:50');
```

Notice that we can chain times together: we can define frequency and specify the day of the week and the time, and of course we can do so much more.

Table 16-1 shows a list of potential date/time modifiers for use when scheduling a job.

Table 16-1. Date/time modifiers for use with the scheduler

Command	Description
->timezone('America/Detroit')	Set the time zone for schedules
->cron('* * * * * *')	Define the schedule using the traditional cron notation
->everyMinute()	Run every minute
->everyFiveMinutes()	Run every 5 minutes
->everyTenMinutes()	Run every 10 minutes
->everyThirtyMinutes()	Run every 30 minutes
->hourly()	Run every hour
->daily()	Run every day at midnight
->dailyAt('14:00')	Run every day at 14:00
->twiceDaily(1, 14)	Run every day at 1:00 and 14:00
->weekly()	Run every week (midnight on Sunday)
->weeklyOn(5, '10:00')	Run every week on Friday at 10:00
->monthly()	Run every month (midnight on the 1st)
->monthlyOn(15, '23:00')	Run every month on the 15th at 23:00
->quarterly()	Run every quarter (midnight on the 1st of January, April, July, and October)
->yearly()	Run every year (midnight on the 1st of January)
->when(closure)	Limit the task to when closure returns `true`
->skip(closure)	Limit the task to when closure returns `false`
->between('8:00', '12:00')	Limit the task to between the given times
->unlessBetween('8:00', '12:00')	Limit the task to any time except between the given times
->weekdays()	Limit to weekdays
->sundays()	Limit to Sundays
->mondays()	Limit to Mondays
->tuesdays()	Limit to Tuesdays
->wednesdays()	Limit to Wednesdays
->thursdays()	Limit to Thursdays
->fridays()	Limit to Fridays
->saturdays()	Limit to Saturdays

Most of these can be chained one after another, but of course, any combinations that don't make sense chained can't be chained.

Example 16-33 shows a few combinations you could consider.

Example 16-33. Some sample scheduled events

```
// Both run weekly on Sunday at 23:50
$schedule->command('do:thing')->weeklyOn(0, '23:50');
$schedule->command('do:thing')->weekly()->sundays()->at('23:50');

// Run once per hour, weekdays, 8am-5pm
$schedule->command('do:thing')->weekdays()->hourly()->when(function () {
    return date('H') >= 8 && date('H') <= 17;
});

// Run once per hour, weekdays, 8am-5pm using new Laravel 5.3 "between"
$schedule->command('do:thing')->weekdays()->hourly()->between('8:00', '17:00');

$schedule->command('do:thing')->everyThirtyMinutes()->skip(function () {
    return app('SkipDetector')->shouldSkip();
});
```

Blocking and Overlap

If you want to avoid your tasks overlapping each other—for example, if you have a task running every minute that may sometimes take longer than a minute to run—end the schedule chain with the `withoutOverlapping()` method. This method skips a task if the previous instance of that task is still running:

```
$schedule->command('do:thing')->everyMinute()->withoutOverlapping();
```

Handling Task Output

Sometimes the output from your scheduled task is important, whether for logging, notifications, or just ensuring that the task ran.

If you want to write the returned output of a task to a file, use `sendOutputTo()`:

```
$schedule->command('do:thing')->daily()->sendOutputTo($filePath);
```

If you want to append it to a file instead, use `appendOutputTo()`:

```
$schedule->command('do:thing')->daily()->appendOutputTo($filePath);
```

And if you want to email the output to a designated recipient, write it to a file first and then add `emailOutputTo()`:

```
$schedule->command('do:thing')
    ->daily()
    ->sendOutputTo($filePath)
    ->emailOutputTo('me@myapp.com');
```

Make sure that your email settings are configured correctly in Laravel's basic email configuration.

> **Closure scheduled events can't send output**
>
> The `sendOutputTo()`, `appendOutputTo()`, and `emailOutputTo()` methods only work for `command` scheduled tasks. You can't use them for closures, unfortunately.

You may also want to send some output to ensure that your tasks ran correctly. There are a few services that provide this sort of uptime monitoring, most significantly Laravel Envoyer (*https://envoyer.io*) (a zero-downtime deployment service that also provides cron uptime monitoring) and Dead Man's Snitch (*https://deadmanss nitch.com/*), a tool designed purely for monitoring cron job uptime.

These services don't expect something to be emailed to them, but rather expect an HTTP "ping," so Laravel makes that easy with `pingBefore()` and `thenPing()`:

```
$schedule->command('do:thing')
    ->daily()
    ->pingBefore($beforeUrl)
    ->thenPing($afterUrl);
```

If you want to use the ping features, you'll need to pull in Guzzle using Composer: `"guzzlehttp/guzzle":"~5.3|~6.0"`.

Task Hooks

Speaking of running something *before* and *after* your task, there are hooks for that, with `before()` and `after()`:

```
$schedule->command('do_thing')
    ->daily()
    ->before(function () {
        // Prepare
    })
    ->after(function () {
        // Cleanup
    });
```

Testing

Testing queued jobs (or anything else in the queue) is easy. In *phpunit.xml*, which is the configuration file for your tests, the `QUEUE_DRIVER` environment variable is set to `sync` by default. That means your tests will run your jobs or other queued tasks synchronously, directly in your code, without relying on a queue system of any sort. You can test them just like any other code.

However, if you'd just like to check that a job was fired, you can do that with the `expectsJobs()` method, as in Example 16-34.

Example 16-34. Asserting that a job of the specified class was dispatched

```
public function test_changing_number_of_subscriptions_crunches_reports()
{
    $this->expectsJobs(App\Jobs\CrunchReports::class);

    ...

}
```

Or, in Laravel 5.3 and later, you can assert against the specific job itself, as in Example 16-35.

Example 16-35. Using a closure to verify that a dispatched job meets given criteria

```
use Illuminate\
public function test_changing_subscriptions_triggers_crunch_job()
{
    ...

    Bus::assertDispatched(CrunchReports::class, function ($e) {
        return $e->subscriptions->contains(5);
    });

    // Also can use assertNotDispatched
}
```

To test that an event fired, you have three options. First, you can just test that the behavior you expected happened, without concerning yourself with the event itself.

Second, you can explicitly assert that the event fired, as in Example 16-36. This works in Laravel 5.2.

Example 16-36. Asserting that an event of the specified class was fired

```
public function test_usersubscribed_event_fires()
{
    $this->expectsEvents(App\Events\UserSubscribed::class);

    ...

}
```

Finally, you can run a test against the event that was fired, as in Example 16-37. This is new in Laravel 5.3.

Example 16-37. Using a closure to verify that a fired event meets given criteria

```
public function test_usersubscribed_event_fires()
{
    ...
```

```
        Event::assertFired(UserSubscribed::class, function ($e) {
            return $e->user->email = 'user-who-subscribed@mail.com';
        });

        // Also can use assertNotFired()
    }
```

Another common scenario is that you're testing code that incidentally fires events, and you want to disable the event listeners during that test. You can disable the event system with the withoutEvents() method, as in Example 16-38.

Example 16-38. Disabling event listeners during a test

```
public function test_something_subscription_related()
{
    $this->withoutEvents();

    ...
}
```

TL;DR

Queues allow you to separate chunks of your application's code from the synchronous flow of user interactions out to a list of commands to be processed by a "queue worker." This allows your users to resume interactions with your application while slower processes are handled asychronously in the background.

Jobs are classes that are structured with the intention of encapsulating a chunk of application behavior so that it can be pushed onto a queue.

Laravel's event system follows the pub/sub or observer pattern, allowing you to send out notifications of an event from one part of your application, and elsewhere bind listeners to those notifications to define what behavior should happen in response to them. Using WebSockets, events can also be broadcast to frontend clients.

Laravel's scheduler simplifies scheduling tasks. Point an every-minute cron job to php artisan schedule:run and then schedule your tasks with even the most complex of time requirements using the scheduler, and Laravel will handle all the timings for you.

## CHAPTER 17

Helpers and Collections

We've already covered many global functions throughout the book: little helpers that make it easier to perform common tasks, like `dispatch()` for Jobs, `event()` for Events, `app()` for dependency resolution, and many more. We also talked a bit about Laravel's collections, or arrays on steroids, in Chapter 8.

In this chapter we'll cover some of the more common and powerful helpers and some of the basics of programming with collections.

Helpers

You can find a full list of the helpers Laravel offers in the helpers docs (*https://lara vel.com/docs/helpers*), but we're going to cover a few of the most useful functions here.

Arrays

PHP's native array manipulation functions give you a lot of power, but sometimes there are common manipulations we want to make that require unwieldy loops and logic checks. Laravel's array helpers make a few common array manipulations much simpler:

`array_first($array, $closure, $default = null)`
> Returns the first array value that passes a test, defined in a closure. You can optionally set the default value as the third parameter:

```
$people = [
    [
        'email' => 'm@me.com',
        'name' => 'Malcolm Me'
    ],
    [
```

```
        'email' => 'j@jo.com',
        'name' => 'James Jo'
    ]
];

$value = array_first($people, function ($key, $person) {
    return $person['email'] == 'j@jo.com';
});
```

array_get(*$array, $key, $default = null*)

Makes it easy to get values out of an array, with two added benefits: it won't throw an error if you ask for a key that doesn't exist (and you can provide defaults with the third parameter), and you can use dot notation to traverse nested arrays. For example:

```
$array = ['owner' => ['address' => ['line1' => '123 Main St.']]];

$line1 = array_get($array, 'owner.address.line1', 'No address');
$line2 = array_get($array, 'owner.address.line2');
```

array_has(*$array, $key*)

Makes it easy to check whether an array has a particular value set using dot notation for traversing nested arrays:

```
$array = ['owner' => ['address' => ['line1' => '123 Main St.']]];

if (array_has($array, 'owner.address.line2')) {
    // Do stuff
}
```

array_pluck(*$array, $key, $indexKey*)

Returns an array of the values corresponding to the provided key:

```
$array = [
    ['owner' => ['id' => 4, 'name' => 'Tricia']],
    ['owner' => ['id' => 7, 'name' => 'Kimberly']],
];

$array = array_pluck($array, 'owner.name');

// Returns ['Tricia', 'Kimberly'];
```

If you want the returned array to be keyed by another value from the source array, you can pass that value's dot-notated reference as the third parameter:

```
$array = array_pluck($array, 'owner.name', 'owner.id');

// Returns [4 => 'Tricia', 7 => 'Kimberly'];
```

Strings

Just like with arrays, there are some string manipulations and checks that are possible with native PHP functions, but can be cumbersome. Laravel's helpers make a few common string operations faster and simpler:

e(*$string*)

An alias to htmlentities(); prepares a (often user-provided) string for safe echoing on an HTML page. For example:

```
e('<script>do something nefarious</script>');

// Returns &lt;script&gt;do something nefarious&lt;/script&gt;
```

starts_with(*$haystack, $needle*), ends_with(*$haystack, $needle*), *and*
str_contains(*$haystack, $needle*)

Return a boolean of whether the provided "haystack" string starts with, ends with, or contains the provided "needle" string:

```
if (starts_with($url, 'https')) {
    // Do something
}

if (ends_with($abstract, '...')) {
    // Do something
}

if (str_contains($description, '1337 h4x0r')) {
    // Run away
}
```

str_limit(*$string, $numCharacters, $concatenationString = '...'*)

Limits a string to the provided number of characters. If the string is less than the limit, just returns the string; if it's greater, trims to the number of characters provided and then appends either ... or the provided concatenation string. For example:

```
$abstract = str_limit($loremIpsum, 30);

// Returns "Lorem ipsum dolor sit amet, co..."

$abstract = str_limit($loremIpsum, 30, "&hellip;");

// Returns "Lorem ipsum dolor sit amet, co&hellip;"
```

str_is($pattern, $string)

Returns a boolean of whether or not a given string matches a given pattern. The pattern can be a regex pattern, or you can use asterisks to indicate wildcard positions:

```
str_is('*.dev', 'myapp.dev');          // true
str_is('*.dev', 'myapp.dev.co.uk');    // false
str_is('*dev*', 'myapp.dev');          // true
str_is('*myapp*', 'www.myapp.dev');    // true
str_is('my*app', 'myfantasticapp');    // true
str_is('my*app', 'myapp');             // true
```

How to pass a regex to str_is()

If you're curious about what regex patterns are acceptable to pass to str_is(), check out the function definition here (shortened for space) to see how it works. Note that it's an alias of Illuminate \Support\Str::is:

```
public function is($pattern, $value)
{
    if ($pattern == $value) return true;

    $pattern = preg_quote($pattern, '#');
    $pattern = str_replace('\*', '.*', $pattern);
    return (bool) preg_match(
        '#^' . $pattern . '\z#u',
        $value
    );
}
```

str_random($length)

Returns a random string of alphanumeric mixed-case characters of the length specified:

```
$hash = str_random(64);
```

```
// Sample: J40uNWAvY60wE4BPEWxu7BZFQEmxEHmGiLmQncj0ThMGJK705Kfgptyb9ulwspmh
```

str_slug($string, $separator = '-')

Returns a URL-friendly slug from a string—often used for creating a URL segment for a name or title:

```
str_slug('How to Win Friends and Influence People');
```

```
// Returns 'how-to-win-friends-and-influence-people'
```

Application Paths

When you're dealing with the filesystem, it can often be tedious to make links to certain directories for getting and saving files. These helpers give you quick access to find the fully qualified paths to some of the most important directories in your app.

Note that each of these can be called with no parameters, but if a parameter is passed, it will be appended to the normal directory string and returned as a whole:

app_path(*$append* = '')
:   Returns the path for the *app* directory:

    ```
    app_path();

    // Returns /home/forge/myapp.com/app
    ```

base_path(*$append* = '')
:   Returns the path for the root directory of your app:

    ```
    base_path();

    // Returns /home/forge/myapp.com
    ```

config_path(*$append* = '')
:   Returns the path for configuration files in your app:

    ```
    config_path();

    // Returns /home/forge/myapp.com/config
    ```

database_path(*$append* = '')
:   Returns the path for database files in your app:

    ```
    database_path();

    // Returns /home/forge/myapp.com/database
    ```

storage_path(*$append* = '')
:   Returns the path for the *storage* directory in your app:

    ```
    storage_path();

    // Returns /home/forge/myapp.com/storage
    ```

URLs

Some frontend file paths are consistent but at times annoying to type—for example, paths to assets—and it's helpful to have convenient shortcuts to them, which we'll cover here. But some can actually vary as route definitions move or new files are versioned with Elixir, so some of these helpers are vital in making sure all of your links and assets work correctly:

action(*'Controller@method'*, *$params* = *[]*, *$absolute* = *true*)

> Assuming a controller method has a single URL mapped to it, returns the correct URL given a controller and method name pair (separated by @):

```
<a href="{{ action('PeopleController@index' }}">See all People</a>

// Returns <a href="http://myapp.com/people">See all People</a>
```

> If the controller method requires parameters, you can pass them in as the second parameter (as an array, if there's more than one required parameter). You can key them if you want for clarity, but what matters is just that they're in the right order:

```
<a href="{{ action('PeopleController@show', ['id' => 3] }}">See Person #3</a>
// or
<a href="{{ action('PeopleController@show', [3] }}">See Person #3</a>

// Returns <a href="http://myapp.com/people/3">See Person #3</a>
```

> If you pass `false` to the third parameter, your links will generate as relative (*/people/3*) instead of absolute (*http://myapp.com/people/3*).

route(*$routeName*, *$params* = *[]*, *$absolute* = *true*)

> If a route has a name (using `as` in the route definition), returns the URL for that route:

```
<a href="{{ route('people.index') }}">See all People</a>

// Returns <a href="http://myapp.com/people">See all People</a>
```

> If the route definition requires parameters, you can pass them in as the second parameter (as an array if more than one parameter is required). Again, you can key them if you want for clarity, but what matters is just that they're in the right order:

```
<a href="{{ action('people.show', ['id' => 3]) }}">See Person #3</a>
// or
<a href="{{ action('people.show', [3]) }}">See Person #3</a>

// Returns <a href="http://myapp.com/people/3">See Person #3</a>
```

If you pass `false` to the third parameter, your links will generate as relative instead of absolute.

url(*$string*) *and* secure_url(*$string*)

Given any path string, converts to a fully qualified URL. `secure_url()` is the same as `url()` but forces HTTPS.

```
url('people/3');
```

```
// Returns http://myapp.com/people/3
```

If no parameters are passed, this instead gives an instance of `Illuminate\Routing\UrlGenerator`, which makes method chaining possible:

```
url()->current();
// Returns http://myapp.com/abc
```

```
url()->full();
// Returns http://myapp.com/abc?order=reverse
```

```
url()->previous();
// Returns http://myapp.com/login
```

```
// And many more methods available on the UrlGenerator...
```

elixir(*$filePath*)

If assets are versioned with Elixir's versioning system, given the nonversioned path name, returns the fully qualified URL for the versioned file:

```
<link rel="stylesheet" href="{{ elixir('css/app.css') }}">
```

```
// Returns something like /build/css/app-eb555e38.css
```

Misc

There are a few other global helpers that I'd recommend getting familiar with. Of course, you should check out the whole list (*https://laravel.com/docs/helpers*), but the ones mentioned here are definitely worth taking a look at:

abort(*$code, $message, $headers*), abort_unless(*$boolean, $code, $message, $headers*), *and* abort_if(*$boolean, $code, $message, $headers*)

Throw HTTP exceptions. `abort()` throws the exception defined, `abort_unless()` throws it if the first parameter is `false`, and `abort_if()` throws it if the first parameter is `true`:

```
public function controllerMethod(Request $request)
{
    abort(403, 'You shall not pass');
    abort_unless($request->has('magicToken'), 403);
```

```
        abort_if($request->user()->isBanned, 403);
    }
```

auth()

Returns an instance of the Laravel authenticator. Like the Auth facade, you can use this to get the current user, to check for login state, and more:

```
$user = auth()->user();

if (auth()->check()) {
    // Do something
}
```

back()

Generates a "redirect back" response, sending the user to the previous location:

```
Route::get('post', function () {
    ...

    if ($condition) {
        return back();
    }
});
```

collect($array)

Takes an array and returns the same data, converted to a collection:

```
$collection = collect(['Rachel', 'Hototo']);
```

We'll cover collections in just a bit.

config($key)

Returns the value for any dot-notated configuration item:

```
$defaultDbConnection = config('database.default');
```

csrf_field() *and* csrf_token()

Return a full HTML hidden input (csrf_field()) or just the appropriate token value (csrf_token()) for adding CSRF verification to your form submission:

```
<form>
    {{ csrf_field() }}
</form>

// or

<form>
    <input type="hidden" name="_token" value="{{ csrf_token() }}">
</form>
```

dd(*$variable...*)

Short for "dump and die," runs var_dump() on all provided parameters and then exit() to quit the application (this is used for debugging):

```
...
dd($var1, $var2, $state); // Why is this not working???
```

env(*$key, $default = null*)

Returns the environment variable for the given key:

```
$key = env('API_KEY', '');
```

Using env() outside of config files

Certain features in Laravel, including some caching and optimization features, aren't available if you use env() calls anywhere outside of config files.

The best way to pull in environment variables is to set up config items for anything you want to be environment-specific. Have those config items read the environment variables, and then reference the config variables anywhere within your app:

```
// config/services.php
return [
    'bugsnag' => [
        'key' => env('BUGSNAG_API_KEY')
    ]
];

// in controller, or whatever
$bugsnag = new Bugsnag(config('services.bugsnag.key'));
```

dispatch(*$job*)

Dispatches a job:

```
dispatch(new EmailAdminAboutNewUser($user));
```

event(*$event*)

Fires an event:

```
event(new ContactAdded($contact));
```

factory(*$entityClass*)

Returns an instance of the factory builder for the given class:

```
$contact = factory(App\Contact::class)->make();
```

old(*$key, $default = null*)

Returns the old value (from the last user form submission) for this form key, if it exists:

```
<input name="name" value="{{ old('value', 'Your name here') }}"
```

redirect(*$path*)

Returns a redirect response to the given path:

```
Route::get('post', function () {
    ...

    return redirect('home');
});
```

Without parameters, generates an instance of the `Illuminate\Routing\Redirec tor` class.

response(*$body, $status, $headers*)

If passed with parameters, returns a prebuilt instance of Response. If passed with no response, returns an instance of the Response factory:

```
return response('OK', 200, ['X-Header-Greatness' => 'Super great']);

return response()->json(['status' => 'success'], 200);
```

view(*$viewPath*)

Returns a view instance:

```
Route::get('home', function () {
    return view('home'); // Gets /resources/views/home.blade.php
});
```

Collections

Collections are one of the most powerful and yet underappreciated tools Laravel provides. We covered them a bit in "Eloquent Collections" on page 174, but here's a quick recap.

Collections are essentially arrays with superpowers. The array-traversing methods you normally have to pass arrays into (array_walk(), array_map(), array_reduce(), etc.), all of which have confusingly inconsistent method signatures, are available as consistent, clean, chainable methods on every collection. You can get a taste of functional programming and map, reduce, and filter your way to cleaner code.

We'll cover some of the basics of Laravel's collections and collection pipeline programming here, but for a much deeper overview, check out Adam Wathan's book *Refactoring to Collections* (Gumroad).

The Basics of Collections

Collections are not a new idea within Laravel. Many languages make collection-style programming available on arrays out of the box, but with PHP we're not quite so lucky.

Using PHP's array*() functions, we can take the monstrosity shown in Example 17-1, and turn it into the slightly less monstrous monstrosity shown in Example 17-2.

Example 17-1. A common, but ugly, foreach loop

```
$users = [...];

$admins = [];

foreach ($users as $user) {
    if ($user['status'] == 'admin') {
        $user['name'] = $user['first'] . ' ' . $user['last'];
        $admins[] = $user;
    }
}

return $admins;
```

Example 17-2. Refactoring the foreach loop with native PHP functions

```
$users = [...];
return array_map(function ($user) {
    $user['name'] = $user['first'] . ' ' . $user['last'];
    return $user;
}, array_filter($users, function ($user) {
    return $user['status'] == 'admin';
}));
```

Here, we've gotten rid of a temporary variable (+$admins+) and converted one confusing foreach loop into two distinct actions: map and filter.

The problem is, PHP's array manipulation functions are awful and confusing. Just look at this example; array_map() takes the closure first and the array second, but array_filter() takes the array first and the closure second. In addition, if we added any complexity to this, we'd have functions wrapping functions wrapping functions. It's a mess.

Laravel's collections take the power of PHP's array manipulation methods and give them a clean, fluent syntax—and they add many methods that don't even exist in PHP's array manipulation toolbox. Now, using the collect() helper method that turns an array into a Laravel collection, we can do what's shown in Example 17-3:

Example 17-3. Refactoring the foreach loop with Laravel's collections

```
$users = collect([...]);

return $users->filter(function ($user) {
    return $user['status'] == 'admin';
})->map(function ($user) {
    $user['name'] = $user['first'] . ' ' . $user['last'];
    return $user;
});
```

This isn't the most extreme of examples. There are plenty where the reduction in lines of code and the increased simplicity would make an even stronger case. But this right here is *so common.*

Look at the original example and how muddy it is. It's not entirely clear until you understand the entire code sample what any given piece is there for.

The biggest benefit collections provide, over anything else, is breaking the actions you're taking to manipulate an array into simple, discrete, understandable tasks. You can now do something like this:

```
$users = [...]
$countAdmins = collect($users)->filter(function ($user) {
    return $user['status'] == 'admin'
})->count();
```

Or something like this:

```
$users = [...];
$greenTeamPoints = collect($users)->filter(function ($user) {
    return $user->team == 'green';
})->sum('points');
```

A Few Methods

There's much more you can do than what we've covered here. Take a look at the Laravel Collection docs (*https://laravel.com/docs/collections*) to learn more about all the methods you can use, but to get you started, here are just a few of the core methods:

all() *and* toArray()
> If you'd like to convert your collection to an array, you can do so with either all() or toArray(). toArray() flattens not just the collection, but also any Eloquent objects underneath it, to arrays. all() *only* converts the collection to an

array; any Eloquent objects contained within the collection will be preserved as Eloquent objects. Here are a few examples:

```
$users = User::all();

$users->toArray();

/* Returns
    [
        ['id' => '1', 'name' => 'Agouhanna'],
        ...
    ]
*/

$users->all();

/* Returns
    [
        Eloquent Object { id : 1, name: 'Agouhanna' },
        ...
    ]
*/
```

filter() *and* reject()

When you want to get a subset of your original collection by checking each item against a closure, you'll use filter() (which keeps an item if the closure returns true) or reject() (which keeps an item if the closure returns false):

```
$users = collect([...]);
$admins = $users->filter(function ($user) {
    return $user->isAdmin;
});

$paidUsers = $user->reject(function ($user) {
    return $user->isTrial;
});
```

where()

where() makes it easy to provide a subset of your original collection where a given key is equal to a given value. Anything you can do with where() you can also do with filter(), but it's a shortcut for a common scenario:

```
$users = collect([...]);
$admins = $users->where('role', 'admin');
```

first() *and* last()

If you want just a single item from your collection, you can use first() to pull from the beginning of the list or last() to pull from the end.

If you call `first()` or `last()` with no parameters, they'll just give you the first or last item in the collection. But if you pass either a closure, they'll instead give you the first or last item in the collection *that returns `true` when passed to that closure.*

Sometimes you'll do this because you want the actual first or last item. But sometimes it's the easiest way to get one item even if you only expect there to be one:

```
$users = collect([...]);
$owner = $users->first(function ($user) {
    return $user->isOwner;
});

$firstUser = $users->first();
$lastUser = $users->last();
```

You can also pass a second parameter to each method, which is the default value and will be provided as a fallback if the closure doesn't provide any results.

each()

If you'd like to do something with each item of a collection, but it doesn't include modifying the items or the collection itself, you can use `each()`:

```
$users = collect([...]);
$users->each(function ($user) {
    dispatch(new EmailUserAThing($user));
});
```

map()

If you'd like to iterate over all the items in a collection, make changes to them, and return a new collection with all of your changes, you'll want to use `map()`:

```
$users = collect([...]);
$users = $users->map(function ($user) {
    return [
        'name' => $user['first'] . ' ' . $user['last'],
        'email' => $user['email']
    ];
});
```

reduce()

If you'd like to get a single result from your collection, like a count or a string, you'll probably want to use `reduce()`. You can define an initial value for the "carry," and a closure that accepts the current state of the "carry" and then each item as parameters:

```
$users = collect([...]);

$points = $users->reduce(function ($carry, $user) {
    return $carry + $user['points']
}, 0); // Start with a carry of 0
```

pluck()

If you want to pull out just the values for a given key under each item in a collection, you can use pluck() (formerly lists()):

```
$users = collect([...]);

$emails = $users->pluck('email')->toArray();
```

chunk() *and* take()

chunk() makes it easy to split your collection into groups of a predefined size, and take() pulls just the provided number of items:

```
$users = collect([...]);

$rowsOfUsers = $users->chunk(3); // Separates into groups of 3

$topThree = $users->take(3); // Pulls the first 3
```

groupBy()

If you want to group all of the items in your collection by the value of one of their properties, you can use groupBy():

```
$users = collect([...]);

$usersByRole = $users->groupBy('role');

/* Returns:
    [
        'member' => [...],
        'admin' => [...]
    ]
*/
```

You can also pass a closure, and whatever you return from the closure will be what's used to group the records:

```
$heroes = collect([...]);

$heroesByAbilityType = $heroes->groupBy(function ($hero) {
    if ($hero->canFly() && $hero->isInvulnerable()) {
        return 'Kryptonian';
    }

    if ($hero->bitByARadioactiveSpider()) {
        return 'Spidermanesque';
    }

    if ($hero->color === 'green' && $hero->likesSmashing()) {
        return 'Hulk-like';
    }
```

```
    return 'Generic';
});
```

reverse() *and* shuffle()

reverse() reverses the order of the items in your collection, and shuffle() randomizes them:

```
$numbers = collect([1, 2, 3]);

$numbers->reverse()->toArray(); // [3, 2, 1]
$numbers->shuffle()->toArray(); // [2, 3, 1]
```

sort(), sortBy(), *and* sortByDesc()

If your items are simple strings or integers, you can use sort() to sort them:

```
$sortedNumbers = collect([1, 7, 6, 4])->sort()->toArray(); // [1, 4, 6, 7]
```

If they're more complex, you can pass a string (representing the property) or a closure to sortBy() or sortByDesc() to define your sorting behavior:

```
$users = collect([...]);

// Sort an array of users by their 'email' property
$users->sort('email');

// Sort an array of users by their 'email' property
$users->sort(function ($user, $key) {
    return $user['email'];
});
```

count() *and* isEmpty()

You can see how many items there are in your collection using count() or isEmpty():

```
$numbers = collect([1, 2, 3]);

$numbers->count();   // 3
$numbers->isEmpty(); // false
```

avg() *and* sum()

If you're working with a collection of numbers, avg() and sum() do what their method names say, and don't require any parameters:

```
collect([1, 2, 3])->sum(); // 6
collect([1, 2, 3])->avg(); // 2
```

But if you're working with arrays, you can pass the key of the property you'd like to pull from each array to operate on:

```
$users = collect([...]);

$sumPoints = $users->sum('points');
$avgPoints = $users->avg('points');
```

Using collections outside of Laravel

Have you fallen in love with collections, and do you want to use them on your non-Laravel projects? With Taylor's blessing, I split out just the collections functionality from Laravel into a separate project called Collect (*http://bit.ly/2f1It7n*), and developers at my company keep it up-to-date with Laravel's releases.

Just use the `composer require tightenco/collect` command and you'll have the `Illuminate\Support\Collection` class ready to use in your code—along with the `collect()` helper.

TL;DR

Laravel provides a suite of global helper functions that make it simpler to do all sorts of tasks. They make it easier to manipulate and inspect arrays and strings, they make it easier to generate paths and URLs, and they provide simple access to some consistent and vital functionality.

Laravel's collections are powerful tools that bring the possibility of collection pipelines to PHP.

Glossary

Accessor

A method defined on an Eloquent model that customizes how a given property will be returned. Accessors make it possible to define that getting a given property from a model will return a different (or, more likely, differently formatted) value than what is stored in the database for that property.

ActiveRecord

A common database ORM pattern, and also the pattern that Laravel's Eloquent uses. In ActiveRecord the same model class defines both how to retrieve and persist database records *and* how to represent them. Additionally, each database record is represented by a single entity in the application, and each entity in the application is mapped to a single database record.

Application test

Often called acceptance or functional tests, application tests test the entire behavior of the application, usually at an outer boundary, by employing something like a DOM crawler—which is exactly what Laravel's application test suite offers.

Argument (Artisan)

Arguments are parameters that can be passed to Artisan console commands. Arguments aren't prefaced with -- or followed by =, but instead just accept a single value.

Artisan

The tool that makes it possible to interact with Laravel applications from the command line.

Assertion

In testing, an assertion is the core of the test: you are *asserting* that something should be equal to (or less than or greater than) something else, or that it should have a given count, or whatever else you like. Assertions are the things that can either pass or fail.

Authentication

Correctly identifying oneself as a member/user of an application is the act of authentication. Authentication doesn't define *what* you may do, but simply *who* you are (or aren't).

Authorization

Assuming you've either succeeded or failed at authenticating yourself, authorization defines what you're *allowed* to do given your particular identification. Authorization is about access and control.

Autowiring

When a dependency injection container will inject an instance of a resolvable class without a developer having explicitly taught it how to resolve that class, that's called autowiring. With a container that doesn't have autowiring, you can't even inject a plain PHP object with no dependencies until you have explicitly bound it to the container. With autowiring, you only have to explicitly bind something to the container if its dependencies are too complex or vague for the container to figure out on its own.

beanstalkd

Beanstalk is a work queue. It's simple and excels at running multiple asynchronous tasks—which makes it a common driver for Laravel's queues. *beanstalkd* is its daemon.

Blade

Laravel's templating engine.

Carbon

A PHP package that makes working with dates much easier and more expressive.

Cashier

A Laravel package that makes billing with Stripe or Braintree, especially in subscription contexts, easier and more consistent and powerful.

Closure

Closures are PHP's version of anonymous functions. A closure is a function that you can pass around as an object, assign to a variable, pass as a parameter to other functions and methods, or even serialize.

CodeIgniter

An older PHP framework that Laravel was inspired by.

Collection

The name of a development pattern and also Laravel's tool that implements it. Like arrays on steroids, collections provide map, reduce, filter, and many more powerful operations that PHP's native arrays don't.

Command

The name for a custom Artisan console task.

Composer

PHP's dependency manager. Like Ruby Gems or NPM.

Container

Somewhat of a catchall word, in Laravel "container" refers to the application container that's responsible for dependency injection. Accessible via app() and also responsible for resolving calls to controllers, events, jobs, and commands, the container is the glue that holds each Laravel app together.

Contract

Another name for an interface.

Controller

A class that is responsible for routing user requests through to the application's services and data, and returning some form of useful response back to the user.

CSRF (cross-site request forgery)

A malicious attack where an external site makes requests against your application by hijacking your users' browsers (with JavaScript, likely) while they're still logged in to your site. Protected against by adding a token (and a check for that token on the POST side) to every form on the site.

Dependency injection

Instead of instantiating dependencies in a class, expect them to be injected in from the outside—usually through the constructor.

Directive

Blade syntax options like @if, @unless, etc.

Dot notation

Navigating down inheritance trees using . to reference a jump down to a new level. If you have an array like: ['owner' => ['address' => ['line1' => '123 Main St.']]], you have three levels of nesting. Using dot notation, you would represent "123 Main St." as "owner.address.line1".

Eager loading

Avoiding *N*+1 problems by adding a second smart query to your first query to get a set of related items. Usually you have a first query that gets a collection of thing A. But each A has many B, and so every time you get the B from an A, you need a new query. Eager loading means doing two queries: first you get all the A's, and second you get *all* the B's related to all those A's, in a single query. Two queries, and you're done.

Echo

A Laravel product that makes WebSocket authentication and syncing of data simple.

Elixir

Laravel's build tool; a wrapper around Gulp.

Eloquent

Laravel's ActiveRecord ORM. The tool you'll use to define something like a `User` model.

Environment variable

Variables that are defined in an *.env* file that is expected to be excluded from version control. This means they don't sync between environments and they're also kept safe.

Envoyer

A Laravel product for zero-down-time deployment.

Event

Laravel's tool for implementing a pub/sub or observer pattern. Each event represents that an event happened: the name of the event describes what happened (e.g., `User Subscribed`) and the payload allows for attaching relevant information. Designed to be "fired" and then "listened" for (or published and subscribed, if you prefer the pub/sub concept).

Facade

A tool in Laravel for simplifying access to complex tools. Facades provide static access to core services in Laravel. Since every facade is backed by a class in the container, you could replace any call to something like `Cache::put();` with a two-line call to something like `$cache = app('cache'); $cache->put();`.

Flag

A parameter anywhere that is on or off (boolean).

Fluent

Methods that can be chained one after another are said to be fluent. In order to provide a fluent syntax, each method must return the instance, preparing it to be chained again. This allows for something like `People::where('age', '>', 14)->orderBy('name')->get()`.

Flysystem

The package that Laravel uses to facilitate its local and cloud file access.

Forge

A Laravel product that makes it easy to spin up and manage virtual servers on major cloud providers like DigitalOcean and AWS.

FQCN (fully-qualified class name)

The full namespaced name of any given class, trait, or interface. `Controller` is the class name; `Illuminate\Routing\Con troller` is the FQCN.

Gulp

A JavaScript-based build tool.

Helper

A globally accessible PHP function that makes some other functionality easier—for example, `array_get()` simplifies the logic of looking up results from arrays.

Homestead

A Laravel tool that wraps Vagrant and makes it easier to spin up Forge-parallel virtual servers for local Laravel development.

Illuminate

The top-level namespace of all Laravel components.

Integration test

Integration tests test the way individual units work together and pass messages.

IoC (inversion of control)

The concept of giving "control" over how to make a concrete instance of an interface to the higher-level code of the package instead of the lower-level code. Without IoC, each individual controller and class might decide what instance of Mailer it wanted to create. IoC makes it so that the low-level code—those controllers and classes—just get to ask for a Mailer, and some high-level configuration code defines *once* per application which instance should be provided to satisfy that request.

Job

A class that intends to encapsulate a single task. Jobs are intended to be able to be pushed onto a queue and run asynchronously.

JSON

JavaScript Object Notation. A syntax for data representation.

JWT (JSON Web Token)

A JSON object containing all of the information necessary to determine a user's authentication state and access permissions. This JSON object is digitally signed, which is what makes it trustworthy, using HMAC or RSA. Usually delivered in the header.

Mass assignment

The ability to pass many parameters at once to create or update an Eloquent model, using a keyed array.

Middleware

A series of wrappers around an application that filter and decorate its inputs and outputs.

Memcached

An in-memory data store designed to provide simple but fast data storage. Memcached only supports a basic key/value store.

Migration

A manipulation to the state of the database, stored in and run from code.

Mockery

A library included with Laravel that makes it easy to mock PHP classes in your tests.

Model factory

A tool for defining how the application can generate an instance of your model if needed for testing or seeding. Usually paired with a fake data generator like Faker.

Multitenancy

A single app serving multiple clients, each of which has its customers. Multitenancy often suggests that each client of your application gets its own theming and domain name, with which to differentiate its service to its customers vis-à-vis your other clients' potential services.

Mutator

A tool in Eloquent that allows you to manipulate the data being saved to a model property before it is saved to the database.

Nginx

A web server similar to Apache.

Option (Artisan)

Like arguments, options are parameters that can be passed to Artisan commands. They're prefaced with - - and can be used as a flag (- - force) or to provide data (- - userId=5).

ORM (object-relational mapper)

A design pattern that is centered around using objects in a programming language to represent data, and its relationships, in a relational database.

Passport

A Laravel package that can be used to easily add an OAuth authentication server to your Laravel app.

PHPSpec

A PHP testing framework.

PHPUnit

A PHP testing framework. The most common and connected to the most of Laravel's custom testing code.

Polymorphic

In database terms, able to interact with multiple database tables with similar characteristics. A polymorphic relationship will allow entities of multiple models to be attached in the same way.

Preprocessor

A build tool that takes in a special form of a language (for CSS, one special form is LESS) and generates code with just the normal language (CSS). Preprocessors build in tools and features that are not in the core language.

Primary key

Most database tables have a single column that is intended to represent each row. This is called the primary key and is commonly named id.

Queue

A stack onto which jobs can be added. Usually associated with a queue worker, which pulls jobs one at a time from a queue, works on them, and then discards them.

Redis

Like Memcached, a data store simpler than most relational databases but powerful and fast. Redis supports a very limited set of structures and data types but makes up for it in speed and scalability.

REST

Representational State Transfer, the most common format for APIs these days. Usually suggests that interactions with an API should each authenticate separately and should be "stateless"; also usually suggests that they use the HTTP verbs for basic differentiation of requests.

Route

A definition of a way or ways the user might visit a web application. A route is a pattern definition; it can be something like /users/5, or /users, or /users/{id}.

SaaS

Software as a Service. Web-based applications that you pay money to use.

Scope

In Eloquent, a tool for defining how to consistently and simply narrow down a query.

Scout

A Laravel package for full-text search on Eloquent models.

Serialization

The process of converting more complex data (usually an Eloquent model) to something simpler (in Laravel, usually an array or JSON).

Service provider

A structure in Laravel that registers and boots classes and container bindings.

Soft delete

Marking a database row as "deleted" without actually deleting it, usually paired with an ORM that by default hides all "deleted" rows.

Spark

A Laravel tool that makes it easy to spin up a new subscription-based SaaS app.

Symfony

A PHP framework that focuses on building excellent components and making them accessible to others. Symfony's HTTP Foundation is at the core of Laravel and every other modern PHP framework.

Tinker

Laravel's REPL, or read–evaluate–print loop. It's a tool that allows you to perform complex PHP operations within the full context of your app from the command line.

TL;DR

Too long; didn't read. "Summary."

Typehint

Prefacing a variable name in a method signature with a class or interface name. Tells PHP (and Laravel, and other developers) that the only thing that's allowed to be passed in that parameter is an object with the given class or interface.

Unit test

Unit tests target small, relatively isolated units—a class or method, usually.

Vagrant

A command-line tool that makes it easy to build virtual machines on your local computer using predefined images.

Valet

A Laravel package (for Mac OS users, but there are forks for Linux and Windows) that makes it easy to serve your applications from your development folder of choice, without worrying about Vagrant or virtual machines.

Validation

Ensuring that user input matches expected patterns.

View composer

A tool that defines that, every time a given view is loaded, it will be provided a certain set of data.

View

A template file that defines HTML to be sent to the end user; often includes accepting data from a controller and formatting it as part of the HTML.

Index

dd() helper, 397
Dead Man's Snitch, 386
decimal() method, Blueprint, 136
decrement() method, Cache, 325
decrement() method, DB, 156
default() method, Blueprint, 137
define() method, Gate, 214
define() method, model factories, 143
delay() method, jobs, 360
delay() method, notification, 349
DELETE method, 45-46
    for resource controllers, 42
    routes based on, 25
delete() method, DB, 149, 156
delete() method, Eloquent, 165
delete() method, Storage, 317
delete() method, TestCase, 269
deleteDirectory() method, Storage, 317
deleted_at column, 166
deletes, soft, 411
denies() method, Gate, 214
dependency injection, 247-249, 408
    constructor injection, 247, 249, 254
    method injection, 247, 255
    setter injection, 247
    testing using, 259
destroy() method, resource controllers, 42
detach() method, Eloquent, 185
development environments, 12-17
DI (dependency injection) container (see con-
    tainer)
directives (Blade), 55, 408
directories() method, Storage, 318
disk() method, Storage, 316, 319
dispatch() helper, 359, 397
DispatchesJobs trait, 359
dissociate() method, Eloquent, 182
distinct() method, DB, 152
dnsmasq tool, 12
domains, top-level, 15
dontSee() method, TestCase, 270
dontSeeInDatabase() method, TestCase, 271
dontSeeInField() method, TestCase, 270
dontSeeIsChecked() method, TestCase, 270
dontSeeIsSelected() method, TestCase, 270
dontSeeJson() method, TestCase, 271
dontSeeLink() method, TestCase, 270
dot notation (.), 408
double() method, Blueprint, 136

down command, Artisan, 114
down() method, migrations, 134, 135
download responses, 235
download() method, Response, 53, 235

E

e() helper, 88, 391
@each directive, Blade, 63
each() method, collection, 402
eager loading, 191-192, 409
Echo, 370, 373, 375-382, 409
    authorization for channels, 376-378
    excluding user from events, 375, 382
    JavaScript package for, 378-382
    listening for events, 379
    presence channels, 381
    private channels, 380
    service provider configuration, 376
    subscribing to channels, 380
    subscribing to notifications, 382
edit() method, resource controllers, 42
Elixir build tool, 75-84, 409
    directory structure for, 77
    documentation for, 78
    extensions for, 83-84
    JavaScript, concatenating, 80
    JavaScript, processing, 81
    multiple files, processing, 78
    preprocessorless CSS, 79
    production mode, 78
    running, 77
    source maps, generating, 79
    tests, running, 82
    versioning, 81-82
    versions of, 77
elixir() helper, 82, 395
Eloquent, 84, 157-193, 409
    accessors, 171, 179, 194, 407
    aggregates, 162
    attribute casting, 173
    collections returned by, 174-176
    customzing route key for, 44
    date mutators, 174
    deletes, 165-168
    eager loading, 191-192, 409
    events, 192-193
    exceptions thrown by, 161
    fillable or guarded properties, 164
    filtering API results, 293

queue.php file, 356
queue:failed command, Artisan, 362
queue:failed-table command, Artisan, 362
queue:flush command, Artisan, 363
queue:forget command, Artisan, 363
queue:listen command, Artisan, 361
queue:retry all command, Artisan, 363
queue:retry command, Artisan, 363
queue:work command, Artisan, 360, 361
Queueable trait, 358
queues, 355-364, 411
    for Artisan commands, 116, 364
    beanstalkd for, 408
    benefits of, 356
    configuring, 356
    creating jobs in, 357-359
    deleting jobs in, 363
    dispatching jobs in, 397
    errors with, handling, 360-363
    for jobs, 356
    for mail, 343, 364
    number of tries for jobs, 361
    providers and drivers for, 356
    pushing jobs onto, 359-360
    releasing jobs back to, 363
    retrying jobs, 363
    workers, 360, 370

R
raw() method, DB, 154
read-evaluate-print-loop (REPL) (see Tinker)
readme.md file, 19
Redirect facade, 48
redirect() helper, 48-52, 237, 398
redirectPath() method, 203
redirects, 48-52
Redis, 133, 373, 374, 411
reduce() method, collection, 402
reflash() method, Session, 323
refresh() method, redirects, 50
regenerate() method, Session, 322
register() method, RegisterUsers, 203
register() method, service providers, 227, 252, 258
RegisterController, 201-203
RegistersUsers trait, 202
regular expressions
    passing to str_is(), 392
    route constraints using, 27

reject() method, collection, 401
relationships, 179-190
    as query builders, 182
    eager loading, 191-192, 409
    inserting related items, 181
    lazy loading, 191, 192
    serialization of, 178
release() method, jobs, 363
remember me access token, 207
remember() method, Cache, 325
rememberForever() method, Cache, 325
rememberToken() method, Blueprint, 137
render() method, pagination, 85
REPL (read-evaluate-print-loop) (see Tinker)
Representational State Transfer (REST), 283-284, 411
Request facade, 95
request headers, 288, 289
Request object, 95-99, 228-233
    accessing, 229-232
    array input, accessing, 98
    capturing directly, 229
    file handling methods, 232
    form requests, 245
    headers for, 288, 289
    JSON input, accessing, 98
    lifecycle of, 225-228
    persistence of, for session interaction, 233
    reading cookies from, 328
    testing, 245-246
    typehinting in constructors, 41, 229-230
    user and request state methods, 231
    user input methods, 230-231
request() helper, 95, 99, 230
reset() method, 204
resetPassword() method, 204
ResetPasswordController, 204
resource controller binding, 42
resource controllers, 41-42, 285-288
resources folder, 19, 77
resources, API, 283, 295-297
resources, online (see online resources)
response headers, 288
Response object, 233-238
    creating, 233-234
    custom, 52
    custom response macros, 238
    download responses, 235
    file responses, 236

times and dates (see Carbon package; scheduler; timestamps)
timestamp() method, Blueprint, 137
timestamps, 137, 160, 174, 190-192
timestamps() method, Blueprint, 137
Tinker, 114, 128, 128, 412
tinker command, Artisan, 114
tinyInteger() method, Blueprint, 136
TL;DR (too long; didn't read), xvi, 412
to() method, 49
toArray() method, collection, 400
toArray() method, Eloquent, 177
toBroadcast() method, notification, 352
toDatabase() method, notification, 351
toJson() method, Eloquent, 177
Tokenizer PHP extension, 11
tokens, CSRF, 46-48
toMail() method, notification, 350-350
toNexmo() method, notification, 352
too long; didn't read (TL;DR), xvi, 412
toOthers() method, events, 375, 382
top-level domains, for local development site, 15
toSearchableArray() method, 329
toSlack() method, notification, 352
transaction() method, DB, 157
transactions, 156
translation (see localization)
Translation component, Symfony, 91
trashed() method, Eloquent, 167
truncate() method, DB, 156
Twig Bridge package, 56
    (see also Blade)
type() method, TestCase, 275
typehint, 40, 412
typehinting, 251, 253

U

uncheck() method, TestCase, 275
union() method, DB, 155
unionAll() method, DB, 155
unique() method, Blueprint, 138
unit tests, 261, 412
universal to, for mail, 345
@unless directive, Blade, 57
unsearchable() method, 331
unsigned() method, Blueprint, 138
up() method, migrations, 134, 135
update() method, DB, 149, 156

update() method, Eloquent, 163, 164
update() method, resource controllers, 42
updateExistingPivot() method, Eloquent, 185
uploaded files, 101-103, 318-320, 331-333
UploadedFile class, 102, 232, 331
url() helper, 28, 29, 395
url() method, Request, 232
URLs
    helpers for, 394-395
    user input from route parameters, 100
    user input from URL segments, 100
user authentication (see authentication)
user authorization (see authorization)
user input
    Artisan commands, 123-125
    Eloquent model, 109
    form requests, 107-109
    getting and handling with controllers, 39-40
    Request object, 95-99, 230-231
    route parameters, 100
    testing, 110
    uploaded files, 101-103
    URLs, 100
    validating, 103-106
User model, 198-201
user() method, 201, 209
username() method, 204
uuid() method, Blueprint, 137

V

Vagrant, 14, 412
    commands for, 16
    mapping Homestead folders to, 15
    migrations with, 141
Valet package, 12-13, 412
validate() method, controller, 52, 103-105
validateLogin() method, 203
validation of user input, 103-106, 412
    error messages from, displaying, 106
    manual validation, 106
    validate() method, controller, 103-105
    validation rules, 105
Validator class, 87, 106
validator() method, 202
vendor commands, Artisan, 117
vendor folder, 19
vendor:publish command, Artisan, 308, 329
versioning, in Elixir, 81-82
versions of Laravel, xvi

About the Author

Matt Stauffer is a developer and a teacher. He is a partner and technical director at Tighten Co., blogs at mattstauffer.co, and hosts The Five-Minute Geek Show and the Laravel Podcast.

Colophon

The animal on the cover of *Laravel: Up and Running* is a gemsbok (*oryx gazella*). This large antelope is native to the deserts of South Africa, Botswana, Zimbabwe, and Namibia, where it is featured on the country's coat of arms.

Gemsbok measure about 5 feet 7 inches tall at the shoulder and can weigh from 250 to 390 pounds. They are typically pale gray or brown, with black and white facial markings and long black tails. A black stripe extends from the chin to the lower edge of the neck. The gemsbok's impressive straight horns, used in defensive maneuvers, average 33 inches in length and are regarded as charms in many cultures. In medieval England, they were often marketed as unicorn horns.

Although these horns make the gemsbok a highly-sought trophy animal, the population remains stable throughout Southern Africa. In 1969, gemsbok were introduced to southern New Mexico, where their current population is around 3,000.

Gemsbok are well-suited to such desert environments, with the ability to survive without drinking water for most of the year. To achieve this, they do not pant or sweat, allowing their body temperature to rise several degrees above normal on hot days. Their lifespan is approximately 18 years in the wild.

Many of the animals on O'Reilly covers are endangered; all of them are important to the world. To learn more about how you can help, go to *animals.oreilly.com*.

The cover image is from *Riverside Natural History*. The cover fonts are URW Typewriter and Guardian Sans. The text font is Adobe Minion Pro; the heading font is Adobe Myriad Condensed; and the code font is Dalton Maag's Ubuntu Mono.

Learn from experts.
Find the answers you need.

Sign up for a **10-day free trial** to get **unlimited access** to all of the content on Safari, including Learning Paths, interactive tutorials, and curated playlists that draw from thousands of ebooks and training videos on a wide range of topics, including data, design, DevOps, management, business—and much more.

Start your free trial at:
oreilly.com/safari

(No credit card required.)

Lightning Source UK Ltd.
Milton Keynes UK
UKOW04f1900171116
287895UK00005B/6/P

9 781491 936085